AF873745

THE STORY OF ZELDA

This is a tale that spans generations: an epic that encompasses goddesses, ancient evil, magical artefacts, a blessed blade, and the intertwined destinies of a young man and woman. *The Legend Of Zelda,* to many videogame fans across its 35-year lifespan, is one of the most revered series of the entire medium. From its humble Famicom beginnings in 1986 to its bold 3D reinvention in *Ocarina Of Time* and the millions-selling epic *Breath Of The Wild, Zelda* games have a universal appeal that captures the imagination of all ages.

Whether your first steps into Hyrule were with 8-bit pixels or into the expansive ruined kingdom portrayed in the most recent games, we've all had a shared experience. There's always a Link, a Zelda and a great evil to overcome. This makes *The Legend Of Zelda* one of the most curious game franchises in existence. Effectively, it's the same story told over and over with embellishments to make each one unique, and in the process, it establishes a familiar connection between its fans no matter which titles they have played.

In this special compendium, we will explore every game in the series, exploring what makes each one so great. *Zelda* creators will also take us behind the scenes and share their insights. If you're a fan, we're sure you'll enjoy the trip through time. If you're a newcomer, we offer you this sage advice: "It's dangerous to go alone, take this!"

FUTURE

THE STORY OF ZELDA

• DISCOVER THE COMPLETE HISTORY OF HYRULE •

Future PLC Quay House, The Ambury, Bath, BA1 1UA

The Story Of Zelda Editorial
Editor **Drew Sleep**
Art Editor **Jon Wells**
Senior Art Editor **Andy Downes**
Head of Art & Design **Greg Whitaker**
Editorial Director **Jon White**

Contributors
Luke Albigés, Ben Graham Alex Dale, Ashley Day, Darran Jones, Stuart Hunt, Leigh Loveday, Dave Meikleham, Matthew Pellett, Aaron Potter, Nikole Robinson,
Chris Schilling, Rich Stanton, Tom Sykes, Nick Thorpe, Alan Wen

Cover images
Nintendo

Photography
All copyrights and trademarks are recognised and respected

Advertising
Media packs are available on request
Commercial Director **Clare Dove**

International
Head of Print Licensing **Rachel Shaw**
licensing@futurenet.com
www.futurecontenthub.com

Circulation
Head of Newstrade **Tim Mathers**

Production
Head of Production **Mark Constance**
Production Project Manager **Matthew Eglinton**
Advertising Production Manager **Joanne Crosby**
Digital Editions Controller **Jason Hudson**
Production Managers **Keely Miller, Nola Cokely, Vivienne Calvert, Fran Twentyman**

Printed in the UK

Distributed by Marketforce, 5 Churchill Place, Canary Wharf, London, E14 5HU
www.marketforce.co.uk Tel: 0203 787 9001

The Story Of Zelda (GAB5056)

FUTURE

Connectors. Creators. Experience Makers.

Future plc is a public company quoted on the London Stock Exchange (symbol: FUTR)
www.futureplc.com

Chief Executive **Zillah Byng-Thorne**
Non-Executive Chairman **Richard Huntingford**
Chief Financial and Strategy Officer **Penny Ladkin-Brand**

Tel +44 (0)1225 442 244

Part of the retro GAMER™ bookazine series

Widely Recycled

ipso. For press freedom with responsibility

108

THE STORY OF ZELDA CONTENTS

052

008

070

080

096

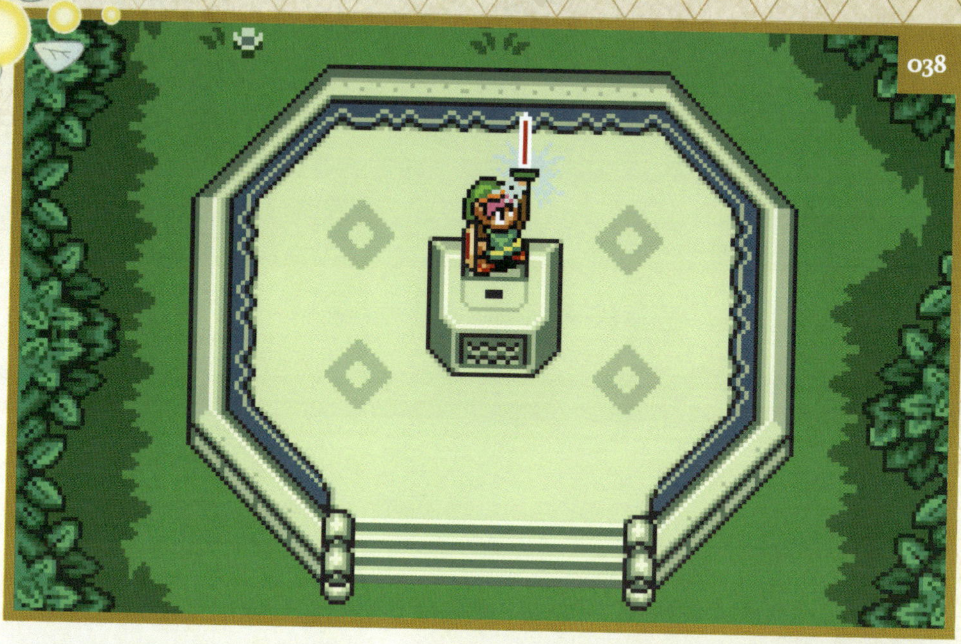
038

030

086

THE LEGEND BEGINS

The story of how an 'Adventure Mario' project evolved to become The Legend Of Zelda

WORDS BY RICH STANTON

It was the morning of 1 February 1985, and Nintendo needed a hit. Shigeru Miyamoto, Takashi Tezuka, and Toshihiko Nakago were working on the first *Mario* game for the Famicom, and *Super Mario Bros* would be finished and released by September of that year. But one killer game was not enough for the Famicom, and its upcoming Famicom Disk System, to be a success: one style of game was not enough. This new title would be different. Work on what would become *The Legend Of Zelda* had begun.

Throughout February, Miyamoto and Tezuka sketched out a design for a new kind of game: where Mario was not linear and all-action, in this new project you could explore and mull over puzzles. Miyamoto and Tezuka worked together, sometimes on the same long piece of graph paper, drawing dungeons, an overworld and a fearsome menagerie of enemies: all of which were bound up in a folder labelled *'Adventure Mario'*.

Though Tezuka's role shouldn't be underestimated, the origins of *The Legend Of Zelda* are inextricably bound to Shigeru Miyamoto, and more specifically to the experiences of his childhood. Miyamoto was born and raised in the small town of Sonobe, in Kyoto – also the home of Nintendo – and by all accounts he was a curious child: poking into cupboards in the family home, rambling over Sonobe's fields and, very occasionally, finding something that he never expected.

In the book *Game Over*, author David Sheff spoke to Miyamoto about these explorations. "When I was a child, I went hiking and found a lake," Miyamoto said. "It was quite a surprise for me to stumble upon it. When I travelled around the country without a map, trying to find my way, stumbling on amazing things as I went, I realised how it felt to go on an adventure like this."

One of the most notable absences in *The Legend Of Zelda* was an overworld map: in dungeons, Link could find a map to help him navigate, but above ground, the player had to rely on memory. Exploration is key to *The Legend Of Zelda* but, more than this, what infused every pixel was Miyamoto's curiosity.

He remembered especially an unfamiliar cave. Young Miyamoto couldn't pluck up the courage to plunge in immediately but returned the next day with a lantern. "The spirit, the state of mind of a kid when he enters a cave alone must be realised in the game. Going in, he must feel the cold air around him. He must discover a branch off to one side and decide whether to explore it or not. Sometimes he loses his way. If you go to the cave now, as an adult, it might be silly, trivial, a small cave. But as a child, in spite of being banned to go, you could not resist the temptation. It was not a small moment then."

Takashi Tezuka's influence on *Zelda* was more straightforward: he'd joined Nintendo in 1984, just before development began, and to Miyamoto's childhood fantasies wedded his love of traditional fantasy – specifically, JRR Tolkien's *Lord Of The Rings*. The rich world of *Zelda* is a ▶

> "The origins of The Legend Of Zelda are inextricably bound to Shigeru Miyamoto, and more specifically to the experiences of his childhood"

patchwork quilt of mythologies: Peter Pan, King Arthur, and most of all, high fantasy.

"Link is a normal boy, but he has a destiny to fight great evil," said Miyamoto. The game, and its creators, understood something fundamental. "Many people dream about becoming heroes."

It is not merely enough to find something: do you have the courage to go further? *The Legend Of Zelda* was known internally, at first, as *'Adventure'* – the *Mario* moniker long since dropped. This game would have no high score to chase or discreet levels to power through. Miyamoto and Tezuka's drawings were of a giant open world, a land full of caves, lakes and forests that the player could explore from the get-go. It was filled with monsters and treasures and, most of all, filled with secrets.

"Miyamoto and Tezuka's drawings were of a giant open world, a land full of caves, lakes and forests that the player could explore from the get-go"

Walls that would crumble with a bomb blast; long grass that hid underground chambers; impassable waters that could be sailed with a raft; enemies that couldn't be defeated through brute force alone. The ideas were ambitious: initially so ambitious that *Zelda* was to be made for the much more powerful arcade machines of its day. But Nintendo's focus as a company was shifting: until the Famicom home console, their most successful games had been arcade cabinets like *Donkey Kong*. The company were introducing the upgraded Famicom Disk System, an add-on that allowed players to use floppy disks that could be erased and rewritten with new games, and it needed a launch game.

The Legend Of Zelda was set to be that flagship: the game, and the Disk System, were released in Japan on 21 February 1986. It had the unwieldy title *The Hyrule Fantasy: Legend Of Zelda*, but for its western release, 17 months later, this was simplified. The Disk System allowed for several tantalising features, one of which sealed *Zelda*'s greatness: saving.

This was one of *Zelda*'s key innovations, most games of the time relying on password systems, though when it reached the west, the game was in cartridge format, the first ever with battery-powered RAM for saving progress. Saving wasn't just an innovation: it also differentiated *Zelda* from arcade games, which were 'fire and forget'. In those days, home consoles couldn't approach the visuals of arcade games, but this was something an arcade game simply couldn't offer. Persistence. Progress. Permanence.

Listing *Zelda*'s innovations today risks underselling the achievement of Miyamoto, Tezuka and the rest of Nintendo's remarkable development team. Its open world, difficulty and even the concept of exploration were alien to gaming.

SKETCHING ZELDA'S WORLD

Miyamoto's first sketches for The Legend of Zelda show he had it all in his head from the start

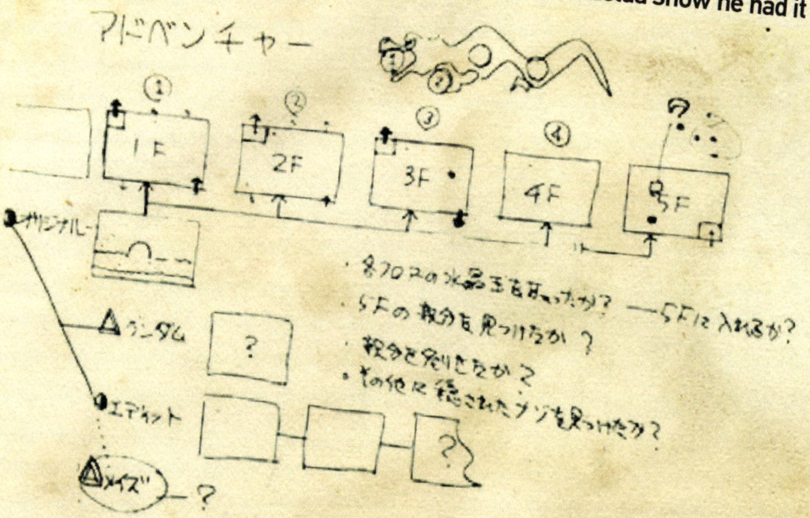

In an 'Iwata Asks' interview with the team who made *The Legend Of Zelda*, Nintendo produced the very first sketches and outlines of the game. Largely drawn by Shigeru Miyamoto, they not only show the outlines but are rich in detail.

The Japanese text at the top of the first image says 'Adventure', and these are the first specifications for the game. From the very start, Miyamoto saw the multilayered dungeons as the cornerstone of the game, and on the left side is the first outline of what would become the Triforce. Perhaps we're pushing things a little here, but doesn't that thing in the top right look a bit like an Ocarina?

The second sheet is fascinating because it shows a different vision for *Legend Of Zelda*: initially, the game consisted only of the dungeon levels, and this was the entrance to all of them, where the player could select where to go next.

The third image is labelled 'enemies', and is interesting not just for the first appearance of many *Zelda* creatures, but also because they're being created to scale: the graph paper indicates what size each enemy should be in the finished game – a useful guide for the programmers tasked with bringing Miyamoto's creations to life. Note also the blade trap and the drawing of the dungeon stairs.

The bottom image shows the first drawing of *The Legend Of Zelda*'s overworld – the left side is by Takashi Tezuka, and the right is by Shigeru Miyamoto. The two worked together, side by side, and completed this in a single sitting – using a permanent marker, hence the correction fluid visible at certain points. The tiny dots are individual rocks and trees, and if you look closely, even the Lost Woods is included here.

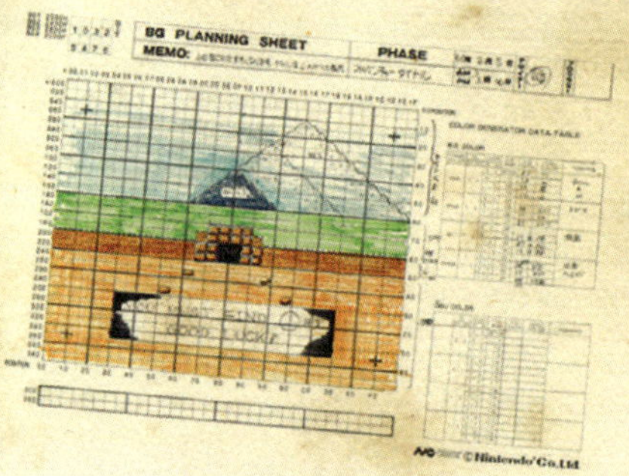

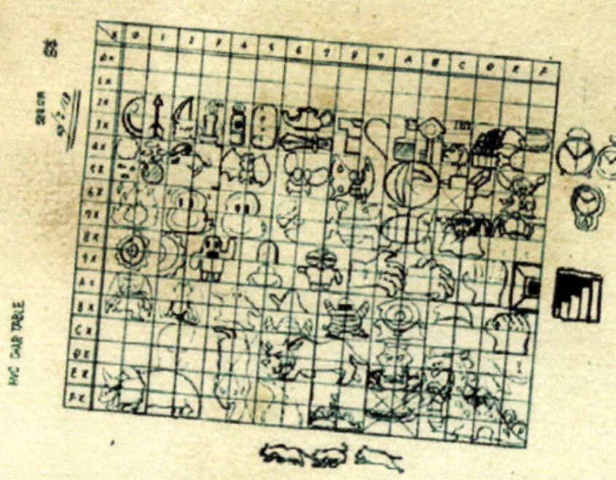

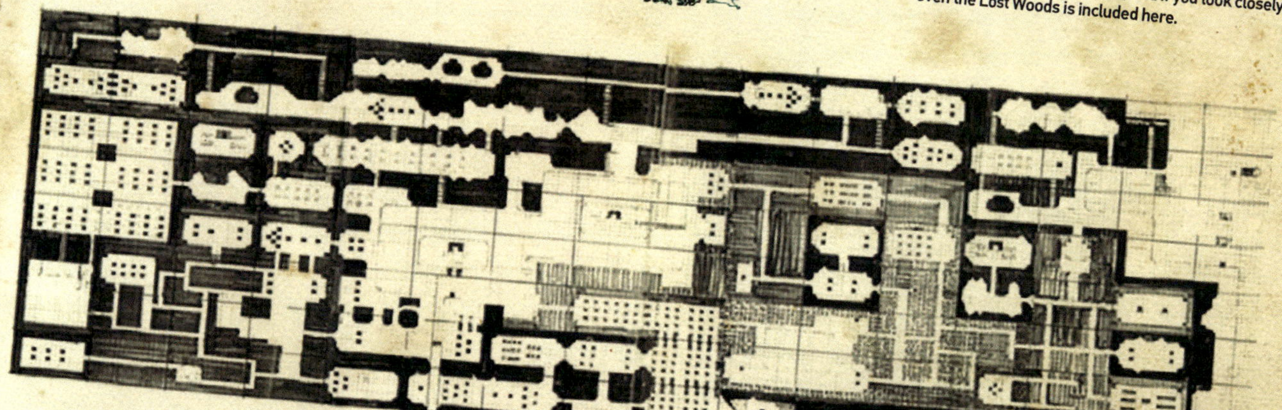

HOW LEGENDS ARE MADE

Amazing facts about gaming's great adventure

Last-minute arrangement

THE THEME TUNE of *Zelda* is one of the most famous in videogame history: but it was a quick fix. Koji Kondo had originally composed a variation on Maurice Ravel's 'Bolero' but, at the last minute, learned that the copyright for the work had not expired. Paying for the rights was out of the question, so Kondo set himself to composing a new theme – and in a day, the *Zelda* overworld tune was complete. Interestingly, the copyright had expired when *Ocarina Of Time* was in development, and Kondo returned to 'Bolero' for the Bolero Of Fire theme in that game.

What's in a name?

ZELDA WAS AN extremely popular name in the US at the turn of the 20th Century, and one of the babies named thus was the future wife of the great novelist F Scott Fitzgerald. It derives from the Old Germanic name Griselda, which roughly translates into 'Dark Battle'. But the appeal for Miyamoto was simpler: "Zelda was the name of the wife of F Scott Fitzgerald. She was a famous and beautiful woman by all accounts, and I liked the sound of her name. So I took the liberty of using it for the very first *Zelda* title."

The Bull Demon King

GANON MAKES HIS first appearance in *The Legend Of Zelda*, but also turns up in the very first concept sketches for the game. The images are called 'Hakkai' – a clear reference to Chohakkai, a piglike character from a Chinese novel called *Saiyuki*, well-known in Japan – though in another note he's called the 'Bull Demon King'. In *The Legend Of Zelda*, Ganon has stolen the Triforce Of Power, and Zelda has broken the Triforce Of Wisdom into eight parts to protect it: it falls to Link to defeat Ganon and unify the sacred relic. In the first game, curiously enough, the Triforce consists of only these two parts: in later instalments, Link is the bearer of the Triforce Of Courage.

An old friend

IMPA, THE NURSEMAID of Princess Zelda first appears canonically in-game with *Skyward Sword* – but she was there from the very start. In the original game's instruction manual, Impa sets out to find Link on Zelda's instructions – "The one who can save them." Ganon sends his men after her, and they finally corner the old woman, but she's saved by a strange boy who chases the villains away. Knowing she has found Link, she tells him the whole story of Ganon's betrayal – and so begins a grand adventure.

The Golden Triangle

THE TRIFORCE RESEMBLES a traditional Japanese kamon, which is the equivalent of a coat-of-arms – and the Triforce is remarkably similar to the kamon of the Hojo clan, a major player in Japan's medieval history. The similarities are obvious, but there's no more to be read into it than that. What is fascinating, however, is that following *Zelda*'s success, Miyamoto, Tezuka and Toshihiko Nagako were nicknamed 'The Golden Triangle' internally, for their knack for producing hits.

Sounds good

THE JAPANESE FAMICOM'S second controller had a built-in mic, not reproduced in its western versions, which could be used to weaken an enemy called Pol's Voices – by shouting (or, more simply, blowing) into it. Confusingly, the western manuals still made reference to this, saying Pol's Voice 'hates loud noise' – when all we had to do was spear it with an arrow. Many players, understandably, made Link blow his recorder till blue in the face – all to no avail.

"The word Link was chosen to indicate that the character is a blank slate, a mute hero defined by the actions of the player"

▶ Miyamoto said he wanted to give players "a miniature garden they can put inside their drawers" and, to that end, its open world really was open – a massive 128 screens, and eight dungeons that could be completed in any order: players ended up exploring because they were unsure where to go next, a new kind of freedom. A new challenge.

It was such a change from the norm that Nintendo worked with a publisher on a 'tips and tricks' book, perhaps the world's first videogame strategy guide, and the Nintendo hotline had dedicated *Zelda* staff. The most-asked question was about a Goriya, a monster with a badly-translated line of dialogue: "Grumble Grumble." What could you do? The answer was simple when you knew: it needed feeding. Callers would be asked what they'd do if their stomach was rumbling. It's not GameFAQs or YouTube, is it?

Zelda's creators were not sure what the reaction would be to a game that demanded such a patient approach: "*The Legend Of Zelda* was our first game that forced the players to think about what they should do next," recalled Miyamoto. "We were afraid that gamers would become bored and stressed by the new concept. Luckily, they reacted the total opposite."

What is most remarkable about *The Legend Of Zelda* now is how fully formed it was: it created a template that the series has followed since with spectacular results. The dungeons and items, the progression and even the bare story outlines – all now seem as inevitable as the morning. Even

the enemies were all there: rock-spitting Octoroks, burrowing Leevers that burst from the sand, boomerang-tossing Goriyas, Gibdo mummies, Peahats with weird propeller heads floating, the Stalfos skeleton warriors, Tektites skittering and hopping around, and Moblins – the grotesque and deadly spear-chucking army of Ganon. And the strangest, most unsettling foe of all was the Wallmaster – a disembodied, ghoulish hand that would grab Link mid-dungeon and deposit him back at the start.

And there is Link himself: one of the greatest characters in the world of gaming. His naming was chosen to indicate that the character is a blank slate, a largely mute adventurer defined by the actions of the player – their own presence and door into the game world. Link is a character, but he's much more of an avatar of the player – Miyamoto wanted players to envision themselves in this exciting world, rather than another bug-eyed cartoon character. Players shouldn't just control Link: they should see a part of themselves, whether a curious child or a wide-eyed adult.

The Legend Of Zelda, a series that has enjoyed almost 40 years in the spotlight, is many things. Loved by critics and players of all ages alike and selling in the millions, it's now arguably the most brilliant jewel in Nintendo's crown and a cultural phenomenon: you can hug a Link plushie, buy a replica of the Ocarina Of Time, or hear an orchestra play its music in the grandest concert hall. However, people love *The Legend Of Zelda* – and that's not too strong a word – for a different reason. They love it because, more than any other game, and from its beginnings, *The Legend Of Zelda* embodied something **that *everyone* wants, something that simply being human makes you ache for. It's an awfully big adventure.**

LEGENDARY INFLUENCES

Two primitive inspirations for Zelda

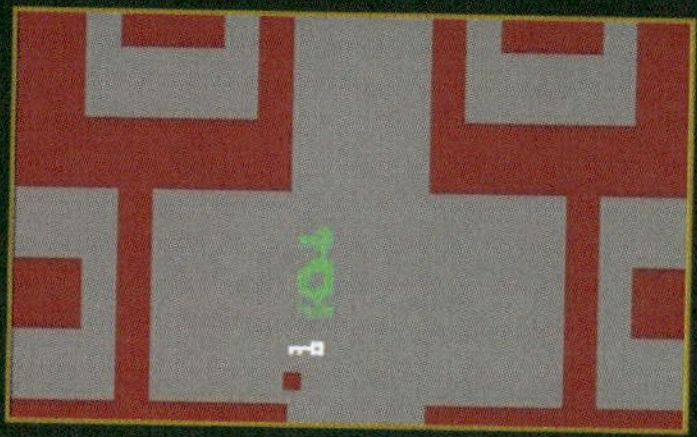

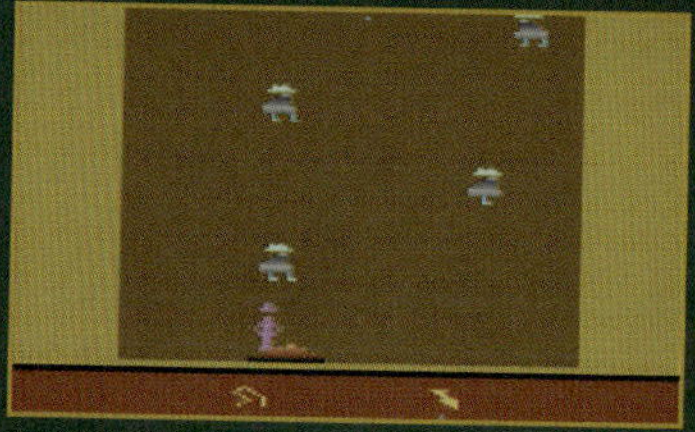

Adventure
(ATARI 2600)

CONSIDERED THE FIRST action adventure game – the genre that *Zelda* would make its own – *Adventure* was inspired by the text game *Colossal Cave Adventure*. Designer Warren Robinett pioneered much in *Adventure*, including gaming's first Easter egg (he wasn't credited for his work, so he slipped his name in secretly), but it's the dungeons and interlocking items that influence *Zelda*. *Adventure* had a simple objective – retrieve the golden chalice – but in order to do this there are a number of items and tricks to discover and use correctly. These days, *Adventure* seems incredibly simple, but its basic principle of building complex systems around seemingly simple items would serve *Zelda* well.

Raiders of the Lost Ark
(ATARI 2600)

THIS SWASHBUCKLING ADVENTURE was one of Shigeru Miyamoto's favourite movies, and the tie-in game for the Atari 2600 was the very first movie licence based on the game: strangely enough, given their subsequent history, it wasn't half bad. The interest here is in its structure and defiance of the Atari 2600's limitations: you had to guide Indiana Jones through a top-down environment while collecting items to progress further, all the while using two joysticks rather than one. The Atari console simply didn't have enough buttons. In truth, it's not a great game to play today, but Miyamoto likely tried it, and its influence on *Zelda*'s dungeon design is clear.

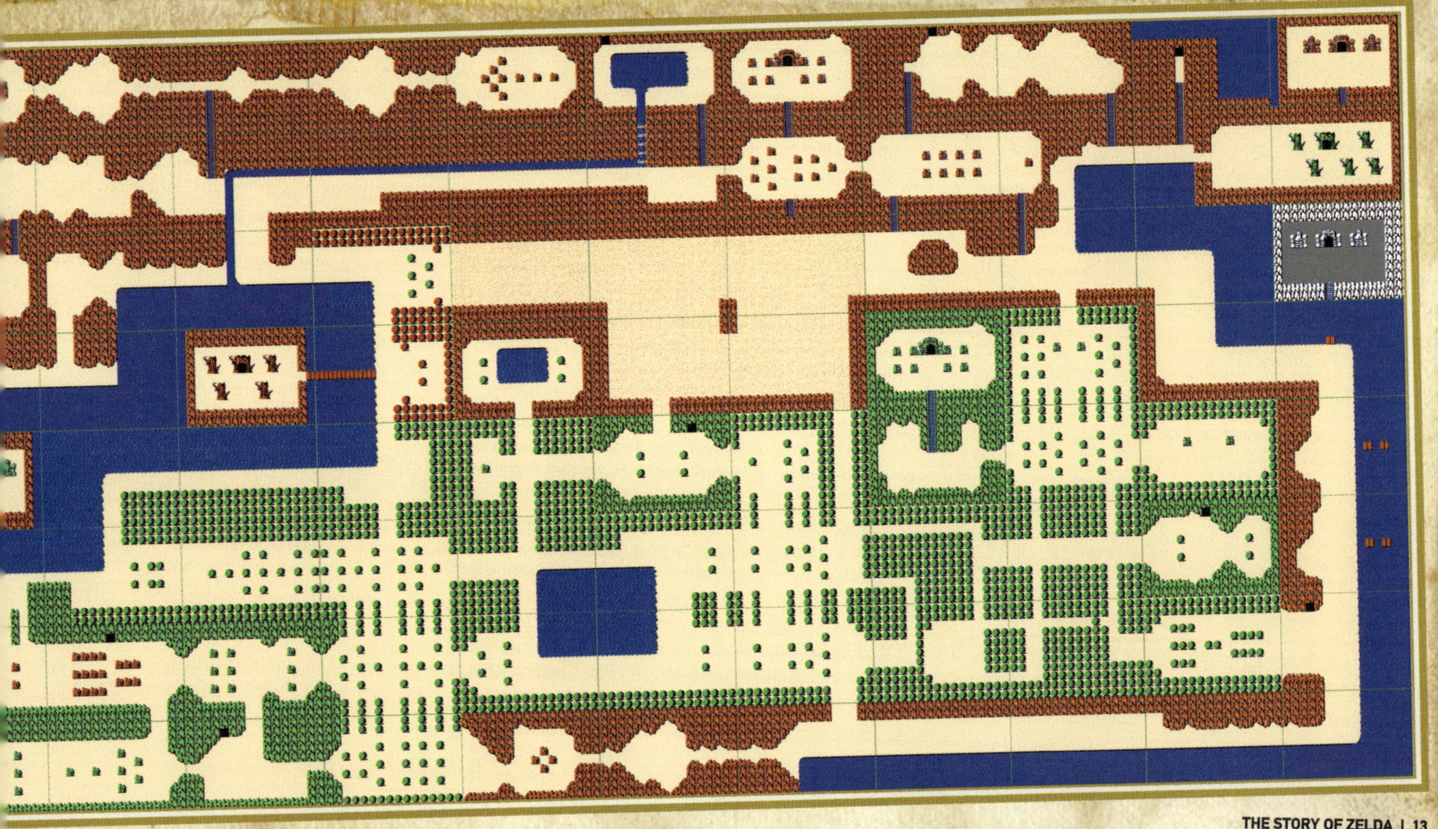

ANATOMY OF LINK

What is it about the hero of Hyrule that makes him one of greatest characters in gaming?

WORDS BY NICK THORPE

HERO PROFILE

NAME: LINK
FIRST APPEARANCE: THE LEGEND OF ZELDA
LAST SEEN IN: TEARS OF THE KINGDOM
FINEST HOURS: A LINK TO THE PAST, OCARINA OF TIME, BREATH OF THE WILD
NOTABLE FOR: GREEN TUNICS, GANON-SLAYING, BREAKING POTS

A persistent evil dwells in the kingdom of Hyrule, an ancient, primordial force of malevolence that rises time and again to claim dominion over the land and all who dwell there. Over the course of centuries, the ordinary people of the kingdom have come to fear and dread the name of Ganon, usually as his previous appearance has faded from living memory. But while this wicked spirit cannot be truly extinguished, there exists a counterpart whose role is to turn back this menace, no matter how bleak the situation may have become – and that personification of virtue is Link.

Link's world-saving adventures often involve common elements: the need to rescue Princess Zelda, the fight against Ganon and the use of items including the Master Sword and the Triforce. But quite often his methods of achieving these goals differ between games – he may time travel, navigate the ocean or even transform into a wolf. That's because Link is not a single hero, but instead the latest in a long line of legendary champions to bear the name. This means that Nintendo has always had a plausible storyline basis to revise Link's appearance and abilities between games, and rarely has to contrive a reason to strip him of his skills and experience, but it's not just useful from a game design perspective.

The fact that you're always playing as a new iteration of Link also serves to level the playing field. Whenever you start a new *Zelda* game, it doesn't matter whether you're an experienced veteran of the series or a brand-new player – everybody starts from the same place. Nobody has to remember what happened in the previous game because Link rarely does; very few games in the *Zelda* series are direct sequels. Whenever you meet a new character for the first time, Link is doing exactly the same. There's a connecting thread that ties the whole story together if you're willing to look for it, and many people have spent a lot of time doing exactly that, but there's no need to concern yourself with it if you just want to have a good time with a *Zelda* game.

But despite the fact that nothing has to be the same from game to game, many elements often are. Very rarely does a game start with Link explicitly given the aim of saving his world. Link is usually young, anywhere from about ten years old to a teenager/young adult, and more often than not, he's considered to be rather lazy by those around him. In fact, it's uncommon for him to even be ready for combat, as in many games one of his first quests will typically involve finding a sword and shield to actually fight with. But before long, he will be drawn into the greater quest, and along the way, he'll usually master a variety of new items and abilities along his long route to victory.

Another thing that seldom changes is Link's verbosity, or lack of it. Link isn't strictly mute a lot of the time, in that other characters can hear what he's saying and respond to him, and he tends to be portrayed as being brave and compassionate in these interactions. But beyond those broad brush strokes of personality, Link's actual words are never revealed to the player, with Nintendo's developers claiming that this is to better allow players to identify with the character and imagine their own interpretation of his conversations.

Indeed, Link is meant to be a character that players can easily project themselves onto, and as the star of action-packed adventures, we can readily identify with Link's accomplishments and development as our own. While he'll grow more resilient by collecting hearts and gain additional power by upgrading his sword, whenever you finally solve a tricky dungeon or best a troublesome boss, it's a shared victory and a shared bit of development. Link's wisdom is your wisdom, and likewise his fighting prowess.

At the most basic of levels, Link's various incarnations over the years have cast him as one of the most enduring heroic archetypes – an ordinary person who does extraordinary things. It's a reminder that heroes are made, not born – we don't have to be told that Link is a hero, because we watch him grow into one over the course of each game, and that's what makes him such an enduring icon of the gaming world. With his youth, he presents a world ripe with potential where you can carve your own path. With his skills, he allows us to perform athletic feats and combat manoeuvres that few of us could hope to pull off in real life. And with his silence, he invites us to step into his shoes – and even if we're just ordinary people playing a videogame, he enables us to become the heroes we wish to be.

> "We don't have to be told that Link is a hero, because we watch him grow into one over the course of each game"

» *Breath Of The Wild* reinvented Link slightly. His hair is longer and his iconic green tunic is missing until you solve all the shrines.

Hat
Link's long, soft hat makes him look a little like Peter Pan. The hair it hides is usually light, ranging from blonde to a sort of auburn shade, but occasionally this has to change for technical reasons – for example, in *The Legend Of Zelda: A Link To The Past*, palette limitations gave him pink hair.

Equipment
Link is something of a scavenger, often acquiring his equipment along the journey rather than setting out with a preferred set of arms. However, he will often find certain mainstay items in a number of his quests, including the Master Sword, the Hylian Shield, boomerangs, bombs and even bows and arrows.

Clothes
Link is most commonly seen wearing simple green clothes and brown boots that suggest an affinity for nature and the world around him – especially in games such as *The Legend Of Zelda: Ocarina Of Time*, where he grew up in a forest. The hue tends to vary, with the relative darkness often reflecting the game's tone.

Ears
While Link appears to be an ordinary human in most respects, his ears give away his Hylian heritage. They're pointy and elf-like, playing into the fantasy themes of the games, and in some games it's explained that his ears are able to hear the gods in a way that most inhabitants of Hyrule cannot.

Face
Link's face is interesting because it evolves so much over the series. He looks quite basic in the original *Zelda*, but as the series progresses more and more, character is revealed on his cute visage. It arguably reaches its height with the *The Wind Waker* where he is super-expressive thanks to the cartoon aesthetic.

HOLDING OUT FOR A HERO

Players were given Link's first sword along with this memorable message.

Link meets many helpful characters, but also odd ones like Tingle and 'Error' here.

Link's first 3D quest, *Ocarina Of Time*, is considered one of the best games ever.

In *The Wind Waker*, Link explored a vast ocean and even partook in combat at sea.

PREPARE FOR ADVENTURE

Link has very few powers or abilities of his own, so his methods of achieving victory over Ganon rest with the equipment and items he carries. Here are some of the notable ones you can find...

MIRROR SHIELD
This rather nifty shield doesn't just block physical attacks – its mirrored surface allows it to reflect light beams and some magic.

PEGASUS BOOTS
These boots allow Link to perform a high-speed dash, enabling him to break things and dislodge objects from tall places.

BOW AND ARROW
A classic piece of weaponry, which has a much longer range than Link's sword but also relies on limited arrows.

BOMB
Bombs also come in limited supplies, and enable Link to blow apart certain objects as well as performing explosive attacks.

BOOMERANG
This classic hunting tool is capable of stunning enemies as well as damaging them. Upgrade it for a magical boomerang that flies further.

MAGIC HAMMER
This speedy weapon has a very short range, making it more effective for bashing pegs – unless your enemy is frozen.

FIRE AND ICE RODS
These rods allow Link to use elemental magic, useful for both lighting torches and freezing enemies.

HOOKSHOT
One of Link's most unique items allows him to drag himself towards certain items, and to also pull enemies towards him.

BUG CATCHING NET
If you want to catch bees and bottle them, this is great – but fairies are much more useful for their healing powers.

LANTERN
The lantern is used to light the way when Link ventures into dark areas – and in some appearances, it's even a weapon.

POWER GLOVE
No, it's not a dodgy NES controller – this gauntlet grants Link the strength to pick up boulders as large as he is.

ZORA'S FLIPPERS
These are incredibly useful items – they enable Link to swim and allow him to make use of the Zora's special shortcuts.

MAGIC MIRROR
When Link visits the Dark World in *A Link To The Past*, this item gives him the power of instantly returning to his own world.

MAGIC CAPE
This useful item turns Link invisible as long as it's being worn – just be careful not to let your magic meter deplete.

BOMBOS MEDALLION
This magical charm allows Link to perform an enormously powerful fire attack sufficient to kill most enemies.

ETHER MEDALLION
When used, this medallion will helpfully freeze every enemy on screen. It's also useful to stop the rain, if you need to.

QUAKE MEDALLION
As you might have guessed by the name, this medallion enables Link to cause enormous earthquakes at will.

BOTTLE
Bottles aren't a particularly glamorous item, but you need them to store potions, fairies and other highly useful things.

HEART CONTAINER
Definitely one of the most useful items you can find as it increases Link's health by a full heart, allowing him to survive longer.

RUPEES
Money can be exchanged for goods and services – and weirdly, can often be found at random when cutting grass.

MASTER SWORD
The sword of legend that has the power to seal Ganon away. This is always an upgrade over Link's default sword.

THE HISTORY OF ZELDA

When a new Zelda title is revealed, the gaming world takes note. Few series in videogames hold a spell over us like Nintendo's epic series, and it is still going strong today as it heads closer towards its 40-year milestone. Join us as we celebrate one of gaming's greatest franchises

WORDS BY STUART HUNT AND NICK THORPE

Since his videogame debut in 1985 (save for the Virtual Boy), Link has always worked his little elfin boots off to ignite interest in every single piece of Nintendo hardware to ever find a release… and even some of the weird and wonderful contraptions that never left his native home ground of Japan. Even through a dark GameCube period, where seemingly infallible Nintendo IPs were somehow failing to capture that Nintendo magic, there was one licence that has always looked after its Nintendo Seal Of Quality. It's apt, then, that a *Zelda* game would close out the GameCube's life, and it was the first licence that Nintendo turned to as a 'proper' launch title for its much-hyped Switch.

Before Hyrule, videogames were usually single-screen worlds filled with bleeping and chirping sprites, where progression and skill were distinguished by stamping three letters into a list. And before *The Legend Of Zelda*, game narratives were generally spared a measly paragraph on an arcade cab or a few dubiously spelt words on a menu screen, and rules and stories would generally play out via easily digestible visuals and an ounce of common sense – escape the ghosts, shoot the crab-looking invader, avoid those asteroids.

Off the back of the unprecedented arcade success of *Donkey Kong*, Nintendo would be able to finance three pivotal projects that would transform it from a Hanafuda card manufacturer dabbling in the world of electronic entertainment, to a leading player in that very market almost overnight: the Famicom, *Super Mario Bros* and *The Legend Of Zelda*.

Zelda's development would begin at around the same time as *Super Mario Bros*, with Shigeru Miyamoto splitting his time between his divided development team and overseeing both projects. His early intention for *The Legend Of Zelda* was to create a sprawling 'virtual garden'; a videogame set inside a lush world that would grow and unfurl. The thinking, at that time, was that *Super Mario Bros* was going to offer an immediately accessible and technically unique gaming experience, and *The Legend Of Zelda* would offer gamers the freedom to essentially shape their own adventure.

Despite this peculiar juxtaposition of projects inside the camp, *Mario* and *Zelda* would both decide to do away with the element of quick-play high-score chasing and instead replace it with the notion of completion – ending the gaming experience and unlocking a reward screen for your troubles. It was a belief that wouldn't hold up inside the money-feeding world of arcade gaming, but one that Miyamoto believed was perfectly viable in the home.

Miyamoto grew up in the small town of Sonobe, in Kyoto, Japan – a picturesque upbringing that would offer the perfect place for his imaginative mind to wander. He was a keen artist with an affinity for music, architecture and design; passions that led him onto an academic road in industrial design and as a staff artist for Nintendo. But it was his fascination for exploration that he would try to impart to the player through *Zelda*.

His inspiration behind the dungeons – now a staple of the *Zelda* series – came from the many hours he would spend playing around the rooms of his home as a boy, and the crystal lakes and bountiful greenery of Hyrule from his recollections of exploring the vast fields nearby. Miyamoto's decision to use the name 'Zelda' was allegedly inspired by the wife of the American author F Scott Fitzgerald. Famously dubbed "the first American flapper", it was her wilful nature that Miyamoto would find so endearing, and persuade him to select her as the muse for the titular princess.

As with *Donkey Kong* and *Super Mario Bros*, Miyamoto would polarise *Zelda*'s story around three central characters: a hero (Link), a heroine (Princess Zelda) and a villain (Ganon). Again it would look to an unusual hero (a young elf-like boy) to embark on the quest. Link's involvement in the story comes about after he spots an old woman being attacked and quickly jumps to her aid. He discovers that the woman's name is Impa and that she is a porter to the Princess Of Hyrule. He then hears news of the ensnared princess at the nefarious trotters of Ganon and learns of the warlord's evil intentions for the Triforce and the land of Hyrule. Link duly agrees to seek out the eight segments of the Triforce Of Wisdom and ventures to the top of Death Mountain where Ganon awaits.

In the first game, the Triforce is described as 'three magical triangles' capable of granting great power to their bearer. But ▶

» *The Legend Of Zelda* satisfied Miyamoto's love of exploring. It remains a superb NES game.

A LINK TO THE PALM

We take a quick look at some of link's best portable adventures

The Legend Of Zelda: Link's Awakening

RELEASED: 1993
SYSTEM: GAME BOY

THE FIRST, AND what many fans consider the best, portable *Zelda* game. *Link's Awakening* was a dazzling GB follow-up to *A Link To The Past* that would mark the first time that the series would ever play an away game, and *Zelda* and the Triforce would get left on the sub's bench. It's also the first *Zelda* game not to be directed by Miyamoto – possibly why it has a lot of Mario imagery in it. Link is marooned on the strange island of Koholint, where he learns of the mysterious Wind Fish; a giant guppy that lives inside an egg sitting aloft a volcano. Legend has it that when the fish is awoken he will be mighty peeved and the island will disappear, so Link and an owl set off to find an orchestra of instruments and aim to wake up the slumbering Fish to put the myth to the test. There's a great Nintendo Switch remake you can try today.

The Legend Of Zelda: A Link To The Past & Four Swords

RELEASED: 2003
SYSTEM: GAME BOY ADVANCE

MARKING THE START of a crossover between the Game Boy Advance and the GameCube, Flagship was at it again with this sublime double-pack that housed a brilliant redux of the SNES classic and a multiplayer add-on in *Four Swords*. *Four Swords* allowed two to four players to link up their GBAs, take control of a Link and work together to crack its clever colour-themed puzzles. Adopting *The Wind Waker*'s chipper 'Toon Link' look, the game would also introduce a new villain in Vaati, who would become an insidious mainstay in the *Four Swords* series.

The Legend Of Zelda: Link's Awakening DX

RELEASED: 1998
SYSTEM: GAME BOY COLOUR

ADDING ITS NAME to the Game Boy Color's Deluxe series, *Link's Awakening DX* is a coloured-in, spruced-up port of the Game Boy original. As well as improving the visuals (which looked pretty fantastic to begin with) Nintendo also added a few new additions to the game, most notably a new 'Color Dungeon', which made use of colour-based puzzles, and a camera shop and photo album function that made use of the Game Boy Printer.

The Legend Of Zelda: The Minish Cap

RELEASED: 2004
SYSTEM: GAME BOY ADVANCE

JUST TO MAKE things confusing for everyone, *The Minish Cap* marks the final game in Flagship's *Four Swords* trilogy, but is actually placed way back in the timeline. In terms of narrative – sages being mysteriously transformed into talking caps, Link shrinking in size and then bafflingly transforming into a large sphere – it is all a little bit strange, but it all makes for another quality *Zelda* caper. Graphically, with a closer camera, picking up the brilliant hues and attention to detail packed into the game, *The Minish Cap* is probably the best-looking *Zelda* handheld game.

The Legend Of Zelda: Oracle Of Seasons/ Oracle of Ages

RELEASED: 2001
SYSTEM: GAME BOY COLOR/ GAME BOY ADVANCE

RELEASED CONSECUTIVELY, *ORACLE Of Ages* and *Oracle Of Seasons* were the first handheld *Zelda* games not to be developed by Nintendo. Instead, the Capcom studio Flagship took reins. The *Oracle* series started out as a planned Triforce trilogy; three games where your actions in one game have an influence on the others. Because of the complexity in achieving this, the idea was later scrapped and the trilogy became a duo. Through use of a password system, the influencing elements would remain.

The Legend Of Zelda: Phantom Hourglass

RELEASED: 2007
SYSTEM: DS

MAKING INSPIRED USE of the Nintendo DS's touchscreen capabilities, *The Legend Of Zelda: Phantom Hourglass* shows us how great a *Zelda* game can be when Nintendo builds it specifically around its hardware. A direct sequel to *Wind Waker*, seafaring elements would again play a strong role, with the stylus being used to plot your journey and jot down notes and reminders on the game map. Couple this with a brilliant story, lush visuals and quirky puzzles and *Phantom Hourglass* maintains *Zelda*'s impeccable handheld lineage.

» *Four Swords Adventures* on the GameCube allowed four friends to link up their GBAs and go off to do their own thing.

» *Four Swords Adventures* introduced a unique strategy element to the combat of *Zelda*. While teamwork was essential, it soon went to pot once everyone started fighting over rupees.

its mythology and origins would continue to evolve throughout the series. Essentially, the Triforce is the catalyst, the object of desire that brings and binds the story and characters together. Inside Hyrule, there exist three parts to the Triforce: the Triforce Of Power that Ganon acquires during his siege on Hyrule castle, the Triforce Of Wisdom, which is the part Link is seeking inside the dungeons beneath Hyrule, and the Triforce Of Courage, which would first make an appearance in *Zelda II: The Adventure Of Link*.

The Legend Of Zelda was first released in 1986 on the Famicom Disk System, a secondary disk drive that made use of rewritable disks, which never found a release outside of Japan. In the west, the game came pressed on majestic gold cartridges that incorporated an internal battery facility to save game data, and it would become the first game cartridge to do this.

Miyamoto's notion to have the game feel completely bilinear was very apparent. Dropped into a huge overhead world, paved with little direction, it would be left to the player to decipher *Zelda*'s modus through consideration and natural exploration alone; a mantra that actually caused a bout of anxiety in the prolific game designer when the game was eventually released.

"I remember that we were very nervous because *The Legend Of Zelda* was our first game that forced players to think about what they should do next," Miyamoto revealed to *Superplay* magazine. "We were afraid gamers would become bored and stressed by the new concept. Luckily, they reacted the total opposite. It was these elements that made the game so popular, and today, gamers tell us how fun the *Zelda* riddles are, and how happy they become when they have solved a task and proceeded with the adventure. It makes me a happy producer!"

But Miyamoto needn't have worried. Graduating with honours alongside its developmental classmate *Super Mario Bros*, *The Legend Of Zelda* would go on to be successful for Nintendo, eventually grossing sales of 6 million copies.

THE MISSING LINKS

We take a look at some of the Zelda titles that slipped through the release net…

The Legend Of Zelda 64

Nintendo 64DD

Originally said to be a launch title for the Nintendo 64DD, *The Legend Of Zelda 64* was rumoured to have been a weird coaxial of *Ocarina Of Time* and *Majora's Mask*. Long delays and a lack of confidence in the hardware would force Nintendo to cram the game on to a large N64 cart and release it as *Ocarina Of Time* instead.

Zelda: Gaiden

Nintendo 64DD

Rumoured to be a very early sequel to *Ocarina Of Time* that would make full use of the Nintendo 64DD's advanced memory system, this Nintendo 64DD *Zelda* project was again switched to standard N64 carts and would be released as *Majora's Mask*.

Ura Zelda

Nintendo 64DD

Picking up where *Ocarina* left off, this add-on pack originally intended for the Nintendo 64DD was to chronicle Link's mission to find the Triforce. It would later find a release in the form of the *Master Quest* bonus disc and was released with *The Wind Waker*.

The Legend Of Zelda

Game Boy Color

Said to be developed by Capcom's studio Flagship, it's believed that inside the vaults of Nintendo headquarters lives an extremely sought-after Game Boy Color port of the original NES game. The rumours are likely untrue and it's probably an incredibly unfinished development build.

The Mystical Seed series/ Triforce Trilogy

Game Boy Colour

The two games from the *Oracle* series would originally be intended to be a series of three games called the *Mystical Seed* series. They were to be named after the three seeds of Power, Courage and Wisdom. One game was eventually dropped and Flagship would release them as two games.

Zelda III

NES

Apparently, before releasing *A Link To The Past* on the Super Nintendo, it's believed that Nintendo was actually working on another *Zelda* game for the NES that was said to marry elements of the first two games. It's believed that its bones were later used to create *Link's Awakening*.

THE MANY LEGENDS OF ZELDA

The Legend Of Zelda 1986

THE EVIL PIG-FACED Ganon has invaded Hyrule Kingdom and kidnapped the Princess Zelda. During the siege, he steals the all-important Triforce Of Power. But it transpires that a cunning Zelda somehow managed to shatter her Triforce Of Wisdom and scatter its parts around the dungeons of Hyrule. When Link gets wind of this, he vows to collect up the pieces, glue them back together and go and save the princess.

Zelda II: The Adventure Of Link 1987

LENDING QUITE A bit from Sleeping Beauty, Link is trying to wake Princess Zelda from a potent sleeping spell cast on her by a powerful sorcerer. The evil mage is holed up inside the ruins of the Great Palace and has locked the door using magic. It's up to Link to seek out the scattered shards of the Magic Crystal in Hyrule, break the seal, fight a doppelgänger and then restore peace to Hyrule Kingdom.

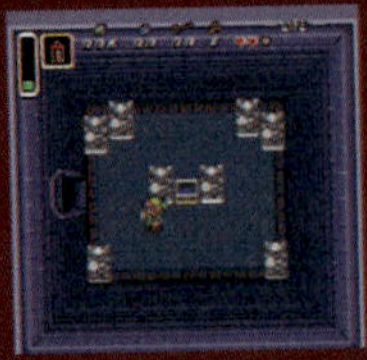

The Legend Of Zelda: A Link To The Past 1991

THANKS TO AN evil sorcerer named Agahnim, Ganon has returned from the darkness – and this time he has a pitchfork with him! Agahnim has also dethroned the king of Hyrule, kidnapped his daughter Zelda and opened up a portal to the Golden Land that has allowed a whole bunch of evil to flood in and wreak havoc in the once peaceful land of Hyrule. It's up to Link to save the day.

The Legend Of Zelda: Ocarina Of Time 1998

GANON'S BACK ONCE again in *Ocarina Of Time*, and this time he's up to his old megalomaniac tricks, so Link's on a mission to banish him to the Dark World forever (well, at least until the next *Zelda* release, that is). To do this, Link requires the power of the Seven Sages, and to find them he must travel in time between child and adult forms making changes in one time that will have a knock-on effect on the next.

The Legend Of Zelda: Majora's Mask 2000

LINK IS CAST into an alternative world known as Termina (picture a slightly more odd version of Hyrule) in his search for his fairy, Navi. But when he arrives, he soon discovers that the world, in only three days time, will be levelled to dust by its gurning moon. With just 72 hours on the clock, Link must work fast to locate Majora's Mask and save the world and its people from an imminent moon-crushing.

The Legend Of Zelda: The Wind Waker 2002

IN THIS NAUTICAL adventure, Link is on a mission to rescue his sister, who has been abducted. Surrounded by miles of water, and using the power of the Wind Waker – which gives Link the power to change the course of the wind – Link must venture out into the big blue ocean and travel to different islands to find out who it is that's holding her captive.

The Legend Of Zelda: Twilight Princess 2006

WHEN LINK AND his friends are attacked by a posse of monsters, Link wakes up to find his pals have been kidnapped. Miffed, he sets off to save them, and steps through the Twilight Realm where he's transformed into a wolf and imprisoned. He soon escapes, but learns that evil sorcerer Zant is trying to merge Hyrule with the Twilight Realm... spelling bad news for everyone, except for Zant.

As with Donkey Kong, Nintendo was quick to churn out a sequel while the popularity of the game was still in its infancy. A year later, *Zelda II: The Adventure Of Link* was released. Although Miyamoto would oversee the game's development, its creation would fall to a new development team, one who would switch the action from overhead to a side-on perspective and bathe it in subtle *Mario*-esque platform undertones – a change that proved to be unpopular with fans of the original. Its structure would remain generally similar to the first, though. It is another 'find several somethings' (nine crystals) to open 'something' (the Great Palace) that holds 'something with wish-granting properties' (the Triforce Of Courage) – and this is a structure that has been mirrored for almost every game in the series.

The Adventure Of Link would also introduce a few staples of the role-playing genre that would never really take off in the series. Link, for instance, could earn experience points to beef up his attacks, raise his stamina and also obtain magic points to cast spells. Additionally, the game also introduced village sections, where Link gathers information from locals wondering around the town, laying down a foundation for the many games that would follow.

» Puzzles are a staple of the series, as are strange statues with huge eyes.

In 1990, a new Nintendo console, the SNES, was breaking into the market rapidly. An early and pivotal partnership with Capcom – securing the machine ports of both *Street Fighter II* and *Final Fight* – bolstered by an impressive debut by *Super Mario Bros* would have everyone eagerly anticipating the end of Link's four-year absence from videogames. And Nintendo certainly wouldn't disappoint. Released in 1991, and into a swathe of praise, *A Link To The Past* is cited by many fans as the seminal game in the prolific *Legend Of Zelda* franchise.

The first two *Zelda* stories were the creations of Shigeru Miyamoto and fellow Nintendo game designer Takashi Tezuka. However, for *A Link To The Past*, Miyamoto would enlist the writing talents of producer Kensuke Tanabe. Link's SNES debut would mark a return of the popular overhead look of the first game, as well as introducing some loving tweaks to the visuals and controls. Link could now move diagonally, run (with the aid of Pegasus Boots), and the range of his sword attack was also improved. Perhaps the most notable aspect came from the game's deft use of its items. There was the new Hookshot, which Link could use to stun his enemies and pull himself across large gaps in the ground, the bow (which made an appearance in the first game but is used to greater effect here) and the Magic Mirror, which Link can use to shift between The Light World: a colourful and lush depiction of Hyrule, and The Dark World: a dank and nightmarish vision painted with skulls, oily looking marshes and menacing-looking trees. The game was packed with a dizzying array of sidequests, subplots and flourishes.

A Link To The Past also marks the first time in the series that the game's three main protagonists: Link, Zelda and Ganon are not the same incarnations seen in the previous games. It's set hundreds of years before the first game – as flipping the back

> "Zelda II introduced a few staples of the role-playing genre that would never really take off in the series"

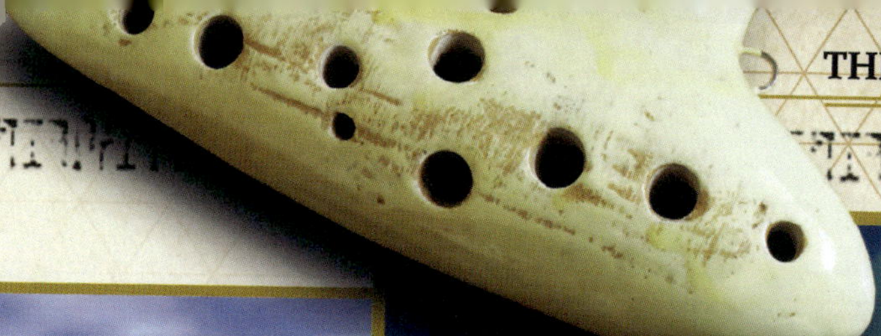

» Despite being the star of the *Ocarina Of Time*, Link's favourite wind instrument first appeared in *Link's Awakening*.

» *The Wind Waker*'s art style has aged better than other *Zelda* titles.

of the box states – our heroes are 'predecessors' to the original Link and Zelda, and this time-fudging has been a running theme throughout the series. This trend which runs through the early games seemed to be for Nintendo to release a *Zelda* game, set it in its own unique time and then follow it up with a quirky direct sequel. *Zelda II: The Adventure Of Link*, *Link's Awakening*, *Majora's Mask* and *Phantom Hourglass* are all direct sequels that adhere to this thinking. But for every third game, generally, the player will always be controlling a spiritual descendant of Link inside a game set in its own unique time; *A Link To The Past*, *Ocarina Of Time* and *The Wind Waker* again all back up this belief. It explains why it is that there's this peculiar sense that Nintendo is occasionally rewriting its story, and why characters in certain sequels react and communicate like they're meeting each other for the very first time.

For many, the series would never better *A Link To The Past*. And yet, despite the huge swathe of popularity that the game would glean, the Super Nintendo would receive only one western *Zelda* game in its lifetime. Nintendo would still cash in on the game's popularity in the east by releasing two *Zelda*-based games on its Satellaview system – a peculiar satellite modem for the SNES co-developed by Nintendo and Bandai. The first game, entitled *BS: The Legend Of Zelda*, was a downloadable four-part episodic remake of the original NES game but with a few subtle differences. First, the graphics and music were given a colourful facelift and a few elements of the gameplay (such as having it play out in real time, and increasing the capacity of Link's rupee purse) were also tweaked. It's often cited as 'The Third Quest', because of the way it messed with the dungeons, items and the size ratio of the overworld.

To cunningly boost awareness of the Satellaview, Nintendo would also opt to supplant the system's two mascots – a boy in a baseball cap and a girl with red hair – in the shoes of protagonists instead of Link. In 1997, Nintendo released a follow-up to the game, *BS The Legend Of Zelda: The Sacred Stones*, which again divided the game into four-weekly downloadable chunks. *Sacred Stones* is considered to be a sidequest to *A Link To The Past*, owing to the look and feel of the game. It retained the two Satellaview mascots as before and would set the player on a quest to find eight pieces of hallowed masonry and defeat a resurrected Ganon. Perhaps the most interesting aspect of the Satellaview games is that, like an interactive television show, they could only be played while the game was being aired. This allowed Nintendo to broadcast hints and tips to the player while they played to help assist them on their quest. As well as the Satellaview, it was always Nintendo's intention to produce a CD add-on for the Super Nintendo. Sony had developed the sound chip for the SNES (the SPC700) and had experience and grounding in CD technology, therefore, Nintendo's looking to Sony to get the project off the ground was really a case of natural selection. However, as the story goes, Sony was determined to break into the videogame market itself and had seen an ideal opportunity to do so when that early contract with Nintendo was drawn up. During that deal, Nintendo signed an agreement that would give Sony the rights to work on a CD-based console that would run both the planned SNES-CD games and also be backwards compatible with Super Nintendo carts. When Nintendo eventually realised this, it decided to attempt to sever ties with Sony and instead strike a deal with one of Sony's rivals: Philips.

After a messy legal battle, Nintendo successfully found a way to pull out of the contract. Eventually dropping the idea of releasing a CD component for the Super Nintendo, Nintendo would give Philips use of two of its IPs for a series of videogames for its CDi machine. Mario and Luigi would cordially appear in the puzzle game *Hotel Mario*, and Link and pals in three interactive movie-games: *Link: The Faces Of Evil*, *Wand Of Gamelon*, (released concurrently in 1993), and *Zelda's Adventure* (released a year later). The first two games (*Faces Of Evil* and *Wand Of Gamelon*) were side-scrolling action games, in the same vein of *Zelda II: The Adventure Of Link*, but spliced up with dated-looking cartoon sequences. For *Zelda's Adventure*, the original top-down approach was adopted but the game filled its boots with poorly prerendered computer-generated ▶

sprites and absolutely dire acting. Not surprisingly, given the games' prolific heritage, the Philips games were lambasted by the gaming press and fans of the series. Today they stand as weird curious entries, oddities amongst a collection of classics.

"Instead of thinking of it as making a game, think of it as nurturing a miniature garden called Hyrule," Miyamoto once about the making of *The Legend Of Zelda: Ocarina Of Time*. Ironically, many fans of the popular series would view *Ocarina* not as a brilliant nurturing of Hyrule but as a brilliant nurturing of Link. Released in 1998, and built from a drastically modified version of the *Super Mario 64* engine, *Majora's Mask* chronicled the biggest shift in the series to date, the transition from a 2D to a 3D realm, and a longer period in Link's life. Starting out as a boy, between the age of eight and nine, we would see Link's quest lead him into adulthood. But it's clear what Miyamoto was hinting at. Technically jaw-dropping draw distances, real-time light sourcing and expansive environments that could be covered effortlessly on Link's steed Epona and an almost faultless camera and control system; it's true that the world of Hyrule was never so brilliantly fleshed out.

The sequel to *Ocarina Of Time*, *Majora's Mask* (2000) introduced many firsts to the series. Originally titled '*Zelda: Gaiden*' in 1999, it was the first time, inside the main canon of games, that Nintendo would really break its 'Triforce Of Characters' (the first game to do so was *Link's Awakening* on the Game Boy). *Majora's Mask* doesn't include any physical incarnation of Ganon (although his name is mentioned) and Zelda's appearance is relatively brief in relation to the prevailing games in the series. Beginning life as an intended extra section of *Ocarina Of Time* (had the game been released on the Nintendo 64DD as originally intended), it heavily tweaked the *Zelda* structure and messed with the series' familiar Hylian setting. As a result, many fans viewed it as the most jarring game in the series. The graphic style of *Majora* is essentially *Ocarina* refined, with many of the same elements wholesaled across. The biggest difference between the two Nintendo 64 games is that in *Majora's Mask*, Link doesn't age (although there's a mask in the game that makes it possible) and the whole episode is set over just three videogame days. Link's mission is to prevent the destruction of Termina (a slightly more sophisticated alternative vision of Hyrule) from an ominous moon that in three days will destroy the town. With only three 'days' until the game ends it was necessary for Link to keep travelling back

THE DARK, THE PIG AND THE FABERGÉ EGG

Here's our rundown of Link's most common adversaries

Dark Link

Appeared as a villain in: *The Adventure Of Link, Ocarina Of Time, Oracle Of Ages, Four Swords Adventures and Twilight Princess.*

Dark Link (aka Shadow Link) is an ominous and mysterious villain that makes its first appearance as the final boss in *The Adventure Of Link*. Taking many different guises over the years – he's essentially an evil version of Link draped in darkness with glowing red eyes. Little is known about the origins of Dark Link, but if his appearance in *Ocarina Of Time* is anything to go by, then he seems symbiotic. So, if *Spider-Man* is anything to go by, we can assume it's an alien from outer space.

Ganon

Appeared as a villain in: *The Legend Of Zelda, The Adventure Of Link, A Link To The Past, Ocarina Of Time, the Oracle series, The Wind Waker, Four Swords Adventures, Twilight Princess, A Link Between Worlds and Breath Of The Wild.*

Ganon is Link's first and most prolific adversary. Kicking things off at the end of *The Legend Of Zelda* as a giant pig, he would retain this porky form up until *Ocarina Of Time*, where he would show his humanoid form: Ganondorf Dragmire. Ganondorf was the only male born into a guild of women thieves known as the Gerudo clan. Being the only male, he would become the 'King of Thieves' and would lead the Gerudo into taking over Hyrule. Without the power of the Moon Pearl to protect him, the Dark Realm would transform him into a powerful demon who resembles a pig, and he would take vengeance on Hyrule.

Vaati

Appeared as a villain in: *The Minish Cap, Four Swords and Four Swords Adventures.*

Vaati is the recurring villain of the *Four Swords* series, who, like Ganon, appears in many different forms. Beginning life as a Minish (a race of fairy-like creatures, also called the Picori) he would betray his master, Ezlo, by stealing his power cap and turning himself into a sorcerer. During the *Four Swords* series he can be seen in his original Minish form, his sorcerer shape and also three different variations of his demonic state: which look like a cluster of Fabergé eggs with demonic eyeballs painted on them. Absolutely terrifying.

"Wind Waker had a sense of humour, and took many aspects from the portable Zelda games"

THE A-Z OF ZELDA

A is for *A Link To The Past*
Link's seminal Super Nintendo *Zelda* adventure and a firm fan favourite

B is for Ballad Of The Wind Fish
The song which Link must play to rouse the Wind Fish in *Link's Awakening*.

C is for Crossbow Training
Link's Crossbow Training is a peculiar lightgun spin-off of *Twilight Princess* that comes bundled with the Wii Zapper.

D is for Death Mountain
The home of Link and Zelda's evil arch nemesis Ganon.

E is for Epona
The name of Link's noble steed that features in many of his adventures.

F is for *Four Swords* trilogy
A series of three spin-off *Zelda* games – *A Link To The Past & Four Swords, Four Swords Adventures* and *The Minish Cap* – that are all linked by The Four Sword.

G is for Ganon
The big bad of the series. He's initially a Gerudo schemer called Ganondorf before turning into the evil boar-like form of Ganon.

H is for Hyrule
The fictional land where the majority of *Zelda* games take place.

I is for Impa
Impa is the caretaker of Princess Zelda, and the old woman that Link saves in the original *The Legend Of Zelda*.

J is for Jabber Nut
The nut that Link must eat to understand the Minish language.

K is for Koholint
The setting of *Link's Awakening*, marks the first time a *Zelda* game wouldn't be set in the kingdom of Hyrule.

L is for Link
Steadfast, brave, full of gusto and dressed in green: the pointy-eared Link is the saviour of Hyrule.

» *Wind Waker* played musical flourishes whenever Link landed a sword strike, giving the adventure a swashbuckling feel.

» Many fools moaned about *Wind Waker's* cartoon aesthetic, so *Twilight Princess* went back to dark, muddy visuals.

in time, to the start of the first day, until his quest was complete. Oddly, despite the notion of time travel and rebirth being a strong mantra for the *Zelda* series, some would find it difficult to warm to *Majora's* confining time-travel structure and oppressive tone. That said, others consider it to be one of the most inventive and atmospheric games in the entire series.

If there were some fans that found it difficult to warm to the direction of *Majora's Mask*, then the next *Zelda* game was always destined to put a few noses out of joint. After the infamous *Legend Of Zelda: Space World* GameCube demo in 2000, which showed an impressively rendered sword fight between Link and Ganon, its sinewy graphical style of an adult Link had many fans believing they were going to get a darker *Zelda* adventure. However, the game they eventually got would look nothing like the teasing demo unveiled to Space World attendees. Taking the biggest shift in terms of visual style, *The Wind Waker*'s cel-shaded graphics would disgruntle fans who were expecting an epic and mature *Zelda* appendage. Ironically though, perhaps the biggest shift in the game came from its scrapping of certain *Zelda* gameplay elements. Instead of time travel, *The Wind Waker* uses the wind and the ocean for its puzzle and explorative elements, and rather than one large land to explore, it's split into islands connected by miles of sea that Link must traverse by sailboat. But *Wind Waker* also had a sense of humour, and took many aspects from the portable *Zelda* games, with more emphasis on characters and a feeling of being more accessible for newcomers. Its effusive and simple anime-style graphics captured the facial expressions of its characters better than any *Zelda* game before it, going lengths to invoke emotion, a real connection with Link, and cleverly serving as subtle hints to the player to help them solve puzzles. In a bid to perhaps soften that visual blow to its fans, Nintendo would accompany the game with a bonus disc containing the original *Ocarina Of Time* and *Ocarina Of Time/Master Quest* – a more arduous version of the N64 game that was intended to be released for the Nintendo 64DD.

Perhaps due to its basic look, the next *Zelda* game to appear on the GameCube came and went with generally little fanfare. Developed by Nintendo, *The Legend Of Zelda: Four Swords Adventures* took visual and multiplayer elements from the GBA game, *A Link To The Past & Four Swords* (see 'A Link To The Palm'), and brought an entirely new squad-based dynamic to the series. Slotting weirdly between two Game Boy Advance games, *Four Swords Adventures* would form the second game of *Zelda*'s *Four Swords* trilogy. It allowed one to four players (if you had a link-up cable and knew three people with a GBA) to control four differing coloured Links, position them into various formations and tier off to work together to solve the game's colour and teamwork-themed puzzles. The multiplayer emphasis of the game was further bolstered by a unique battle mode that allowed four friends to select a Link and duel to the death.

The next game to appear in Nintendo's popular series was the engaging *Twilight Princess*, a game that famously carried the weight of two consoles on its shoulders. After a one-year delay, *Twilight Princess* would prove a fantastic farewell to the GameCube, but sadly a tepid and awkward debut for the Wii. With *The Wind Waker*, Nintendo's intention was to make a *Zelda* game that anyone could finish, and as a result, many fans would bemoan the game for being far too easy. So Nintendo looked back to *Ocarina* as the blueprint for the style and direction of *Twilight Princess*. Running from a heavily tweaked *Wind Waker* engine, *Twilight Princess* looks to be the polar opposite to its GameCube sibling. In hindsight, it's actually a culmination of ideas and themes from the later *Zelda* games. It clearly borrows from *Ocarina Of Time* in terms of its visuals, adopts the darker tone of *Majora's Mask*, and boasts the scale and gameplay tweaks of *Wind Waker* – with regard to its cinematic look and continued use of facial expressions.

It was decided, mid-development, that the graphical style of the game would be altered. Early shots of the game showing ▶

M is for Master Sword
A purple-hilted heroic blade that Link wields in many of his adventures

N is for Navi
Link' companion throughout his adventure in *Ocarina Of Time*.

O is for Ocarina
The flute-type musical instrument that makes its first appearance in the Game Boy adventure, *Link's Awakening*.

P is for Picori
Also called Minish, these are sprite-like creatures that help link in *The Minish Cap*.

Q is for Queen Gohma
A larger version of the spider Gohmas that serves as a boss fight in the Deku Tree.

R is for Rupees
The ruby-like currency of *Zelda* that Link can acquire by killing enemies and cutting the grass.

S is for Satellaview
The SNES equivalent of Xbox Live or PlayStation Network, only released in Japan, home to two *Zelda*-based games.

T is for Triforce
This is the sacred triangular relic that binds the characters and events of *Zelda* together.

U is for Urbosa
Champion of the Gerudo tribe and controller of the Divine Beast Vah Naboris.

V is for Vaati
Is the villain in the *Four Swords* series. Like Ganon he takes two shapes: a human sorcerer and a monstrous form.

W is for Wind Waker
Wind Waker was the first *Zelda* game for the GameCube, and marked a dramatic shift in the visual style of the franchise.

X is for X-Shaped-Jewel
One of the relics needed to open up Holodrum's Tarm Ruins.

Y is for Yoshi
Yoshi appears in *Link's Awakening* as a sought-after cuddly toy that Link must win.

Z is for *Zelda: Gaiden*
Was the original working title for *Majora's Mask*.

Link inside a grey and desaturated **world would reaffirm to** fans that *Twilight Princess* was to **be a darker direction for the** series. However, the eventual graphical style would shift to a hazy world made of warm serene palettes, but that darker direction was kept. The game also contained more dungeons and more items than *Ocarina Of Time*, as was the intention by Nintendo to finally offer the hardcore *Zelda* fan a game to really test their mettle. While the Wii version is essentially an enhanced port of the GameCube release, the game would actually play out slightly differently; the game worlds were mirrored. Link has always been left-handed in the game, and if you were to look closely at the series, you'll notice that whatever direction Link is facing he will hold his sword in his left hand. With the advent of the Wii-remote controls in *Twilight Princess*, Nintendo realised that many players would be right-handed so would make Link a mirror to the player in the Wii version, and the game world would follow suit.

» *Link's Crossbow Training* was a pack-in title designed to show off the capabilities of the Wii Zapper.

With the exception of *Link's Crossbow Training*, a short game packed in with the Wii Zapper as a means of demonstrating the peripheral, Link would not return to the Wii for several years. In the meantime, the cartoonish Link of *Wind Waker* and *Minish Cap* continued to adventure on the Nintendo DS. The first of these was *Phantom Hourglass*, a successor to *Wind Waker* which retained much of the game's seafaring action. Link's pirate pal Tetra goes missing after the pair happen upon a ghost ship, which kickstarts a quest to save the girl and uncover the mystery of the phantom vessel. The biggest change was a touchscreen control method that saw players directing Link and performing combat moves using the stylus. Though some players disliked the lack of traditional controls using the d-pad and buttons, *Phantom Hourglass* received critical acclaim and sold over 4.1 million copies.

Given that success, it's unsurprising that the *Zelda* series returned to the DS in 2009 with *Spirit Tracks* – and once again, the stylus was the main input device. Instead of sailing the high seas, Link now found himself riding the rails as a train engineer with a mean sideline in swordplay, trying to discover why the titular *Spirit Tracks* that connected the kingdom were disappearing. Though this might seem a little out of place in a series that has usually had a fantasy focus and not drawn too much attention to technology, director Daiki Iwamoto was deliberately aiming for a different feeling to a regular *Zelda* game. The result was another success, though with 2.6 million sales it didn't quite match up to its predecessor's popularity.

Though Link's next game was not a new one, it generated considerable excitement as it was a remake of the game many still considered to be the greatest in the series. *Ocarina Of Time 3D* was a full visual overhaul of the N64 game for the 3DS, designed to take advantage of the added sense of depth offered by the new handheld hardware. The game was both a critical triumph and a sales success, selling over a million copies, but bigger things were coming as the *Zelda* series was about to return to the home console arena.

The Wii received *Skyward Sword* in 2011, making it a relatively late release in the console's life. Though *Skyward Sword* was not nearly as dark in tone as *Twilight Princess*, it didn't veer back into the overt cartoonishness of the cel-shaded *Wind Waker*. The tone was pitched closest to that of *Ocarina Of Time*, with a slightly more vibrant colour palette. The game is also the earliest in the *Zelda* story chronology, with Link and Zelda cast as childhood friends. When Zelda is kidnapped and taken down to the Surface, Link becomes entangled in the evil Ghirahim's plot to free the demon king Demise, and must prevent it to save Zelda and the world.

In order to add extra precision to the Wii controller's motion-sensing capabilities, *Skyward Sword* made use of the Wii MotionPlus add-on. The more accurate tracking played heavily into combat, with the Wii controller used for the sword itself and the shield controlled using the Wii Nunchuk. Likewise, the bow was now fired by pulling the remote back as you would the string in actual archery, and bombs could be rolled towards targets like bowling balls. Despite some reservations over the implementation of this new scheme, as well as a feeling that the rest of the game development community was finally beginning to catch up to the 3D *Zelda* mechanics, most reviewers were overwhelmingly positive about the game and it sold millions in short order.

Though the Wii was succeeded by the Wii U in late 2012, there was no early *Zelda* release, so GameCube remasters were released to plug the gap, *Wind Waker HD* in 2013 and *Twilight Princess HD* in 2016. Instead, new developments would take place on the 3DS, though they would also mine the past for inspiration. *A Link Between Worlds* was released in 2013 and served as a successor to *A Link To The Past*. Link's task was to prevent the theft of Hyrule's triforce by the inhabitants of the parallel world of Lorule, who seek to restore their kingdom after it falls into decay due to the destruction of their own Triforce. One fun mechanic introduced here was the ability to merge onto walls as a mural, allowing Link to cross otherwise impassable gaps. It was an excellent game and went on to sell over 4.2 million copies.

» *Hyrule Warriors* is actually pretty good fun. Plus, it gives Zelda a more active role in the action.

EVOLVING ZELDA

The Legend Of Zelda: Breath Of The Wild has reinvented the series for a new age – here's how…

1 Climbing is a major part of traversing the new open world – but Link will need enough stamina to reach the summit.

2 If you see an enemy with a deadly weapon, you can steal it once they're defeated, but it might not last long.

3 These items can be picked up and used to craft new items, for example by cooking delicious and health-replenishing meals.

4 Hyrule is bigger than ever, and you'll need to climb towers in order to reveal new points of interest on the map.

5 Link's clothes can be changed, both to increase his defence and to guard against the elements in harsh weather conditions.

6 If it gets too hot or too cold, Link will begin to take damage, but this can be mitigated by using the right items.

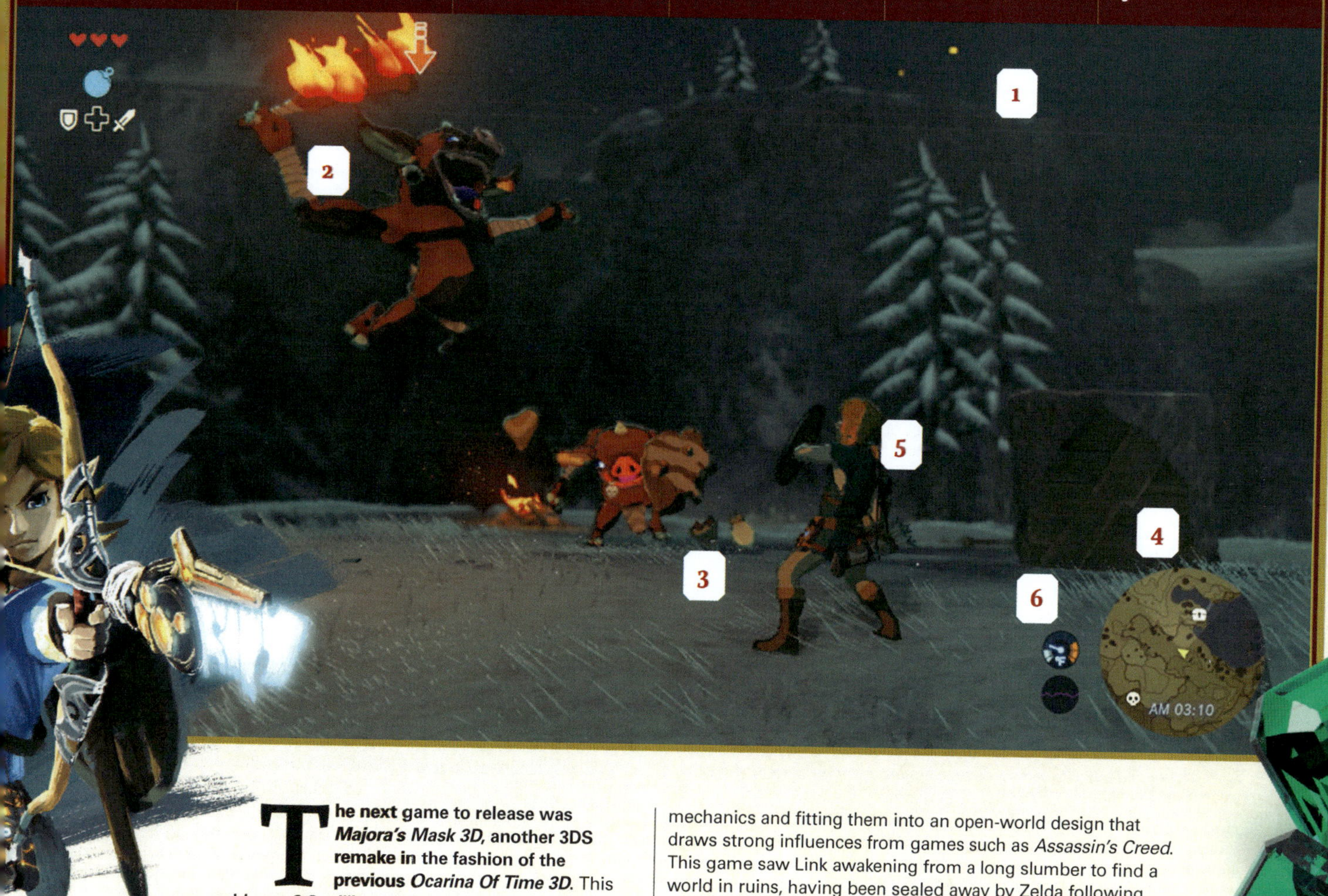

The next game to release was *Majora's Mask 3D*, another 3DS remake in the fashion of the previous *Ocarina Of Time 3D*. This sold over 3.3 million copies and was easily the most exciting *Zelda* development of 2015, as the year's other 3DS release was a rare misstep for the series. *Tri Force Heroes* focused on multiplayer cooperation in a similar manner to the prior *Four Swords* games and allowed players the option to play alone, via local wireless and even online. However, the game was stifled by its need to cater to the friendless, with few challenges truly testing a truly organised team. Additionally, much of the design was lifted from prior *Zelda* games with little innovation. Likewise, the spin-off *Hyrule Warriors* on Wii U was little more than the *Dynasty Warriors* games with a new skin, though it was popular enough to see a few sequels.

A lack of innovation is not something that troubled the most recent major game. Though it began life as a Wii U game and was revealed as such in 2014, *Breath Of The Wild* ended up carrying a new piece of hardware to glory, as the Nintendo Switch ended up as the system that most players would use to experience it. Released in 2017, the game was a radical reinvention of the series, taking the game's trademark mechanics and fitting them into an open-world design that draws strong influences from games such as *Assassin's Creed*. This game saw Link awakening from a long slumber to find a world in ruins, having been sealed away by Zelda following a heavy defeat by Ganon. To end the tyrant's influence over Hyrule, Link's goal was to defeat the Divine Beasts that had been corrupted by Ganon, release the spirits of the kingdom's champions and then slay Ganon himself. *Breath Of The Wild* was a critical success and also the bestselling *Zelda* game ever. A anticipated sequel, *Tears Of The Kingdom* is due this year.

So what is it that makes the *Zelda* series so popular? Why does every new chapter create such an air of excitement surrounding? Why do people meticulously dissect every screenshot, analyse and pore over every *Zelda*-related rumour and await the next chapter more so than any other videogame franchise to date? Miyamoto sums it up perfectly. "I think many people dream about becoming heroes", he told *Superplay* magazine in 2003. "For me it has always been important that the gamers grow together with Link, that there is a strong relationship between the one who holds the controller and the person on the screen. I have always tried to create the feeling that you really are in Hyrule. If you don't feel that way, it will lose some of its magic."

HYRULE HISTORY

Did you know the games have an established timeline? Here's a guide to Zelda's calamitous canon

WORDS BY DREW SLEEP

Nintendo didn't have plans for an overarching story to its *The Legend of Zelda* series. Originally, the games felt like a reinterpretation of the same tale, thanks to their similar stories and design. After all, this is a legend, and legends often change over time in real life.

Fans have debated about an established timeline within the *Zelda* series for decades, and in 2011 Nintendo revealed its official interpretation of the franchise's canon. It can get a bit convoluted, and now with the modern popularity of multiverses, you could say it was a little ahead of its time.

Here, we'll provide a guide to what happens when in the world of Hyrule.

THE LEGEND OF THE GODDESSES AND THE HERO

Skyward Sword 2011

The origin story of the Master Sword and the goddess Hylia's champion, Link. It also features Zelda awakening to her generations-long destiny as the mortal reincarnation of Hylia. At the end, the kingdom of Hyrule is established.

The Minish Cap 2004

Many years after *Skyward Sword*, the evil mage Vaati plots to unleash evil on Hyrule. The titular Minish, a race of tiny creatures also called the Picori, aid Link in his battle against Vaati by granting him the power to wield the Four Sword.

Four Swords 2002

Vaati escapes from imprisonment and kidnaps Zelda. Link unsheathes the Four Sword once again to save her, but in doing so, he splits into four. Vaati is defeated, and Link is made whole by returning the Four Sword to its resting place.

Ocarina Of Time 1998

Ganondorf arrives in Hyrule and threatens to conquer the world. Link travels between his future and present to overthrow the evil entity. At the climax, the timeline splits into three directions: one where Link fails to defeat Ganondorf, and two where he is successful – in one, he is absent, having journeyed back to his original time, and in the other, he remains in Hyrule, regaining his youthful form.

LINK IS VICTORIOUS

LINK IS DEFEATED

The Wind Waker 2002
Ganon returns, but there is no Link to defeat him. In response, the gods flood Hyrule to seal Ganon away. Generations later, a new Link and Zelda awaken to their destinies and discover a sunken Hyrule.

Phantom Hourglass 2007
Link and Tetra (the alter ego of Zelda) set sail in search of a new continent. On the way, they find a ghost ship that whisks Tetra away. Link embarks on a voyage to find Tetra and defeat a new foe, Bellum.

Spirit Tracks 2009
Link and Tetra establish a new Hyrule populated with trains. Many generations later, a new Link and Zelda investigate why the titular Spirit Tracks are vanishing. Together, the duo adventure across the land to defeat an ancient evil called Malladus.

CHILD TIMELINE

ADULT TIMELINE

Majora's Mask 2000
Following on from *Ocarina Of Time*, Link embarks on a quest to find his missing fairy Navi. On the way, he encounters Skull Kid, who transports him to the land of Termina. Link thwarts Skull Kid's apocalypse and continues to search for Navi.

Twilight Princess 2006
Imprisoned in the Twilight Realm, Ganon forces Midna, the Twilight Princess to flee to Hyrule. She encounters a ranch-hand, a descendant of Link, and together the two begin a journey to save the Twilight Realm and put an end to Ganon.

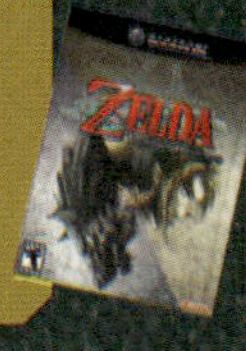

Four Swords Adventures 2004
Years after Ganon's defeat, Hyrule has made peace with the Gerudo tribe. However, a reincarnation of Ganondorf frees Vaati, and Link again separates into four heroes when he draws the Four Sword. Together, they defeat Vaati and seal Ganon within the Four Sword.

A NEW ERA

THE GREAT CALAMITY

Breath Of The Wild 2017
Millennia after the other stories, Hyrule prospers with new technology. Calamity Ganon awakens, however, and lays waste to Hyrule. Link is sealed away for 100 years, awakening to a ruined land. Together with Zelda, Link defeats Dark Beast Ganon, and the two vow to restore the land.

Tears Of The Kingdom 2023
Link and Zelda explore the ruins beneath Hyrule castle and inadvertently cause the Upheaval by awakening Ganondorf. Later, Link awakens on Great Sky Island with a new arm and discovers the kingdom below in crisis once again.

THE DECLINE OF HYRULE AND THE LAST HERO

A Link To The Past 1991
Seven sages seal Ganon and the completed Triforce into the Dark World. Years later, Agahnim, a dark wizard, deposes Hyrule's king and unleashes Ganon. Zelda calls out to a slumbering Link to save Hyrule. Ganon is defeated and the Triforce is restored.

Link's Awakening 1993
Link embarks on a journey to strengthen himself and is shipwrecked on Koholint island. To leave, Link assembles a series of instruments to awaken the Wind Fish. His adventure concludes as he wakes up clinging to some driftwood.

The Oracle Of Ages & Oracle Of Seasons 2001
Twinrova and their minions plot to resurrect Ganon by gathering magic flames and offering a human sacrifice. Link heads to two new lands to avert a calamity and rescue Princess Zelda from certain death.

A Link Between Worlds 2013
The wizard Yuga traps the Seven Sages in paintings. It's revealed Hilda, a dark counterpart of Zelda, sent Yuga to save her world of Lorule but the dark wizard had designs of his own. Link and Zelda restore the worlds of Hyrule and Lorule.

Tri Force Heroes 2015
Link adventures beyond Hyrule to the fashion-conscious land of Hytopia, where he encounters Princess Styla. Lady Maud, an evil witch, curses Styla to wear a brown bag and Link teams up with lookalikes to restore her fashion sense.

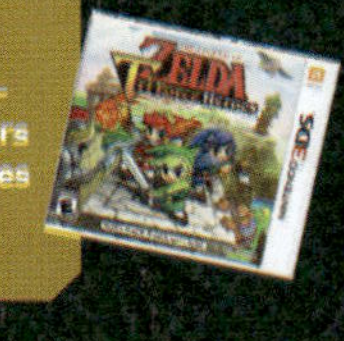

The Legend Of Zelda 1986
A revived Ganon leads an army upon Hyrule and steals the Triforce Of Power. Zelda splits her Triforce Of Wisdom into eight pieces, and Link begins a quest to assemble it again. Ganon is defeated by Link in Death Mountain.

Zelda II: The Adventure Of Link 1987
Link remains in Hyrule and six years after Ganon's defeat, the Triforce Of Courage awakens. Link travels to claim the Triforce and awaken (a confusingly different) Princess Zelda, who is suffering from a sleeping curse. Zelda wakes up, and Hyrule prospers.

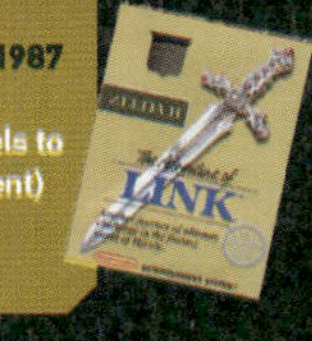

THE LEGEND OF ZELDA

STALFOS

Nintendo's masterpiece has enthralled us for almost 40 years. The original Legend Of Zelda isn't just an important piece of history but it's also a game that's still great to play today

WORDS BY ASHLEY DAY

OLD MAN

You really have to hand it to Miyamoto and his band at Nintendo. To make one of the greatest and most important videogames of all time, in the shape of *Super Mario Bros*, was one thing. But to repeat the same trick just a year later, and in a completely different genre, is just incredible.

In fact, there isn't even a year between *Super Mario Bros* and *The Legend Of Zelda*. There were only five months between the Japanese release dates of each game, yet the latter represents a giant stride from the former in terms of game design. Where Mario was brilliantly simple, placing you at the start of a linear journey and merely asking you to move a little plumber to the right, *Zelda* offered a world of possibility by comparison.

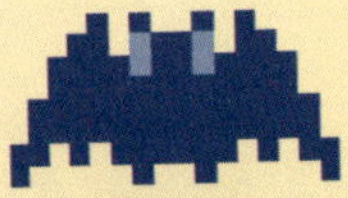
KEESE

Starting off in the middle of the vast land of Hyrule, it put you in control of an elf-like boy named Link, with three possible exits standing before him, and then... did nothing. No instructions, no dialogue and no hints. Just the promise of adventure and an invitation into the unknown. Which way should you go? Well, that was entirely up to you, and that was the entire point of the game. There was an ultimate goal, of course – to collect the eight scattered pieces of the Triforce Of Wisdom, defeat the evil warlord Ganon and rescue the titular Princess Zelda – but it was the open nature of how you approached this task that really made *The Legend Of Zelda* so compelling.

It's a well-known story that Miyamoto's inspiration for *Zelda* came from his childhood memories of exploring the Japanese countryside without a map and the pleasure that he got from discovering places he had no previous knowledge of. The goal of the *Zelda* project

LINK

LIKE LIKE

» The beginning moments are some of the most difficult. That tiny life bar won't get you far!

PEAHAT

» You're not told where to go, so it's up to you to locate and clear the game's dungeons.

DARKNUT

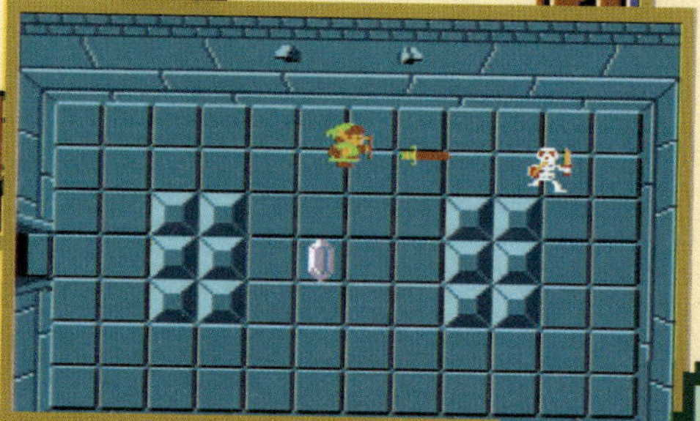

» Mercifully, if you die in a dungeon, you'll be placed at its beginning and not the start point in the overworld.

was to capture that childlike fascination with the unknown, the sense of wonder that the world can provoke when everything around you is so new and unusual. And that project also happened to fortuitously coincide with the development of the Famicom Disk System, Nintendo's Famicom add-on that side-stepped the rising cost of ROM chips and allowed developers to create much bigger games than before.

The Disk System's re-writable media also allowed for game progress to be permanently saved without the need for cumbersome passwords, and this was a crucial technological advantage that enabled Nintendo to further distinguish its console games from those of the arcades. Coin-operated arcade games were still the dominant form of videogaming in 1986 and were focused very much on short-term challenge, cyclical and repetitive gameplay, and the thrill of chasing a high score. But Nintendo wanted its games to be something different; something you played over a long period of time, returning to like a good book to enjoy an ever-evolving experience; a journey, rather than the same few setup over and over again.

This is very much how the modern videogame can be described over 35 years on, of course, but *The Legend Of Zelda* was one of the first games to truly offer that kind of deep, long-term experience. And it did it very well indeed. So many early videogames can be credited as the first to do one thing or another, but *Zelda* did it all, establishing the rules of the modern adventure game in such a style that, alongside its sequels, it remains brilliantly fun almost four decades later, while Nintendo's competitors were still playing catch-up.

It's not just the tantalising nature of Hyrule's open world that makes *Zelda* so appealing. It's the way Link's ever-increasing inventory and abilities open up new routes through that world, ensuring that it rewards progress with a steady stream of surprises and discoveries right up to the end. There's the contrast between the freedom of the overworld and the tightly focused structure of the dungeons beneath the ground. There's the way each weapon Link acquires has more than one obvious use, forcing you to experiment and be creative with the way you play. And, of course, there's the wealth of secrets ▶

ZOL

DODONGA

INSTANT EXPERT

■ *The Legend Of Zelda* is the most nonlinear adventure in the series, even compared to *Breath Of The Wild*. You can tackle the dungeons in almost any order you like, and the game can be finished without ever collecting the sword.

■ It was the first NES title to sell over a million copies and went on to sell 6.5 million in total.

■ Though the map for *Zelda*'s third dungeon resembles a swastika, it is actually the much more innocuous manji, an ancient religious symbol used by Japanese Buddhists, which is the reverse of the infamous emblem and is common in Eastern philosophy.

■ Link is an unusual hero in that, in the first game and canonically throughout the series, he is left-handed. Perhaps by coincidence, the word 'links' is German for 'left'.

■ Complete *The Legend Of Zelda* and you can play a second quest with different dungeon layouts and item placements. If you want to skip straight to it, enter your name as 'ZELDA' at the start.
Princess Zelda is named after Zelda Fitzgerald, wife of novelist Francis Scott Fitzgerald.

■ When *Zelda* arrived in the US and Europe, it was ported from disk to cartridge and became the first console game to include a battery to store save data.

ROPE

FAIRY

MOBLIN

LEEVER

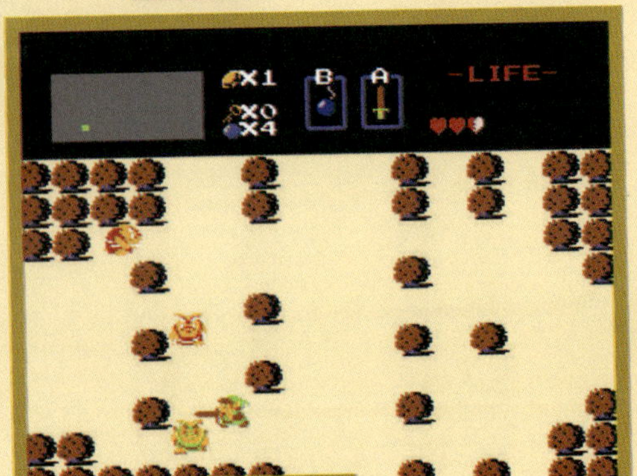

» Some areas of the overworld are packed with Moblins. Watch out for their spears!

that permeate the world, not just rewarding the player but encouraging them to dig deeper, play harder and uncover hidden treasures that make you feel like the best player in the world. It's a deeply personal feature that makes you feel special for finding those secrets and personalises the experience, even though those secrets are, in reality, accessible to everyone.

With almost four decades under its belt, the *Zelda* series has since gone from strength to strength, and many people have a favourite entry in the series that isn't the first one. *A Link To The Past*, *Link's Awakening*, *Ocarina Of Time* and *Breath Of The Wild* could all legitimately lay claim to the title of 'Greatest *Zelda*', but there's something pure about that first game that sets it apart from its successors. Right from *Zelda II* onward, the series began to change. It still retained the core features of an overworld, a series of dungeons and an expanding bag of tricks, but it also lost something along the way. As the series has become increasingly preoccupied with telling a story, you could argue that it has also limited itself, weighing its opening moments down with unnecessary dialogue and lengthy tutorials that

» This dragon boss is pretty easy to vanquish: just lay a few bombs at its feet and you'll be on your way to a Triforce piece.

actually distance you from Link instead of doing the opposite.

The Legend Of Zelda's real brilliance is that it has the confidence to just drop you into its world and leave you to explore, experimenting with its mysteries without any real hand-holding. Instead of simply telling you a story, it allows you to live the adventure; its events are driven by your decisions and actions. It feels unique, it rewards those who jump in at the deep end to go see what they can find, and it's a quality that the *Zelda* series would do well to nurture as it evolves.

ARMOS

POWER-UPS

Some of The Legend Of Zelda's pick-ups have endured throughout the series' history, while it never quite happened for others…

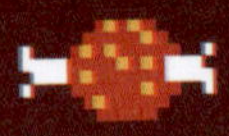

Bait

THIS MEAT IS bought from a shop and used to feed any Goriyas that block your path.

Bombs

THE BOMB CAN be used to hurt just about any enemy but can also be used to blast open secret entrances.

Boomerang

THE BOOMERANG HAS two uses. One to damage enemies, the other to retrieve distant objects.

Bow

THE BOW IS the only thing that can kill Ganon, at least once you've acquired the silver arrows for it.

Candle

THIS CAN LIGHT your way, but it can also be used to burn bushes, sometimes revealing secrets.

Ladder

THIS ITEM ALLOWS you to cross sections of river to take shortcuts and is essential for some dungeons.

Magic Book

AN OPTIONAL ITEM that upgrades the wand so that it can shoot fireballs, making candles redundant.

Magic Wand

IT'S A WAND! What more do we have to tell you? It uses your magic energy to shoot beams.

Potions

POTIONS COME IN two varieties: blue and red. Blue restores some of your life while the red replenishes it all.

Raft

ALLOWS LINK TO get around the waterways of Hyrule. He can embark or disembark the raft at any dock.

Rings

THESE, MUCH LIKE other magic items, can be found in two colours. Each increases Link's strength.

Shield

THE WOODEN SHIELD just repels ordinary attacks. The magic shield, however, can block fireballs.

Swords

THERE ARE THREE swords – Wooden, White and Magical – each one more powerful than the last.

Whistle

A SINGLE-USE ITEM that is essential for beating Digdogger, the boss of the fifth dungeon.

VIRE

MEMORABLE MOMENTS

We present the best bits of the best NES game Nintendo ever made

Signature tune

THE NOW-ICONIC *Zelda* theme slowly plays and builds up speed as a waterfall pours down the title screen. Koji Kondo's composition is yet another classic, leading to his involvement in every game in the series up until *Ocarina Of Time*.

Good advice

ONE OF THE few pieces of dialogue is also the most memorable. Though you can play the whole game without a sword, the old man's advice is right. You'll do much better with it, and what's a *Zelda* game without a sword? Later, you can obtain more powerful weaponry.

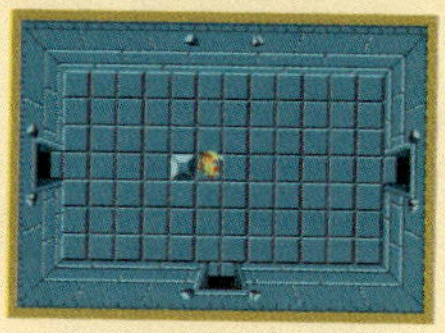

Secret exit

FINDING SECRETS IS one of *Zelda* series' greatest pleasures, not to mention one of its inspirations, and here's one of the earliest you can find in the game. A door without a keyhole is opened by pushing a seemingly ordinary block to the left.

Fairy godmother

FIND AN ENCLOSED pool and a fairy will pop out and rejuvenate Link's health with a swirl of hearts. It's another feature that has cropped up time and again through the series, with the fairies' abilities and applications expanding as the games have evolved.

WIZZROBE

AQUAMENTUS

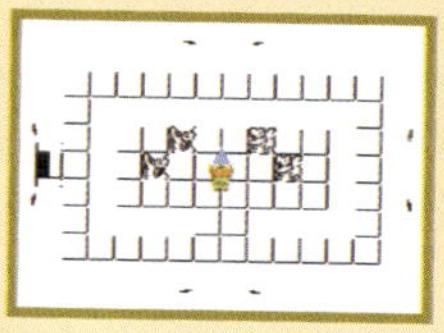

Triforce get!

LINK FINDS HIS first piece of the Triforce and holds it above his head in a way that has now become an identifiable characteristic of the little lad. The Triforces of Wisdom and Power appear in the original, with Courage debuting in the next.

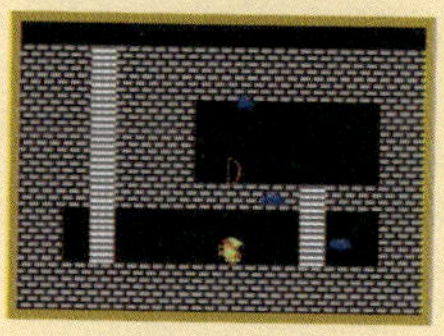

Side story

SOME DUNGEON SCREENS switch perspective to a side view, a trick that was adopted wholesale for *Zelda II: The Adventure Of Link* and would return for some brief sequences in the Game Boy's *Link's Awakening*.

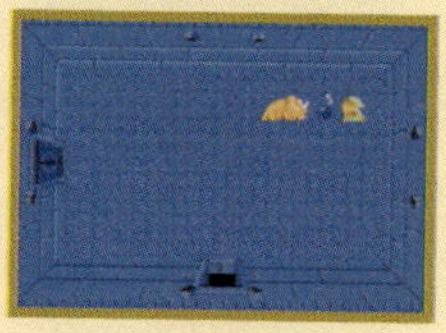

Hard to swallow

THE BRILLIANT DODONGO boss is defeated by getting him to eat and swallow a bomb, causing him some nasty indigestion when it explodes in his belly. A similar boss, King Dodongo, became an iconic sequence in *Ocarina Of Time*.

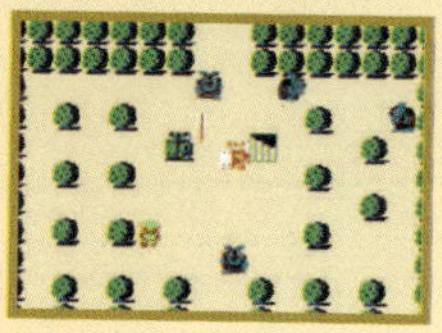

Hidden stairs

ANOTHER GREAT SECRET. Touch a statue and it will come to life to attack you. Some statues stand over stairways that lead to secret underground rooms, tempting players to engage them in combat in the hope of some reward.

ZELDA

GANON

Boss hog

THE FINAL SHOWDOWN with Ganon reveals him to be some kind of grotesque demon pig, much more monstrous than the humanoid reinterpretation in *Ocarina Of Time*. Recent games tend to give him a hideous second form.

Loud noises!

IN THE JAPANESE release of *Zelda*, you can shout into the Famicom microphone to hurt Pols Voice enemies. But you can't in the western NES release. So in Japan it's a memorable setpiece. Over here, it's barely even a regular moment.

Feeding time

THIS GORIYA ISN'T having a moan. Strangely, that noise is actually his stomach rumbling. Feed him some meat and he'll let you pass. The first time a *Zelda* enemy defies expectations of simply being sword fodder and not the last.

POLS VOICE

LEEVER

TEKTIKE

THE VERSIONS OF ZELDA

There have been many more versions of the original Legend Of Zelda than you probably think. Here's every one and the differences between them

PATRA

PROTOTYPE

(1985, ESTIMATED)

A PROTOTYPE VERSION of the original Famicom Disk System game, only recently discovered in late 2010. The prototype differs from the real thing in several ways, most notably that it's a lot easier thanks to a higher distribution of rupees and slightly different enemy arrangements. The disk image is available to download from www.lostlevels.org.

GHINI

FAMICOM DISK SYSTEM

(1986)

THE FIRST OFFICIAL release of the game was titled The *Hyrule Fantasy: Zelda No Densetsu* and was a launch title for the Famicom Disk System. This release used the extra capabilities in the FDS to play sounds not present in the NES cartridge version. It also used the microphone built into the second controller of the Famicom. Blowing into it was a secret way to kill the sound-sensitive Pols Voice enemy, which was technically impossible on the standard western NES.

ZELDA NO DENSETSU: TEIKYOU CHARUMERA

(1986)

MADE TO PROMOTE Myojo Foods' charumera noodles, this special release of the Famicom Disk System game is identified by a different label design and is considered a rare Famicom collector's item, selling for hefty prices in Japanese retro stores.

SHOPKEEPER

NINTENDO ENTERTAINMENT SYSTEM

(1987)

AS WELL AS translating the game into English, the US and European release of *The Legend Of Zelda* was the first to arrive on cartridge. Though the Famicom Disk System had been introduced to reduce the cost of ROMs, the add-on never made it outside Japan so Nintendo used a new type of chip. The MMC1 (Memory Management Controller) used bank-switching to make bigger games possible and allowed *The Legend Of Zelda* to be released worldwide. And boy did Nintendo milk it, releasing the game on a special gold cartridge and cutting a window into the packaging so that everyone could see for themselves. Classy.

FAMICOM CARTRIDGE

(1994)

ZELDA EVENTUALLY GOT its Japanese cartridge release in 1994, eight years after the disk release and a staggering 11 years after the launch of the Famicom console. The game is virtually the same except that it's renamed *Zelda No Densetsu 1*, given that the second, third and even fourth *Zelda* games had been released by 1994.

BS ZELDA NO DENSETSU

(1995)

A 16-BIT REMAKE of the original *Zelda*, broadcast on the Super Famicom's Satellaview add-on between August 1995 and January 1997. As well as the advanced graphics, *BS Zelda No Densetsu* also made use of the hardware's SoundLink feature to provide a live narration throughout the broadcast quest.

GIBDO

GOHMA

BS ZELDA NO DENSETSU MAP 2

(1996)

BASICALLY THE SAME game but based on the second quest from *The Legend Of Zelda*, this *BS Zelda* is much more elusive and was broadcast one time only in March 1996.

GAME BOY COLOR REMAKE

(2000, CANCELLED)

IN 1999, YOSHI Okamoto of Capcom negotiated a deal to develop six new *Zelda* titles for the Game Boy Color. Flagship worked on the remake for a year but encountered a number of problems. One was that the GBC's resolution was too different to that of the NES, meaning the game had to be redrawn to fit the more narrow screen, and another was that the team wanted to rebalance the game to make it less difficult. The remake was eventually scrapped in 2000 as Flagship changed direction. At Miyamoto's request, the studio started work on three interlinked games in the 'Triforce' series, named *Mystical Seed Of Wisdom*, *Mystical Seed Of Power* and *Mystical Seed Of Courage*. This idea proved too ambitious, however, and had to be downgraded to the two games that were eventually released: *Oracle Of Ages* and *Oracle Of Seasons*. The latter evolved directly from *Mystical Seed Of Power*, which was developed off the back of the remake project, and you can still find similarities between *Seasons* and *The Legend Of Zelda* today.

ANIMAL CROSSING

(2001)

BOTH THE NINTENDO 64 and GameCube editions of *Animal Crossing* allowed players to enjoy a series of NES games in their virtual homes. The *Legend Of Zelda* was one of those games although, weirdly, it was buried in the code and couldn't be accessed without using cheat devices.

THE LEGEND OF ZELDA: COLLECTOR'S EDITION

(2003)

A PROMOTIONAL GAMECUBE disc that was never officially sold but given away to Nintendo customers to promote the upcoming release of *The Wind Waker*. The disc includes emulated versions of *Zelda II*, *Ocarina Of Time*, *Majora's Mask* and, of course, *The Legend Of Zelda*, which featured a new translation that corrected some of the spotty localisation in the NES version, as well as changing the name of Gannon to the more canonical Ganon.

NES CLASSICS: THE LEGEND OF ZELDA

(2004)

IN 2004 NINTENDO released a series of Game Boy Advance games called Famicom Minis, which recreated favourite Famicom games on yellow cartridges that came packaged in tiny, cute boxes. When the series came to Europe and America, it was re-envisioned to evoke nostalgia for the NES and sadly lost the cute boxes, but we did get some cool NES games. This version was reformatted for the GBA's wide screen and featured the same new translation as the GameCube remake.

VIRTUAL CONSOLE

(2006)

THE LEGEND OF Zelda was one of the first big Nintendo games to be distributed on the Wii's Virtual Console service. Sadly, the European version ran in 50Hz as part of Nintendo's ludicrous policy of remaining faithful to the version each territory remembers, despite the fact that it used the updated 2003 translation.

THE LEGEND OF ZELDA: MASTERPIECE DEMO

(2008)

NINTENDO'S ALL-STAR Wii fighting game *Super Smash Bros Brawl* contains a Vault section that celebrates the history of the playable characters that appear in the game, and the Vault includes a selection of Masterpieces – timed demos of old games so that you can go hands-on with history yourself. With five *Zelda* characters, three of them different versions of Link, appearing in *Brawl*, it's only natural that *The Legend Of Zelda* appears on the disc.

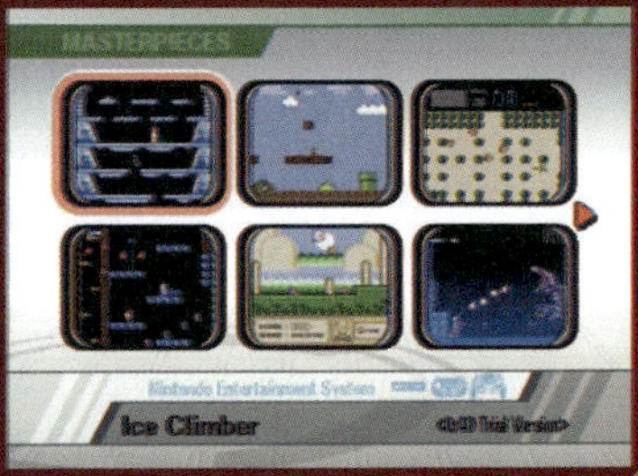

CLASSICS EDITIONs

(2012)

WHEN THE 3DS was shown off at E3 2010, one of the tech demos was a series of 'Classic Games' redrawn to take advantage of the 3D display, and one of the games in that showreel was *Zelda*. It took a while, but *The Legend Of Zelda* arrived on Nintendo 3DS December 2012. Also, as part of the Nintendo Switch Online service, several NES games were made available, including *Zelda*. If you were to pick between the two, we'd opt for the Switch one thanks to the functionality of the modern console's emulation.

ZELDA II
THE ADVENTURE OF LINK™

Meet the unfairly-maligned sequel that dared to be different

WORDS BY ALEX DALE AND DREW SLEEP

Quick pop quiz: until *Breath Of The Wild* arrived, which *Legend Of Zelda* game boasted the largest explorable world of all? *Twilight Princess*? *Wind Waker*? *Ocarina Of Time*? No, no and thrice no. It might be a little-known (and quite astonishing) fact, but that honour belongs to the NES's *Zelda II: The Adventure Of Link*.

Despite the technical progress made over the years, no other instalment pieced together a land of *Zelda II*'s scale until 2017's *Breath Of The Wild*. Sprawled across five islands, this version of Hyrule takes in sights ranging from mountains to deserts, from caves to forests, and from water palaces to winding rocky labyrinths. They all exist side-by-side on a gargantuan continent that makes *The Ocarina Of Time*'s overworld look like a bonsai garden. But if this is so, then why is *The Adventure Of Link* often considered the black sheep of the *Zelda* family?

It's not because it isn't any good. As it happens, *Zelda II* is very good. The answer, simply put, is that this sequel plays quite unlike any other *Zelda* game there has ever been, or likely ever will be again. And that can put off many *Zelda* enthusiasts before they get the chance to discover this epic 8-bit iteration of Hyrule has a charm all of its own.

The most notable difference between this and the other *Zelda* games is the shift in perspective. Although the overworld is, once again, presented from a top-down perspective, this section of the game exists solely to allow Link to travel between points of interest on the map, much like in Square's early *Final Fantasy* games. These points of interest include dungeons, caverns, and towns where Link can pick the locals' brains for hints and tips on how to progress. When he stumbles upon one of these areas, the game transitions to a very un-*Zelda*-like side-on view as if it were a *Super Mario* platformer. There have been side-on segments in other *Zelda* games, of course, most notably in *Link's Awakening*, but never at this level of prominence. Although *Zelda II* is still a role-playing game at heart (Link can level up by accruing experience points, for instance), it looks and plays more like an action game. The new perspective allows for a more complex kind of swordplay that just isn't possible in the top-down *Zelda* games. Knights, for example, can block Link's thrusts, meaning you have to dart between standing and crouching attacks; bats will swoop down onto our hero's undefended green hood, causing you to duck and quickly retaliate; projectiles are flung with reckless abandon, forcing you to dodge, dip and dive to stay alive. This level of action could not be achieved with the traditional top-down viewpoint.

This was all by design, of course. When sketching out plans for a follow-up to *The Legend Of Zelda*, Shigeru Miyamoto wanted to make it

» Like its predecessor, Link's quest has him journeying across the world to find dungeons to plunder.

SECOND TO NONE

What the first sequel bought to the series

Error

ONE OF *ZELDA II*'s most famous characters. Start up a conversation with him and he'll declare "I AM ERROR". This odd dialogue has been retained in subsequent re-issues.

Healing lady

HAVE A NATTER with this helpful housekeeper in any of the villages and she'll invite you inside. After a few moments, you step back outside with a full complement of health.

Link doll

ADVENTURE OF LINK is the only *Legend Of Zelda* game to have a traditional lives system. Link could grab an all-important extra life by hunting out one of these cute dolls.

Link

OUR GREEN-HOODED hero is a little different compared to his first incarnation on the NES. He's a little taller, perhaps a little wiser, and is viewed entirely with a side-on perspective.

Carock

THE GAME'S FOURTH boss is allegedly related to the magician who places Princess Zelda in a deep sleep at the very beginning of the game.

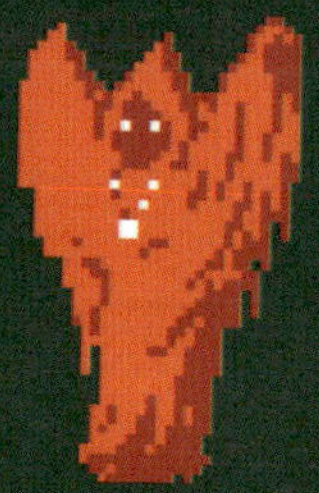

Raft

SEVERAL ITEMS, SUCH as the flute and the hammer, can be used in the overworld to open new areas. The raft lets you travel across bodies of water without fuss.

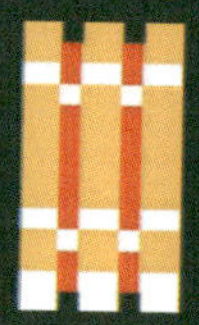

stand apart from the original game, even going as far as assembling a new team for the sequel. Tadashi Sugiyama and Yasuhisa Yamamura took over directing duties, while Takashi Tezuka penned the story and script.

In that respect, the sweeping changes made by Nintendo EAD seemed logical at the time, and the game was well-received by fans, shifting an impressive 4.3 million copies worldwide. It was just unfortunate (from *Zelda II*'s point of view, not ours) that Nintendo chose to revisit the original's top-down template rather than this sequel's ambitious design when it came to developing the SNES successor, *A Link To The Past*. It was a decision that proved so successful that the series never really looked back on its side-on offerings.

This left *Zelda II* looking like an anachronism. Some buffoons would even consider it an oddity or outcast – something which, regardless of any merits it might have, did not deserve to be regarded as part of the wider *Zelda* canon. Such criticism is grossly unfair, as *Zelda II* left a legacy that continues to be felt by the series today. It was here that Link first gained the ability to learn new moves, and it was here that the pointy-eared hero first dabbled in magic.

Some changes were more subtle, though. This sequel was the first *Zelda* game to lay down the now-sacred rule that keys can only be used in the dungeon the player finds them in. The change stopped the exploit of players hoarding keys and using them to blast their way through the harder dungeons. It also introduced a grander ambition for the series: NPCs that populated villages that could offer information, facilities or abilities to Link. For these small but critically important contributions to *Zelda* design alone, this unorthodox legend lives on.

» You'll be rudely accosted by enemies while exploring the overworld, placing you into an encounter screen like this.

» *Zelda II*'s palaces are dangerous to clear and look to take inspiration from Ancient Greek architecture.

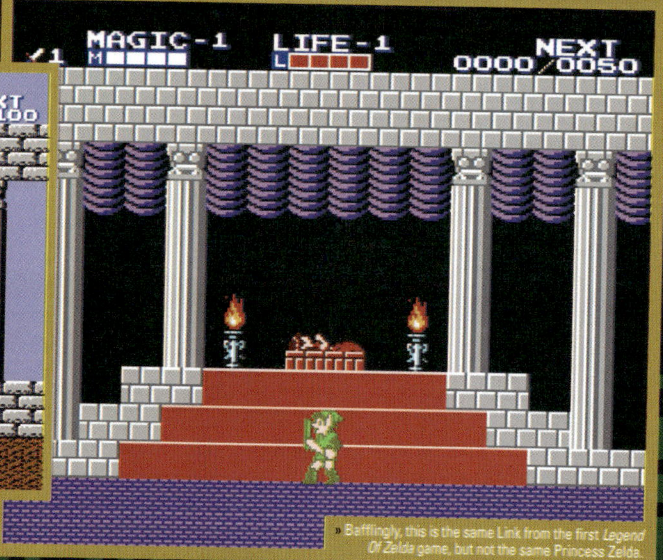

» Bafflingly, this is the same Link from the first *Legend Of Zelda* game, but not the same Princess Zelda.

THE LEGEND OF ZELDA
A LINK TO THE PAST

Refreshing a series for a new generation is tough, especially when it's a Zelda title. Takashi Tezuka and Kensuke Tanabe reveal the hard work that went into this action-RPG SNES classic…

WORDS BY NICK THORPE

When you look back at the history of the series, *The Legend Of Zelda* occupies a funny space in Nintendo's planning processes. If a *Zelda* game arrives in time for a console launch, it's because the game was heavily delayed on the previous generation of hardware. Yet *Zelda* is never overlooked when a new Nintendo console is being planned – in fact, it's often one of the very first things considered for a new machine. Our first look at *The Legend Of Zelda: The Wind Waker* came before the GameCube had hit the shelves, but the game launched over a year into the life of the machine. A demo of what would eventually become *The Legend Of Zelda: Ocarina Of Time* was shown to attendees of Nintendo's Shoshinkai 1995 expo, but the game didn't materialise until 1998. But the game that started this tradition was *The Legend Of Zelda: A Link To The Past*, the game that marked Link's move off of 8-bit platforms.

In planning the launch of the 16-bit SNES console, Nintendo identified two basic software needs: new properties that could demonstrate the power of the new hardware, and more of what had made the NES successful. For the former category, Nintendo chose racing and flight games that would be impossible to achieve on rival consoles, and delivered a one-two punch of *F-Zero* and *Pilotwings* in November and December 1990. For the latter, Nintendo chose to immediately develop follow-ups to its most popular NES properties – the *Super Mario Bros* and *The Legend Of Zelda* series.

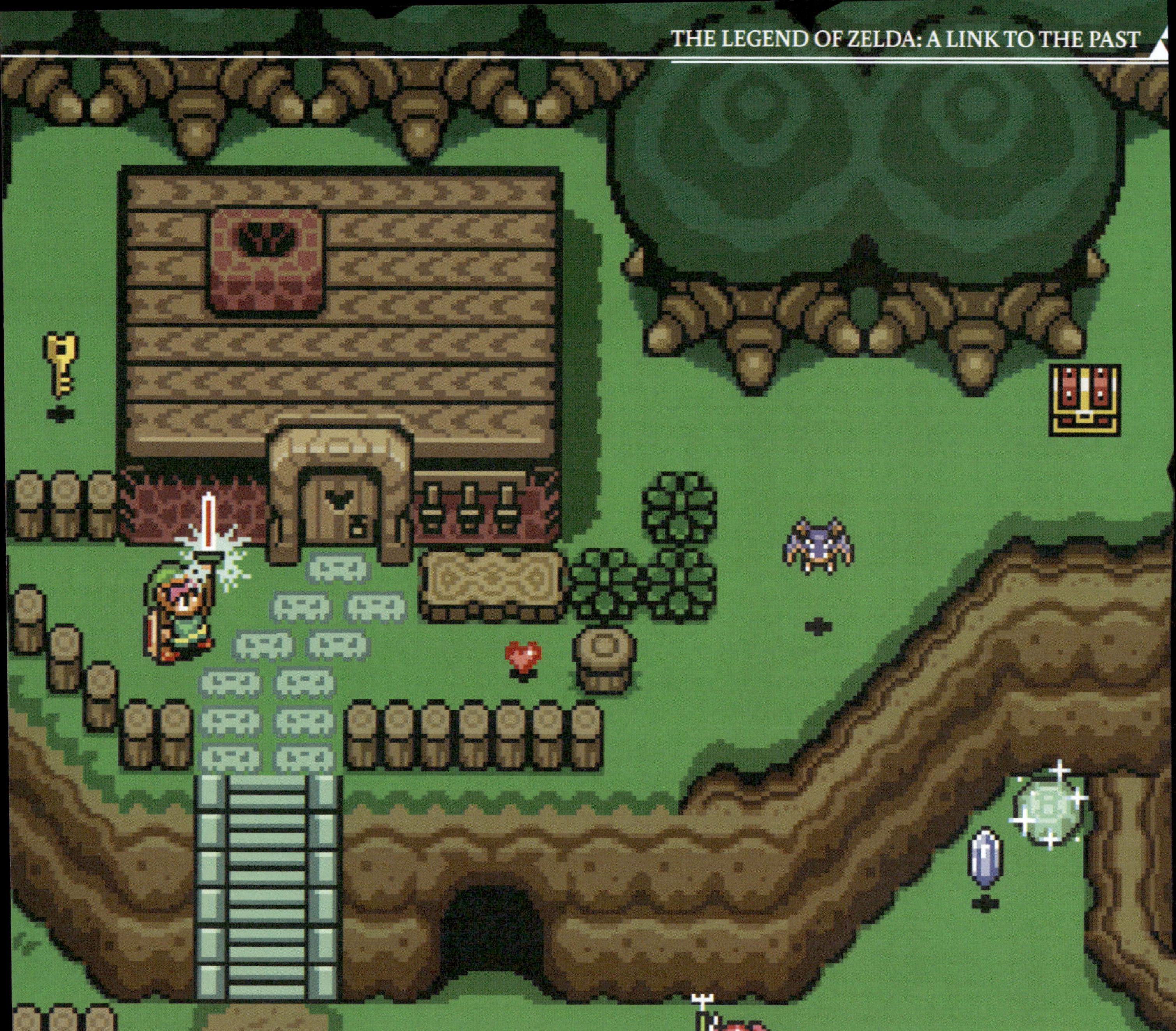

However, creating a new *Zelda* was a bit more difficult than creating another *Mario* game – *Mario* games were all very similar, but *The Legend Of Zelda* and *Zelda II: Link's Adventure* were very different games. This left the Nintendo EAD team with some big decisions to make regarding its approach to the new game. "In *Zelda II: The Adventure Of Link*, we wanted to include sword combat with a variety of different moves into the gameplay, and so decided the project would use a side-scrolling view that made use of our experience from *Super Mario* games," explains Takashi Tezuka, a veteran Nintendo developer who served as director for both *The Legend Of Zelda* and *The Legend Of Zelda: A Link To The Past*. "We made two *Zelda* games for the NES, both making the most of that hardware. But then with the next *Zelda* for the SNES, we were able to add even more new things to the gameplay."

The final decision on which structure to use was driven by the concept of the game, according to Tezuka. "When we were starting the project, we experimented to see if it was possible to include a multi-world structure into the game. Our plan was that events in the hub world would have an effect on the other, overlapping worlds," he explains. "We decided it would be best for us, the developers, as well as for players to have this as two worlds. We felt the best way to represent this overlap of light and dark, and to represent the changes between them, was to use the same slanted top-down view used in the original *The Legend Of Zelda* game."

It's rare for a company to discard the major changes made to a sequel, but it would prove to be a wise decision. Quite apart from the fact that *Zelda II* has become known as one of the weaker games in the series as time has passed, there was still a lot that Nintendo could change and improve in going back to the old top-down format. Even very basic things were overhauled, such as the way Link moved around the environment – for the first time, he was able to move diagonally as well as in the four cardinal directions. Rather than using a simple thrust, Link would actually swing his sword in a more realistic arc.

LINK'S ARSENAL A hero can't get the job done without the right tools…

Bow & Arrow
■ A good ranged weapon, although you have a limited supply of arrows.

Boomerang
■ This doesn't just hurt enemies, it retrieves far-off items too.

Hookshot
■ This item can pull Link across dangerous gaps, or grab baddies.

Bomb
■ Does what it says on the tin – place it and run away!

Ether Medallion
■ An enormous blast of lightning fries flying enemies and stuns the rest.

Quake Medallion
■ A mighty tremor reduces grounded enemies to either nothing or slime.

Lamp
■ Useful for lighting up the game's many dark rooms by igniting torches.

Magic Hammer
■ This versatile tool and weapon is useful against frozen enemies.

Cane Of Somaria
■ This is used to instantly create blocks – good for weights and shielding.

Cane Of Byrna
■ This awesome item shields Link and hurts enemies in the process!

Magic Cape
■ This fashionable item makes Link both invisible and invincible.

Magic Mirror
■ An important item, as it's Link's path between the Light and Dark Worlds.

LINK SHRINKS

The only port of Link's 16-bit adventure received some major upgrades…

The prospect of SNES-quality games on the Game Boy Advance was one that intrigued gamers around the world, and Nintendo set about making sure that a number of them would be available for dedicated fans, with *The Legend Of Zelda: A Link To The Past* being one of the earlier examples. The game ran at the slightly lower screen resolution of 240x160 (as opposed to 256x224), but received slightly more accurate translation and some minor bug fixes.

However, the game also received a major new mode in the form of the co-operative game *Four Swords*, which allowed up to four players to quest together as various coloured Links using the GBA's Link Cable. If you finished that quest, it was then possible to play through a new single-player dungeon as a reward, facing numerous stronger versions of the Dark World bosses before coming face to face with a surprising final enemy.

Not only did the GBA game sell an impressive 1.8 million units, but *Four Swords* left its own legacy, spawning the dedicated multiplayer GameCube sequel *The Legend Of Zelda: Four Swords Adventures* and the 3DS game *The Legend Of Zelda: Tri-Force Heroes*. *Four Swords* was also rereleased as a limited anniversary edition downloadable game for the Nintendo DSi and 3DS handhelds.

▶ According to a 1992 *Famitsu* interview with Miyamoto, this combo of new features actually gave way to another new feature. With the addition of diagonal movement, the Nintendo EAD team had made the logical assumption that Link should be able to attack diagonally, too. However, in practice it made the controls feel somewhat worse, and Link was once again saddled with the ability to move in eight directions but face only four. Undeterred, the team found a way to add a multi-directional attack in the form of a spin attack, activated by holding the sword button down for a couple of seconds. This elegant solution would go on to feature in many subsequent *Zelda* games and become a staple of the series.

Other changes to the use of weaponry and items were considered too, according to Tezuka. "At the start of development, we wanted players to be able to freely choose which weapons to hold, not just the sword and shield," explains the game director. "We also thought about having these weapons combine, say, for example, having the Bow & Arrows set to the A Button and a Bomb to B Button so that when you use them together (i.e. press both the buttons), Link would shoot an arrow with a bomb attached." This would have revolutionised *Zelda*'s combat system, but ultimately didn't come to pass – however, it might sound familiar to fans of the series. "In the end, we didn't use this in *A Link To The Past*, as Shigeru Miyamoto requested that Link always have the sword equipped," Tezuka recalls. "We were able to implement this system in the next title, *Link's Awakening*, though."

Working with the SNES also opened up a world of new possibilities for the team. "The hardware allowed us to do things we hadn't been able to until that point. I'd only been drawing four-colour pixel images up until then, so even simply just increasing the number of colours available to use to 16 or 256 colours, as well as being able to use high-quality sounds, was really exciting for me," explains Tezuka. "Figuring out how best to effectively reflect the features of the hardware into a game is always a challenge that Nintendo's game designers face, and not limited to this game," notes Kensuke Tanabe, the scriptwriter for *A Link To The Past*. "For me, who'd studied visuals at university, being able to use two 'animation cells' and having the possibility to scroll them separately was a huge deal."

The technique that Tanabe refers to above is that of using multiple background layers. On the NES, it was only possible to draw a single layer of background graphics and a single layer of sprite graphics. With the SNES, developers had the luxury of multiple background layers. For example, in *A Link To The Past*, one layer is used to display the stage layout and a second layer is reserved for special effects. A third layer is used to display the HUD, which never moves. "Using it allowed us to create the raining scene at the very start of the adventure, as well as show sunlight filtering down through the leaves in the forest," Tanabe recalls of the special effects layer. "It's the effect of the sunlight in the forest that I'm particularly fond of. I'm also really pleased that we were able to

» The memorable rainy intro to A Link To The Past was only possible with the power of the SNES.

Magic Powder
This can transform enemies into weak or even helpful creatures!

Fire Rod
Use this to send a burning blast in the direction of your foes.

Ice Rod
Freeze the enemy with this vital piece of magical weaponry.

Bombos Medallion
Hit everything on screen with fire magic, at great magical cost.

Flute
This ocarina-shaped object can summon a bird for fast travel.

Bug-Catching Net
If you want to put a bee or fairy in a bottle, you'll need this.

Book Of Mudora
This allows Link to read Ancient Hylian, often used in magical places.

Bottle
These handy containers can hold potions, fairies and even bees.

Pegasus Shoes
Footwear that allows Link to perform a speedy dash attack.

Power Glove
No dodgy NES peripherals here – this lets Link lift some heavy objects.

Flippers
Worth the 500 Rupees the Zora charges, as you'll be able to swim!

Moon Pearl
Without it, Link would lose his human form in the Dark World.

> **"Shigeru Miyamoto requested that Link always have the sword equipped"**
> Takashi Tezuka

display which floor a player is on by using two 'animation cells'. This was actually a suggestion from the engineering team."

Despite the new possibilities, technical issues were rare. "Our designers had a pretty good idea of what could be done on the hardware back then, so I don't believe we had any unexpected implementations," Tezuka confirms, though he does note one important exception. "Having said that, though, we had a long battle with the memory size, and I remember that the engineering team worked extremely hard to optimise it."

Prior to *The Legend Of Zelda: A Link To The Past*, all of Nintendo's first-party SNES games had used a minimal ROM size of just four megabits. Not only did the new *Zelda* require eight megabits of storage, it was pushing that limit. A simple graphical compression routine was brought over from *Super Mario World* to combat this, which saved space by limiting many graphical tiles to eight colours, rather than the standard 16 that the SNES is capable of. With data duplication cut to an absolute minimum, the game was able to fit into the ROM allocated. Even then, translating the game from Japanese once again challenged this limit. In his 1992 *Famitsu* interview, Miyamoto explained that the original plan was to use a higher capacity cartridge for the translated game, and use what extra space remained afterwards to make some improvements to the Western releases. However, further compression rendered increased capacity unnecessary.

The dastardly wizard Agahnim has got Zelda, and now he's zapping her into the Dark World!

The 16-bit versions of both *Mario* and *Zelda* had entered development at the same time, but while *Mario* stuck to its planned trajectory and made it out for the November 1990 launch of the console, *Zelda*'s planned arrival in March was going to be impossible. In fact, by the time eager gamers in Japan were trying out the new Super Famicom for the first time, Nintendo EAD was only just confident of the game system it had settled upon! The next step was to add additional staff to complete the work by adding in enemies, a scenario and more. In an interview for the official *Super Mario World* guidebook in Japan, Miyamoto estimated that the game would be completed by Children's Day (May 5th) in 1991 in anticipation of a summer release, but this turned out to be an underestimation. According to Miyamoto's 1992 *Famitsu* interview, implementing these final features took about eight months, pushing the game back further from summer to winter.

If there's any reason that *A Link To The Past* took longer than expected, it might well be because of how much attention was paid to the plot of the game. Right from the start, it was clear that it would be told in more detail and with greater dramatic flair than the NES *Zelda* games were capable of, and that item acquisition would be closely tied to story progression. A clear example of this comes in the game's opening sequence – by contrast to the earlier games, the SNES game offered a far more structured introduction to Link's quest. "In *A Link To The Past*, the game starts with a dark, rainy scene, with Link being just a regular village boy who, in the same situation as the player, doesn't really know what's going on, but just follows Princess Zelda's voice and works to save her. However, in doing this he somehow ends up becoming an outlaw. We wanted players to start feeling excited and wonder what will happen next," explains Tezuka. It's a dramatic opening, but finding and rescuing the princess so early on surprised some players, who felt that the game was going to end suddenly. "We didn't intend to make players feel like the game was going to end there," admits Tezuka, who always saw Link's ascension to heroism in a rather different way.

The moment when Link gains the Master Sword is a pivotal and iconic scene in the game.

The previous games had just dropped the player into the world and allowed them to get on with it, but this would not be an approach that would be repeated in *A Link To The Past*. "We didn't have Link start out as a sword-wielding

hero right from the start, because we had already decided at the beginning of the project that we wanted him to awaken as a hero when he pulls out the Master Sword," explains Tezuka. "We did make a number of adjustments to the placement and ordering of the weapons and items so that we could get the ideal flow for the game, no matter the player or playstyle," he continues. Instead of starting out as a bonafide hero, Link would acquire a variety of items over the course of the game and experience his development naturally. "We thought that players would form an emotional connection with Link as they play and by the time he ultimately becomes a hero, it would just be natural that he can use a variety of different weapons," Tezuka confirms.

The most memorable weapon to be introduced in *A Link To The Past* was the Master Sword, a weapon that has endured over the decades as a key piece of the *Zelda* mythology. As Tezuka alluded to earlier, the scene where Link obtains this blade was one of the most crucial parts of the project. "Kensuke Tanabe had an idea for a truly memorable hero-awakening scene when we started this project," recalls the director, crediting the scriptwriter. "In the midst of a forest, with light filtering down through the leaves, the sword stood waiting for someone worthy of wielding it to arrive. Link draws the sword out as the light trickles through the leaves.

"In order to draw the sword, one needs to have both inherited the blood of the family of knights who protect Princess Zelda, as well as possess the three pendants. From the moment Link pulls the sword out, it recognises him as a hero, and grants him its power," says Tezuka, with his accurate recall of the plot standing as a testament to the importance with which it was treated. The Master Sword was also given its mythological importance at this early stage, as Tezuka recalls, "We also decided then that the Master Sword was a sword that alone holds the power to repel evil, and I suspect this is why it continues to carry such an important role in the rest of the series."

However, the Master Sword scene isn't just symbolic. "It's at this point that the game's real battle starts," the director notes. "Our main aim was to show the birth of a hero in a scene fitting of *The Legend Of Zelda*, and overlap this with a sense of achievement for the player that they have been recognised as a hero after having overcome many challenges." Instead of being a moment of triumph, it's a turning point which ultimately leads to the introduction of the game's dual-world concept. "What we had decided on from the start was that Link would first become a hero in the Light World and defeat the first boss," says Tezuka. "From that point is when his battle to defeat the real enemy, Ganon, in the Dark World begins."

The Legend Of Zelda: A Link To The Past was released on 21 November 1991 in Japan, with North American and European releases following on 13

BOSS RUSH

While many foes stand in Link's way, these bosses are easily the deadliest dozen...

Armos Knights

■ These six knights attack in a regimented formation, no matter where they're pushed in combat. When they attack in a full row, make sure to slow one knight down with arrows to break the line.

Lanmolas

■ It's hard to predict the movements of this trio of burrowing sandworm-like enemies. Their heads are their weak points – the sword is effective, but try arrows or the Ice Rod if you need distance.

Moldorm

■ THIS NASTY PIECE of work likes to push you off the stage onto the floor below, which resets the battle completely. Try your hardest to avoid being hit as you swing your sword at its tail, which is its weakness.

Agahnim

■ THE WIZARD BEHIND Zelda's kidnap looks unthreatening, but wields potent magic attack spells. Some of these can be reflected back by swinging the Master Sword, so get ready to return service!

Helmasaur King

■ THIS FIERY-TEMPERED individual will give any hero a warm welcome with his hot breath. To cool him off, first smash his mask with the hammer and then hit him with the sword until he's dead.

Arrghus

■ THIS FLOATING FOE is a tricky one to hit, and brings an entourage of meanies with it. Pull away the smaller Arrgi with the Hookshot, and then get to work with the sword when Arrghus crashes to the floor.

> "Our main aim was to show the birth of a hero in a scene fitting of a Zelda [game]"
> Takashi Tezuka

April 1992 and 24 September 1992 respectively. No matter where you were in the world, the game was regarded as a classic. Critical praise was unanimous – *Computer & Video Games* awarded the game 89%, noting that "the elements of strategy and adventure are added treats rather than annoying extras." A review in *Mean Machines* scored the game 95% and declared it "simply the greatest exploration/adventure game available for a console," while *Super Play Gold*'s 93% review noted that "you're unlikely to want to switch the game off". The game sold a massive 4.61 million copies on the SNES, and ultimately spawned both a successful re-release on the Game Boy Advance as well as a successor for the Nintendo 3DS, *The Legend Of Zelda: A Link Between Worlds*.

Despite the excellent quality of *A Link To The Past*, it would ultimately prove to be the end of the line for the *Zelda* series as players had known it, as the series was about to undergo a radical change. The next home console sequel was *The Legend Of Zelda: The Ocarina Of Time*, which transformed the series with open 3D spaces and more. While smaller 2D *Zelda* games would continue to appear on the Game Boy platforms, including the excellent *Link's Awakening*, *Oracle Of Ages*/*Oracle Of Seasons* and *The Minish Cap*, there was never another 2D *Zelda* game to get the big-budget treatment that *A Link To The Past* received.

But that's not to say that *A Link To The Past* hasn't had a lasting influence, not by a long shot. Elements from the game including the spin attack, the Hookshot and the Master Sword have become series regulars, and that dual-world concept has been revisited very frequently – just look at young and adult Link in *Ocarina Of Time*, or human and wolf Link in *Twilight Princess*. The third *Zelda* game is as tightly woven into the legacy of the series as any of the other major entries.

Ultimately, *The Legend Of Zelda: A Link To The Past* is one of those rare games that not only achieved critical and commercial success, but has stood the test of time and continues to attract new fans today. How does the team feel about this sustained success? "We're truly thankful, and consider it a great privilege," Tezuka says, but he's careful not to rest on his laurels. "At the same time, it also drives us to create new games that will surpass this acclaim."

» Soldiers take pig form in the Dark World, and you won't see any other humans.

» Climbing the mountain to Hera Tower is dangerous, thanks to a constant rain of rocks.

I AM ERROR...

The story behind one of gaming's most infamous secrets...

BACK IN THE early Nineties, we can't imagine many American kids turning down the chance to get their name featured in a NES game. With that in mind, a contest ran in *Nintendo Power* during 1990, allowing the winner to win just that prize. The eventual winner was a chap named Chris Houlihan, whose name was eventually incorporated into not a NES game, but a SNES game – *The Legend Of Zelda: A Link To The Past*.

Of course, there was a catch. There's every chance that you might have missed that young Nintendo fan's crowning moment of glory, as Chris Houlihan's secret room only appears as an error handling measure – if the game can't determine Link's next destination, he ends up in this Rupee-filled room and exits to his own house. Plus, if you played the game in any language other than English, Chris Houlihan's name is nowhere to be seen!

Mothula

■ NOT ONLY DOES Mothula move erratically around the stage, it fights you in a room with moving floors. If you're struggling to get close enough for the sword to hit, blast it from afar with the Fire Rod.

Blind The Thief

■ THIS PHOTOSENSITIVE THIEF disguises himself as a maiden before revealing his true formidable form. There's no clever strategy here – hit him with the sword and avoid his floating heads and projectiles.

Kholdstare

■ THERE'S A FROSTY atmosphere in this boss fight, and Link will slide around easily. Melt its icy shield with a fire attack (the Bombos Medallion works well), before finishing it with the sword or Fire Rod.

Vitreous

■ THE SLIME THAT this gaggle of eyeballs lives in is both disgusting and deadly to touch! Slice down each smaller eyeball as it launches itself at you, before taking out the biggest one from afar with the bow.

Trinexx

■ THREE HEADS ARE deadlier than one, as far as this boss is concerned. Stun the red head with the Ice Rod and the blue head with the Fire Rod before attacking, then finish Trinexx off by hitting the glowing orb.

Ganon

■ THE BIGGEST OF big bads, Ganon is the swine behind this whole evil scheme. To finish him off, make sure the room is brightly lit, hit him with the sword to stun him and shoot him with a silver arrow.

THE WORLD

Here's a look at the key locations Link will visit as he becomes a hero in the Light World…

Lost Woods

■ This is where you'll find the Master Sword, truly awakening Link as a hero. But you'll need three pendants to claim it…

Hyrule Castle

■ This is where Princess Zelda is being held at the beginning of the game, and where you'll later fight Agahnim. The boomerang can be found here, too.

Kakariko Village

■ Most of the residents of the town here are terrified of Link, and some will summon guards to attack him. You can grab a bug-catching net here.

Desert Palace

■ The Power Glove here is key to lifting heavy rocks, which you'll need to do to claim the second pendant.

Hera Tower

■ Atop the mountain, this fortress guards the final pendant you'll need to obtain the Master Sword. You'll need the Moon Pearl located here, too.

Zora's Domain

■ Make sure to bring some cash with you here, as you'll be able to pick up some useful flippers that allow Link to swim.

Eastern Palace

■ You can grab the all-important bow here, as well as collecting your first pendant. You'll have to fight for it, though!

Sage's Hideout

■ The man who'll set Link on his path to heroism is taking refuge from the forces of evil here, and is holding onto the Pegasus Boots for you.

Lake Hylia Secret Cave

■ This remote cave holds a particularly useful item, the Ice Rod – it's worth the big detour to claim it as soon as possible.

Link's House

■ This is where you'll start your quest, and where you'll often resume it. You can pick up the lantern here at the very start of the game, too.

THE LEGEND OF ZELDA® LINK'S AWAKENING™

Creating an epic fantasy adventure for a tiny monochrome screen was never going to be an easy task. But, to the surprise of absolutely nobody, Nintendo had the courage, wisdom and power to pull it off flawlessly. We revist one of the most underrated members of the Zelda family

WORDS BY LUKE ALBIGÉS

ANTI-KIRBY

CHEF BEAR

» For some unknown reason, Marin really likes it when you use the Shovel. Some people are just easily pleased, we suppose...

If there's one thing that other games could stand to learn from *Link's Awakening*, it's that the stakes don't need to be absurdly high for a story to be captivating. Having spent three games (and many more after this one) dealing with potential end-of-the-world scenarios, *Link's Awakening* is little more than an escape room by comparison – our hero finds himself marooned on a strange island following a shipwreck and is tasked with simply getting away. And so, under the guidance of a talking owl and with a little help from some of the friendly eccentric islanders, Link sets about attempting to wake the mighty Wind Fish from its slumber, which is apparently the only way he might leave Koholint Island.

Mechanically, *Link's Awakening* feels almost like a greatest hits collection of the best elements of the trio of preceding games. Parallels with *A Link To The Past* are unsurprising given that this game originally started out as a proposed port of the SNES classic, but it clearly helped to influence and inform much of the Game Boy release's design. In terms of the NES games, *Zelda II*'s impact is most apparent from the inclusion of side-scrolling sections, while similarities to the original primarily spring from this being another case of big ideas on hardware that should by rights be too small for them. Literally, in this case – as well as a smaller, monochrome screen to work with, there would also be the button limitations of the Game Boy to consider after *A Link To The Past* had gone beyond what was possible on the two-button NES controller. A handful of talented artists would see to that first issue, but the second would not be so easily resolved.

Despite the Game Boy sharing the same limited control options as the NES, *A Link To The Past* evolved the core systems of the series to a point that made use of more buttons, so a creative solution was required. To that end, *Link's Awakening* became the first *Zelda* game where the sword is not mapped to its own button, with both the A and B buttons able to be assigned to any item Link finds. While this can make for some fiddly item switching (particularly in later, more

MARIN

BOWWOW

» Side-scrolling interludes reminiscent of *Zelda II: The Adventure Of Link* add platforming flair.

» At the time, *Twin Peaks* was *the* TV show in the public zeitgeist, which inspired the team to create a cast of eclectic characters.

ARMOS KNIGHT

ZOL

PIRANHA

OWL

COLOUR US IMPRESSED

Link gets a fresh lick of paint on GBC

ARRIVING SOME FIVE years after the original game's release, *Link's Awakening DX* for Game Boy Color breathed new life into the classic adventure with its vivid palette and suite of new features. Chief among these – aside from the colourful visual upgrade – is a brand-new dungeon for Link to explore. The aptly named Color Dungeon expands on what was possible in the monochrome original, with puzzles and mechanics that rely on the use of coloured objects and enemies. Completing this trial rewards Link with a choice of either the Red Clothes or Blue Clothes, new items that double his attack and defence respectively. In addition, the enhanced port also features support for the Game Boy Printer, with a number of photo opportunities added to the world for Link to find over the course of his adventure. The resulting snapshots can be printed out as cute little *Link's Awakening DX* stickers.

complex dungeons), the flexibility of the system also allows for the use of item combos the likes of which the series hadn't seen before… or since, really. Long gaps can be cleared by combining the Pegasus Boots with the Roc's Feather, for instance, or equipping bombs and the bow and pressing both buttons simultaneously allows Link to loose an explosive arrow. While the former is the only item combo required to beat the game, having those other options in there gives players a chance to be surprised by their own experimental solutions – a rarity in a series so grounded in linear formula, and really something you only otherwise see in the open-world powerhouse, *Breath Of The Wild*.

The differences between *Link's Awakening* and most of its stablemates don't stop there, either. Trading sequences are a staple sidequest in the franchise, but this is the only *Zelda* game where the entire endeavour is mandatory. As such, it's a little more streamlined and obvious than its peers and feels more like helping people

» The Moldorm boss loves to punt you into pits and make you start the fight over.

out along your journey, rather than ditching your main objective and going out of your way to run errands for them. It's strange that would be the case in the game with the least pressing objective in the entire series, but it's a great way of allowing players to meet the weird and wonderful residents of Koholint without it feeling like busywork. But perhaps the most noticeable difference of all is the game's tone, which is much more playful, whimsical and lighthearted than any other game in the series, thanks in no small part to the lack of a Ganon-like big bad looming large and ready to bring an end to the world. There's just this wonderful dreamlike quality to Koholint, apparent in everything from its curious cast of characters and creatures to it having the feel of a slightly misremembered recollection of a *Zelda* adventure, with elements of other Nintendo games seeping in (domesticated Chain Chomps are found in Mabe Village, *Mario* enemies such as Goombas and Piranha Plants inhabit dungeons, as does an evil version of Kirby later on, while the trading sequence includes cameos from Yoshi, Peach and even Prince Richard from *Link's Awakening*'s Japan-only Game Boy forerunner, *Kaeru No Tame Ni Kane Wa Naru*) and lashings

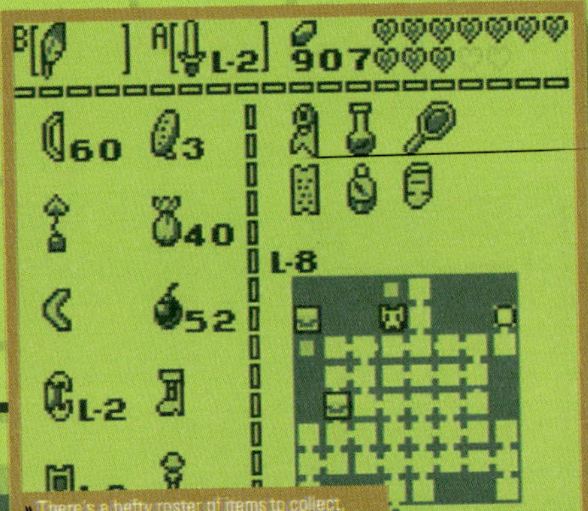

» There's a hefty roster of items to collect, and… wait a second, is that an ocarina?

» Uncover a secret and you'll often find a Piece Of Heart waiting for you.

GENIE

GREAT FAIRY

» Puzzle and dungeon design required the player to make large leaps of logic compared to other games.

» Takashi Tezuka has said that his team approached *Link's Awakening* as if they were making a *Zelda* parody.

» The overworld opens up quickly, especially with the first special item earned in a dungeon being the Roc's Feather, which allows Link to leap over gaps.

LIKE A DREAM

A legend reborn on Nintendo Switch

IT'S BEEN SAID by many that *Link's Awakening* deserves to be enjoyed and adored by a much wider audience, and Nintendo finally seems to agree. A remake is out on the shelves as you read this, and has been for some time, although you may not recognise it at first. The quaint new visual style looks like a diorama come to life, and while it might be a little twee for some people's tastes, there's no denying that it perfectly captures the feel of the original's simple style. A slightly angled top-down viewpoint allows the game's beautiful environments to pop like never before, and it's a joy to revisit the many and varied locations across Koholint Island in this charming new aesthetic.

As with *Link's Awakening DX* before it, Nintendo isn't stopping with just the visuals, either. While most of the Game Boy adventure game has been lovingly recreated for a new audience, there's also another brand-new dungeon to delve into. The Chamber Dungeon is an interesting proposition, as it allows players to piece together their own custom dungeons from a host of premade rooms unlocked as the game progresses. You can even earn rewards by clearing your own custom creations, so be sure to head to where the Camera Shop was in *DX* to check it out.

A LINK TO THE FAST

A few of the tricks speedrunners use to wake the Wind Fish in record time

Save/Quit

A PRETTY COMMON technique in games is to both save and load quickly, since it's often faster to return to the previous position than to have things play out normally. Here, entering and leaving buildings and caves is the usual way to set where you restart after quitting, although you can also use the trick in dungeons to instantly return to the entrance room as well.

Text skip

GOING INTO THE save menu requires bit of work, but by pressing Start+Select+A+B as soon as any text box would pop up then continuing can let you skip most dialogue in the game, from simple item descriptions to longer conversations. It only typically saves a few seconds per instance, but that all adds up over the course of the run – especially when every moment counts.

Super Jump

HOW CONVENIENT THAT the first key item you get allows for some of the most significant skips! By clipping into the corner of a wall and moving along it then swinging your sword while jumping, you can set up jumps that can clear otherwise impossible obstacles and even ignore elevation changes. There are a bunch of spots where this can save significant time.

Instrument skip

JUST AS MOST text can be skipped, so too can the majority of the short musical interludes that occur when you pick up the instrument at the end of a dungeon. This involves setting up Link's position so he's only a pixel away from the instrument and using the map screen to buffer into the save menu as the item is picked up, although this is not what you might call 'consistent'.

Bomb trigger

ODDLY, USING A bomb exactly as a screen transition occurs will result in triggering whatever special scene happens on the new screen. This can be used to skip the walrus blocking the exit to Animal Village, open the Turtle Rock dungeon, break the pillars in Eagle's Tower, and even skip the Wind Fish Egg sequence, although it can be quite fiddly and requires two bombs per skip.

Magic rod despawn

ROUTES THAT DO dungeons out of order can abuse this neat technique, which triggers a glitch that takes advantage of the game's sprite limit. Going into the menu quickly after multiple Magic Rod projectiles are active can cause intense slowdown, and changing the screen straight after this will despawn any sprites on that screen, including bosses.

MOBLIN

» Any Great Fairies you find will fully restore your health. Smaller ones can't be captured, though.

» Link is invincible while the Hookshot is extended, making throwing it out an easy way to avoid damage from certain attacks and enemies.

of self-referential humour in a series that typically tends to play things pretty straight.

All of this combines to give *Link's Awakening* a very different flavour to most other *Zelda* games, and it's perhaps for this reason that it's not treated with the same reverence as notable series highlights such as *A Link To The Past* and *Ocarina Of Time*. For all its charm and whimsy, though, it's somewhat ironic that this clear outlier should be one of the most rigidly linear examples of traditional *Zelda* game structure, to the point where dungeons are literally numbered and cannot be tackled out of sequence. Conversely, the dungeons themselves feature virtually no such handholding after the first few, save for a handful of stone tablets that offer cryptic clues. Crucial items can be hidden in untelegraphed secret rooms, while some of the puzzles require a level of lateral thinking far beyond the standard 'use the last item you picked up to overcome this' nature of so many other games in the genre.

We almost feel bad for *Link's Awakening*, and indeed for so many of the slightly quirkier *Zelda* games that came after it. They're inherently always going to exist in the shadow of the handful of truly genre-defining members of their own family, their own innovations and triumphs dwarfed by those of the two *Zelda* games that have a residency on just about every major all-time top ten list ever compiled. But it's important to remember just how much of an impact these less-discussed classics in the series help shape and evolve the all-time greats – by Eiji Aonuma's own admission in an Iwata Asks piece from 2010, *Ocarina Of Time* would have been a very different game were it not for innovations from *Link's Awakening* in the fields of broad narrative and character development. Interestingly, the same piece also cites *Twin Peaks* as an influence on *Link's Awakening*, which makes a heck of a lot of sense in retrospect. It's important to love and respect these series underdogs, then, since without them, the classics that dominate discussion of both series and genre simply would no exist. As if *Link's Awakening* weren't lovable enough already, that's just another reason it'll always be one of our favourite *Legend Of Zelda* games.

» Broadly speaking, Capcom's Flagship studio took a lot of *Link's Awakening*'s design and used it for the *Oracle* games.

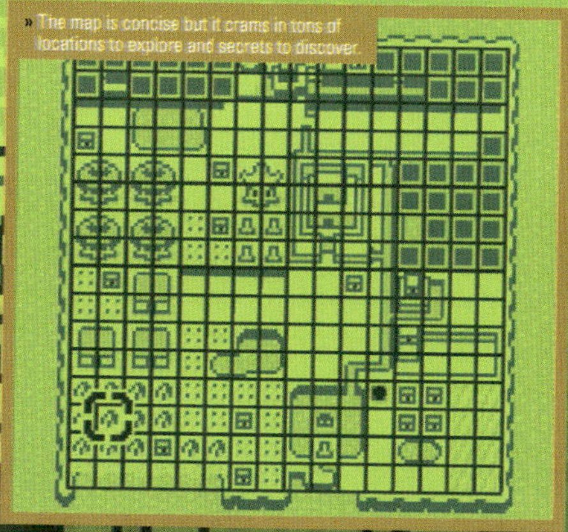

» The map is concise but it crams in tons of locations to explore and secrets to discover.

WALRUS

PEAHAT

SEA URCHIN

GRANDPA ULRIRA

THE LEGEND OF ZELDA OCARINA OF TIME

Link's first Nintendo 64 adventure is often seen as one of the franchise's highest points. An epic quest spanning two eras, featuring unforgettable allies, antagonists and awesome setpieces, it's hard to ignore the brilliance of this ambitious adventure that stands the test of time

WORDS BY STUART HUNT

When all is said and done, a great game is measured simply by the journey you've taken – that moment when you reflect on the hours you've invested and ask yourself, 'Was it really worth it?' The best titles across the history of videogaming have all provided us with memorable adventures we've enjoyed taking a commanding role in, adventures we've felt a strange polarised sense of melancholy and pleasure at seeing the credits roll, enjoyed paying a revisit to once or twice, and have provided us with memories we will likely carry with us forever – because we were 'there', and we made them happen. Perhaps these include something as simple as rescuing Peach from the clutches of Bowser, or maybe you remember specific parts of bigger pictures most fondly – like the time you caught your very first Pokémon and levelled it up enough to evolve, beat your best friend at a game of *Street Fighter* with a perfectly timed dragon punch, or crossed the finish line with mere moments to spare in *OutRun*.

The fact that *Ocarina Of Time* is a game bursting at the seams with memorable moments like these all wrapped up inside one epic adventure makes it not only one of the best *Legend Of Zelda* games, but also one of the greatest videogames of all time. It's a game that takes you on a perfect adventure, one that anyone of any age can relate to: you're the hero, you scale the castle, defeat the villain and in doing all of that, restore peace to the land and become the stuff of legend.

While there can be no question that the original *Legend Of Zelda* was a true watershed moment for videogames, and *Ocarina* owes it a sincere debt of thanks for putting the core pieces in place, it was merely a small portion, a compromise if you like, of what series creator Shigeru Miyamoto had actually envisioned for Link, Zelda, Ganon and the land of Hyrule. Since *Ocarina*'s release, *Zelda*'s creator has revealed that *Ocarina Of Time* marks his true original vision of the world – it is the land of Hyrule he imagined, finally brought to life.

Back in 1986, when that first game in the series was released, technical constraints meant Miyamoto could only project the core themes of *Zelda* on the screen – staples such as the three central characters, the Triforce, Hyrule, the sense of freedom, and of course, the dungeons. And as early as its first sequel, it was clear Miyamoto was beginning to think more about how, having smashed the pegs into the ground, he could start erecting his true image for Hyrule using the modest powers of the NES.

Zelda II: The Adventure Of Link, while widely branded as the 'black sheep' of the series, shares several similarities with the franchise's golden calf. The sequel added side-on platform sections that transported gamers into the heart of Hyrule, with this new viewpoint used to create village sections filled with people with which Link could interact and converse with during his quest. Not only would this help to breathe a greater sense of life and immersion into the world, but also weight a greater sense of responsibility on the shoulders of the player, too.

» As the title implies, Ocarinas play an essential part in the story. Throughout his quest Link learns new songs that he must play to solve puzzles.

» Aiming your weapons became a precise task, using the Nintendo 64's then-sophisticated controller to fine-tune your shots.

» The original plan was for *Ocarina* to be entirely first-person. While this idea was dropped, the perspective was kept for looking and aiming.

The first sequel also had a stronger emphasis on action. Link could now cast spells (in *Ocarina Of Time,* Link can do the same, and a new magic meter enables the hooded hero to perform special charge attacks) and earn experience points to improve his attacks. While this levelling up mechanic was promptly dropped by the series soon after, this aspect of character development still played a big part in *Ocarina Of Time*'s design – just now it was done by the far more interesting means of acquiring new gadgets, items, additional heart containers and better weapons during the quest.

But while *Ocarina* appears to take lessons from *The Adventure Of Link*, the game also borrows a number of popular ideas and themes from other sequels, too. The ocarinas, for example, which play a big part in helping you progress in the story, made their first appearance in the Game Boy game *Link's Awakening*, while *A Link To The Past*'s dark and light realms also returned, with Link ageing seven years in the game to see the devastating effect Ganondorf's rule has had on the kingdom of Hyrule.

Ocarina Of Time was first unveiled at Nintendo's Space World event in December 1995. Shown to a floor of astonished and excited attendees, Nintendo announced that the game would be ready in time to become a launch game for its successor to the Super Nintendo, the Nintendo 64.

"When the project started, the developers working on the game numbered around 15; by the time it neared completion, this number had swelled to 50"

But with the launch just a year away, that projection proved a little ambitious. *Ocarina Of Time* didn't actually appear until the end of November, two years after the launch of the N64 in Japan, following a string of delays.

Designed on a heavily altered version of the *Super Mario 64* engine, *Ocarina*'s creation was handled by Nintendo's EAD branch, with different parts of its creation overseen by various teams headed up by different directors. Each team focused on areas such as scripting and story scenarios, Link's actions and camera controls, and coming up with the various items for the player to use in the game.

As the development progressed, further teams were added, overseeing aspects such as sound and special effects in the game. Finally, Kensuke Tanabe, writer on *A Link To The Past*, returned once again to pen the script for the game based on a story idea that had been hatched by Shigeru Miyamoto and Yoshiaki Koizumi.

Working as producer and supervisor, Miyamoto oversaw the overall production of the game, giving ideas to the directors to develop and also it was his responsibility to see that all the individual components came together. Once *Super Mario 64* was released in 1996, Miyamoto was able to concentrate on *Zelda* to help the teams complete the game. When the

» Link makes friends with Malon and Epona, and in the future, the grown-up steed becomes an invaluable ally for our hero.

project started, the developers working on the game numbered around 15; by the time it neared completion, this number had swelled to an impressive (for the time, at least) 50.

The larger development team helped, of course, however, several inescapable issues delayed *Zelda*'s first Nintendo 64 release. As well as its development moving across to the 64DD at one stage (with the plan to make it a launch game for the N64 disk-drive add-on), when thinking of how best to fully immerse the player in Hyrule like never before, Miyamoto had originally wanted the game to play out entirely in first-person. This idea, however, was dropped after it was decided that during the game the player would control Link both as a boy and then as an adult, and the idea would have lost much of its impact if Link remained out of sight for the majority of the adventure. Surprisingly, the game's memorable ▶

» Pesky Dekus required precise shield blocking to overcome.

TIME FLIES

We relive some of our favourite moments from Ocarina Of Time

Kokiri Forest

YOU START THE game in Kokiri Forest, and can spent ages exploring it before venturing out into Hyrule Field. Acting almost as a training dungeon, Link has to retrieve both a sword and the Deku Shield to be granted an audience with The Great Deku Tree. When both objects are retrieved, Link then enters the tree and embarks on his first dungeon. Once complete, the tree warns Link of Ganondorf, rewards him with the first spiritual stone and tells him to speak with princess Zelda.

Hyrule Field

MANY *ZELDA* FANS remember the first time they set foot onto Hyrule Field in the game as being a special and defining moment in gaming. The point at which *Ocarina* really starts to reveal its size and majesty, the field acts as a hub stage and is surrounded by various different areas, all populated by the different creatures that populate Hyrule. When you make your way to Hyrule Castle and the sunlight in the sky fades, you cannot help but feel both impressed and captivated.

Taming Epona

NAVIGATING HYRULE FIELD by foot is fine to begin with but later on you'll be covering a lot of ground; it's a good idea to pay a stop at Lon Lon Ranch located near the centre of the field. Visiting there as a child, Link meets Malon, who teaches him to play Epona's song on his ocarina. When he returns as an adult, and learns that Ganondorf has handed the ranch to devious range hand Ingo, Link uses the song to tame Epona and bust her out. She then becomes his companion across Hyrule Field.

Meeting The Princess

AFTER AN UNNECESSARY *Metal Gear Solid*-style stealth section, in which Link must avoid the glare of the guards as they patrol the grounds of Hyrule Castle, the child hero finally catches up with Princess Zelda. Their encounters always memorable, she tells Link that she fears that Ganondorf is seeking the Triforce to rule over Hyrule, and so she asks him to retrieve the remaining two spiritual stones and get to its before he does. And Link does just that. Well, she is the princess after all. How can we say no?

Lord Jabu-Jabu

THERE ARE SOME imaginative and brilliantly designed dungeons in *Ocarina* but none more quirky than the belly of Lord Jabu-Jabu. One of the game's trickier dungeons to complete, it sees Link getting swallowed by the giant, sacred whale-like creature after giving him an offering of fish, and then having to travel through his extremely large stomach to find Ruto, the princess of the Zora race, and retrieve the final spiritual stone together.

Using the Ocarina

MUSIC PLAYS A big part in *Ocarina*, as is to be expected from a game with a musical instrument in the title. Not only is the audio in the game dynamic, quickly changing depending on what's happening, but its characters and many areas are also given their own unique motif, too. Music also has a significant part to play in the quest and story, thanks to the eponymous ocarinas. Acquiring his first ocarina from Saria when he leaves Koriki Forest, Link continually learns new songs to aid him on his quest – tunes to open doors, befriend people, even for summoning help.

Becoming Adult

THE SNES SEQUEL *A Link To The Past* was the first game to introduce the dual-realm mechanic to the series. Proving so popular, it was then reintroduced in *Ocarina*. When Link enters the Sacred Realm his concentration is distracted by the Master Sword, allowing Ganondorf to seize the Triforce. When Link awakens seven years later, he's an adult, and Hyrule has been cast into darkness and despair as a result of Ganondorf's abuse of the powerful relic. Link is given a startling glimpse of what the future holds should he fail in his quest.

GAME-CHANGER

It wasn't just about being a 3D Zelda; these elements helped elevate Ocarina Of Time to be one of the greatest games of all time

Enemy targeting

ATTACKING ENEMIES IN a 3D space was always a little cumbersome in early action-adventure games. Or at least, it was until *Ocarina Of Time* arrived with its ingenious lock-on system. A staple of the genre today, it allowed the player to intuitively snap the camera to an enemy, giving Link the freedom to circle and strafe around monsters without losing the ability to follow up and dish out attacks. Where would we be today without such an important game system?

Platforming excellence

SUPER MARIO 64 is a classic, a showcase for the brilliance of Nintendo in the Nineties. But it also showcased some of the pitfalls of navigation in a 3D space. As *Ocarina Of Time* and *Super Mario 64* were developed in tandem, it gave the team plenty of time to make adjustments and tweaks to the controls and camera, ultimately ensuring that – by the time *Ocarina Of Time* was released – it handled far more confidently in the tight dungeon enclosures.

Context-sensitive actions

WITH SO MANY actions available to the player – many of which were new to gaming – Nintendo simplified the control system to ensure play was as smooth as possible. Context-sensitive actions enabled multiple tasks to be assigned to one button, cutting the fuss of learning too many controls and guiding the player around its environments. It let Link adventure without worry, only being given the option to move boxes or climb when it was necessary.

◀ Dungeon design

THE TEMPLES IN *Ocarina Of Time* are a marvel of 3D design and execution, with each offering challenge and reward to players ready to push their understanding of the combat and platforming mechanics. Even the Water Temple, largely considered to be the toughest challenge in the game and a notorious headache even today, has proven itself to be a masterclass in spatial awareness, demonstrating a willingness to challenge convention and take risks in every area of game design.

Sprawling overworld

ONE OF THE ingenious aspects of *Zelda* games was the inclusion of an overworld, a hub that linked all levels, dungeons and areas together. This was expanded for *Ocarina Of Time* to a space large enough to make you feel like you were a small part of the world around you. If you could see it, you could reach it – even if that meant searching out specific items and returning later.

▶ story was actually incorporated and finalised at the latter stages of the game's design.

In keeping with the focus on immersion and displaying the land of Hyrule in the best possible way, it was Miyamoto's intention that the camera in the game had a spotlight on Hyrule rather than Link and his actions. This decision made logical sense in the adventure game setting. In *Mario 64*, players benefited greatly from having fluid and clear sight over Mario at all times, helping them to get accustomed to his new abilities and negotiate platform sections in a new 3D space. It was decided that such requirements were not necessary for a *Zelda* game.

Since the release of *The Legend Of Zelda*, Miyamoto had always wanted to make players feel as if they were really inside Hyrule. With the N64 giving him the power to do this, Miyamoto and his teams thought about how best to make the player feel fully immersed in its world. And, in finding their answer, they came up with another of *Ocarina Of Time*'s best aspects: the controls.

> "Every aspect of Ocarina felt well-considered; it was like the game was trying its hardest to make your stay in Hyrule as pleasurable as possible"

To say the controls in *Ocarina* are attuned perfectly to the game world better than any 3D game that has come before or since is no exaggeration. Making full use of the crazy number of buttons on the Nintendo 64's unique controller, Link was able to effortlessly navigate Hyrule. Simple but very effective inclusions made the game instantly accessible to all – such as having Link jump automatically whenever he was steered off the edge of a platform (considerately saving you the obvious job), and a context-sensitive A button which could be used to make Link wave his sword around, open doors, move objects, climb platforms, and converse with Hyrule's many memorable characters.

Similarly, using items and viewing the world was made a breeze thanks to the clever use of the controller's yellow C (camera) buttons. In third-person mode, items could be assigned to them to enable easy and immediate access during the game, while in first-person mode the same buttons offered total control over the game's camera to help you get your bearings and offer precision aiming for weapons such as the slingshot and boomerang. Combat, like everything else in *Ocarina Of Time*, was also made incredibly simple thanks to an innovative new combat system the game introduced that was called 'Z-targeting'. An automatic aiming mechanic for Link's projectile weapons, it has since become a combat staple in videogames

» Each ocarina tune you learn impacts the world in a meaningful way, a mechanic that was replicated in *The Wind Waker.*

» This odd stealth section, which sees Link avoiding guards to reach princess Zelda, is one of the less impressive sections in the game.

▲ Extended adventuring

THROUGHOUT HIS QUEST, Link will acquire and collect different items and weapons that greatly expand the adventure. Many introduced new abilities, with Nintendo gradually introducing them through well-masked tutorials in the guise of puzzle-solving before letting you loose with them in boss battles and, eventually, the overworld to access new areas. It has proven to be a staple of *Zelda* design, not to mention a process carried across into various other genres and game types.

Heartfelt narrative

UNLIKE MOST OTHER Nintendo games released at the time – in which mechanics took precedence over all else – *Ocarina* had the story at its centre. While joyful to play, it had a dark undertone of loss and tragedy. Link's journey across timelines, to stop a disaster he inadvertently had a hand in creating, has proven to be one of gaming's greatest.

Boss design

BOSS DESIGN IN *The Legend Of Zelda* has always been fairly simple: find the flashing bit of the enemy and hit it with whatever new item has just been gifted to you. That's okay though because *Ocarina* masked this with memorable and striking encounters. *Zelda* bosses made a wonderful transition into 3D, always looking large enough to make the task ahead seem implausibly difficult, with impossibly-tight mechanics making it seem ultimately achievable.

and has been used in many games across many different genres and franchises.

In addition to the game's obliging control scheme, players were also aided on their quest by a fairy helper called Navi. Acting as your guide throughout the adventure, and never away from Link's side, she would point out points of interest during the game as well as offer useful hints and suggestions to help you complete puzzles.

Every aspect of *Ocarina* felt well-considered; it was like the game was trying its hardest to make your stay in Hyrule as pleasurable as possible, so that you'd tell all of your friends to pay it a visit, or maybe even decide to return to it yourself.

The story of *Ocarina Of Time* is set before the events of the first four games in the series, and sticks to the traditional *Zelda* template. Link must venture into a series of enemy-filled dungeons, find a desired object and then make his escape by defeating a gargantuan boss blocking the exit route. However, *Ocarina*, like *A Link To The Past* before it, is split into two very distinct sections. The first, which is set in a lush and vibrant-looking depiction of Hyrule, sees Link as a young boy, under orders from Princess Zelda to retrieve three Spiritual Stones that will grant him access to the Sacred Realm where the Triforce is kept. Simply getting to this point can take players a good amount of time – especially if they embark on many of the sidequests – but this is less than halfway through the adventure. Upon unsealing the Sacred Realm, Ganondorf pilfers the Triforce and Link is sealed away and must work out how to escape.

It is once you reach this point that events take a dramatic turn. Seven years pass by, and when Link awakens he is met by one of seven sages whose job is to protect the Triforce. Now a young adult, Link learns that Ganondorf has used the Triforce to cast the kingdom of Hyrule into darkness. Hope now rests with Link reawakening ▶

» Unlocking Epona is one of the game's must-do side-missions – otherwise you'll make some pretty long treks across Hyrule Field.

» The music in the game was composed by Koji Kondo, who was responsible for creating the music in all of the main *Zelda* games.

five dormant sages, by travelling to five temples in Hyrule to defeat Ganondorf's monsters and break his evil spell. If he succeeds, the sages can trap Ganondorf inside the Sacred Realm and restore the kingdom of Hyrule to its original state.

The moment that Link steps outside and sees the effects Ganondorf's reign has had on Hyrule – sapping it of all life, colour and beauty and turning it into a dark, depressing, shrivelled-up shell of its former self – is one of *Ocarina Of Time*'s many rug-pulling moments. Future Hyrule looks ashen and volcanic; the walking dead replace the fizzy townsfolk, and Kokiri Forest is overgrown with deadly flora and fauna – no longer a safe haven for Link, but the perfect place for evil to thrive.

Like that memorable scene in *Back To The Future 2*, where Marty McFly returns to a bleak and unwelcoming image of the present in which Biff has become a casino magnate, it's an effective plot device that shows the hero an important glimpse at what his future will be should he fail to put things right. In *Ocarina Of Time*, the effect is used just as evocatively, spurring the player on to complete their quest and put things right. Indeed, paying a return visit to many of the familiar locations around Hyrule at this point kicks up a number of surprises for Link and the player. Lon Lon Ranch, the stables where Link finds and (once an adult) wins his trusty horse Epona, is now under new ownership. Walking through its tall gates expecting to find a friendly face, Link learns that its original proprietors, Talon and his daughter Malon, have been mercilessly booted out of their home by Ganondorf, and its ownership has now been handed to Talon's deceitful stablehand, Ingo. This and many other changes for the worse you learn about quickly add mounting weight to the quest, as you see not only the important but also the personal effects of your actions.

With its numerous delays, an almost-switch of platform, and also taking that sometimes tricky step up to 3D, it would be fair to say that *Ocarina Of Time* exceeded almost everybody's expectations at the time, achieving incredible reviews. Nintendo not only appeased long-standing fans of its popular franchise by delivering a brand-new 3D *Zelda* game to surpass the lofty eminence of its 16-bit masterpiece *A Link To The Past*, but also managed to attract a whole new audience to the franchise by delivering one of the greatest adventure games to ever see release. Garnering high acclaim and rave review scores across the board, and making history by scoring the first ever 40/40 in *Weekly Famitsu*, the only other game sequels to have ever had the same kind of impact are perhaps *Street Fighter II* and Nintendo's very own killer app, *Super Mario 64*.

If we want to be incredibly picky, we'd say that there are some weaker aspects of *Ocarina Of Time* that don't live up to the majesty displayed elsewhere, and which leave it looking and feeling fairly dated today. For example, at points, it's not made explicitly clear where you should be going next in the game, and there are sections that only open up to you on the completion of some pretty baffling criteria – such as cleansing a room entirely of bats (which can sometimes mean that the odd wayward one can leave you stumped), or having two conversations with the same character in quick succession. Don't even get us started with the swimming mechanics or the legendary frustration of its slow-motion Water Temple dungeon. However, its lush, beautiful 3D world, fluid controls, masterful storytelling, game

> "The moment that Link steps outside and sees the effects Ganondorf's reign has had on Hyrule is one of Ocarina Of Time's many rug-pulling moments"

» Leaving the safety of Kokiri Forest and stepping into Hyrule was a formative moment for many gamers.

» Locking on to your enemy became so successful that many games borrowed the concept, and you can still see its influence today.

FAVOURITE MOMENTS FROM OCARINA OF TIME

Retro Gamer readers offer us a link to the past by recalling the Ocarina moment that has stayed with them more than any other

theantmesiter
Finishing it. I bought *Ocarina Of Time* on release day back in 1998 and it literally took me ten years to finish it. Looking back, it really was the greatest adventure I ever experienced in gaming. I aged along with Link and almost cried when it was over. And with that, I boxed up the game and haven't touched it since.

ShadowMan
Getting out of the Water Temple. Words cannot describe my joy and relief to finally finish that pain in the backside.

RetroMartin
Pulling out the Master Sword – classic scene, classic tune… and the ability to change from adult to kid!

Shinobi
When you first meet Zelda for the first time and she plays Epona's Song – the best piece of music ever! Also, the art gallery, and the Grim Reaper on the horse that came out of the paintings..

sscott
Walking out onto Hyrule field for the very first time and thinking, 'I can go anywhere I want!'

The Mask Seller
When Link first leaves Kokiri Forest, the parting with Saria on the wooden rope bridge gets me every time. They're just children in the game but the parting is handled so well. It conveys a lot more emotion with its muddy textures, simple character models and purely text script then any FMV-enhanced epic I've played. I also love the bit when the Goron King rocks out to Saria's Song.

StickHead
Got to be escaping Lon Lon Ranch on the back of Epona. I felt like Steve McQueen in *The Great Escape*.

mrmarvelxiii
It has to be the ending. No other game ending has touched me so deeply; the music, the gathering around the Lon Lon Ranch Bonfire and that final shot of young Link and Zelda meeting once again…

Budley Moore
Simply solving some of the fiendishly deceptive puzzles, kicking myself after spending hours and hours trying to solve them, only to realise it was something simple, like firing an arrow into the eye or such. A great game.

learnedrobb
Just one moment? There's no way I can manage it. I'll say the whole damn game!

Reglan
When Link first encounters King Dodongo. I think my jaw hit the floor from being caught off guard by how massive that thing actually was. The ensuing battle is still one of my favourites.

Zapper
Beating the game without picking up any extra heart containers. The atmosphere is generally great in this game but this challenge I set for myself made me feel it a lot more. I had gotten a bit too used to the game after playing it so much, so this made it a lot more exciting.

Miketendo
I think the most important moment in *Ocarina Of Time* isn't just one moment, it's all of the moments. That was one of the last games that I just could not put down until I finished it. I haven't had that feeling since *Ocarina*. The overall feeling of massive exploration was astonishing, and I think that's what ultimately sold me on the game in the first place.

FatTrucker
At the time it was released, probably the standout moment for me was when you finished the first hour or so of god-awful Nintendo handholding and 'practice', and suddenly had access to anywhere you wanted to go. It just seemed so suddenly unscripted and ripe for exploration as you walked out onto Hyrule field for the first time. It was probably the first step toward what's now known as 'sandbox' gaming, and it felt genuinely new and exciting at the time.

dste
I would say, for me, that out of the entire game my favourite moment would be when, after seven years, Link leaves the Temple Of Time and you see how time and evil has destroyed Castle Town. Death Mountain sitting in the background with the light whirring around it just looks immense, and it just introduces the next part of the game so brilliantly.

boggyb68
The beginning; all I do in it is wander around the village throwing rocks all over the place and making a silly whooping noise at the same time… it's marvellous!

design and incredible pacing make it as perfect a game as you could probably ever hope to play.

That its influence and popularity can still be felt to this day is a mark of its impact and legacy. Having already been re-released twice before, first with *Ocarina Of Time: Master Quest* for GameCube in 2003 – a revision of the game featuring new puzzles and tougher dungeons to tackle – and then for Virtual Console, the game was once again thrust back into the spotlight with a new remastered – and, dare we even say, definitive – edition for the 3DS. As well as rendering the Hyrule in stereoscopic 3D, *Ocarina Of Time 3D* has made subtle improvements to the gameplay, full use of the console's in-built touchscreen for item selection, and gyroscopic technology to offer motion-controlled aiming. It also came packaged with both the original Nintendo 64 and *Master Quest* editions of the game, as well as a brand-new boss rush mode for fans to hone their Z-triggering skills with. In short, it's a superb update of a classic game that highlights just how far ahead of the curve the original N64 classic was at the time.

Clearly proud of what it achieved with *Ocarina Of Time* – creating one of the most enchanting and perfect game worlds, and setting an early benchmark for all 3D adventures that has still yet to be bettered in any meaningful way – Nintendo must have hoped the 3DS version would encourage those who missed the game first time around to pick up and experience one of its most finest and accomplished videogames.

The muddy Nintendo 64 visuals may have lost some of their magic since the game was originally released, but that's never been *Zelda*'s formula for success and it never will be, as *Breath Of The Wild* proved when the Nintendo Switch launched. As we said at the start, the mark of whether a game is good or not is always judged by reflecting upon the journey it's taken you on. No game series on any format proves that better than *Zelda*, and few games, if any, offer a journey as magical, memorable and timeless as *Ocarina Of Time*. It remains as enchanting to play now, as it did the very first time we experienced it. A true videogaming classic in every possible way, we'll never get bored of it.

» *Ocarina* features plenty of epic bosses, made more interesting by their imposing shapes filling the screen and clever attack patterns.

» The graphics are quaint today, but they still convey that thoughtful charm as well as they did in 1998.

THE LEGEND OF ZELDA™ MAJORA'S MASK

The Hero Of Time makes his return in a surreal sequel that was never supposed to exist

WORDS BY NIKOLE ROBINSON

The strict time constraints and constant pressure of *Majora's Mask* mirror perfectly the creation and development of the game itself, completed in just one year. After 1998's *Ocarina Of Time* became an instant hit and redefined 3D gaming, series producer Shigeru Miyamoto wanted to both capitalise on its success and further utilise the game's engine; the iconic title originally used the same engine as *Super Mario 64*, but so many modifications were made during *Ocarina*'s three-year development that it became its own beast.

The spawning of a sequel ties in heavily with the failure of the 64DD, a Japan-only peripheral designed to expand the limitations of the Nintendo 64. *Ocarina Of Time* was intended to be a flagship title for this new device, but Link's expansive range of motion was stunted when the game was read from a disc, thus the code found its home on a 32-megabyte cartridge instead. However, this halved the available space, meaning many concepts, enemies and locations went unused in the final release.

The 64DD suffered repeated delays and was still under development at the time of *Ocarina*'s launch. Holding onto the hope that this future technology would find its footing, plans were discussed to bolster *Ocarina Of Time* with a disc expansion. The story would remain the same, but the overworld would be flipped, enemies would hit harder and dungeons would be relocated and redesigned to pose new challenges for returning players. Inspired by the Second Quest mode unlocked after completing *The Legend Of Zelda*, it would ensure that the engine and cut content wouldn't go to waste.

Most of the work of overhauling the dungeons for the 64DD expansion, tentatively titled *'Ura Zelda'*, would fall to Eiji Aonuma, lead dungeon designer for *Ocarina Of Time* and one of its directors. Going back to the drawing board, Aonuma became frustrated. He'd spent a lot of time balancing his dungeons with puzzles, exploration and combat, and believed his creations were already the best they could be. He found himself designing new dungeon concepts instead of remixing his previous work, getting more enjoyment from his secret side project.

Inspired, Aonuma built up the courage to meet with Miyamoto to present his ideas, asking if they ▶

» Not helping Romani with an alien invasion leaves her in a vegetative state.

© Getty

» Under the influence of Majora's Mask, the Skull Kid becomes a powerful adversary for Link.

» This first transformation scene mirrors a nightmare Aonuma had during production.

could instead work on a new *Zelda*. Miyamoto agreed, but with one caveat: the game must be finished within a year. It could make use of *Ocarina*'s engine, assets, models and unused material as a way of speeding up production, but would need all-new dungeons, story elements and quests, as well as some fresh mechanics. Aonuma cautiously accepted the mantle of supervising director of a new *Zelda* story, and the race against the clock began.

Development started in January 1999, just two months after *Ocarina*'s release. With a much smaller team and limited to a third of the time its predecessor had required, Aonuma needed an ambitious idea to continue the legacy of what was being called the pinnacle of game design across the world. Wondering what kind of game could find success as a follow-up to something so critically acclaimed, Aonuma conferred with fellow *Ocarina Of Time* director Yoshiaki Koizumi.

Koizumi had worked on story elements for *A Link To The Past* and created the ethereal dream world of the Wind Fish for *Link's Awakening*. Aonuma hoped he could help with ideas for the new game, given the working title of '*Zelda Gaiden*', meaning 'side story'. At the time, Koizumi was in charge of his own project, a cops-and-robbers board game where the aim was to catch a criminal in under a week. Though this game would never come to fruition, its soul can be found at the heart of *Majora's Mask*.

Taking inspiration from his board game, Koizumi agreed to work with Aonuma on *Zelda* as long as the passage of time was a key element. Since *Ocarina Of Time* already had a day-night cycle, which could even be controlled by the player with the Sun's Song, the foundations were already in place. The pair realised that a week-long time loop could pack a lot into a compact game world, adding depth over breadth. Playing the same days over and over while uncovering more and more secrets was the genesis of a new form of exploration, relying on multiple playthroughs. At the end of a cycle, you'd have to go back to progress forward. Miyamoto approved of the concept, liking how it added replayability.

Zelda Gaiden had its core element, and because the series had already featured time travel, it didn't feel out of place. Now it was time

EXPANDING ON A MASTERPIECE

Majora's Mask presents several elements that differentiate it from its predecessor

On the clock

GIVEN THREE DAYS to save Termina, a constantly ticking clock is present at the bottom of the screen as a reminder of what little time you have. The 72-hour cycle takes about 54 minutes of real time to complete, meaning an in-game hour equates to just over 45 seconds. It's up to you to decide what to do with that precious time.

Manipulating time

DANCING WITH THE Stylin' Scarecrow in the Astral Observatory or Trading Post will skip time to the next dawn or dusk, but he'll also hint about using an instrument to do the same. The Song Of Double Time lets you skip ahead yourself, while the Inverted Song Of Time slows time down to a third of its normal rate.

Social networking

MORE THAN ANY other *Zelda*, talking to the world's inhabitants is an important part of gaining information and finding hints on what you can do to progress, especially in *Majora's Mask*'s many multi-day sidequests. Certain dialogue and events only occur at a specific time, and wearing masks can get a different reaction out of people.

Finding fairies

EACH OF THE four dungeons has 15 Stray Fairies to locate and rescue. Some are in chests or appear after you defeat an enemy, but others are very well hidden. While entirely optional, the power-ups you receive by taking the extra time to find all the Stray Fairies hidden within a dungeon are worth the trouble, staying with you when you restart a cycle.

Coming undone

NOT EVERYTHING YOU do in Termina is permanent. Once you reach the end of a cycle or decide to turn back time, you sacrifice all the progress you've made and the people you've helped in that run, including dungeon completion, and only Link will remember past outcomes. You'll also lose arrows, bombs and any rupees you haven't banked.

to build around that. Taking Link away from the well-travelled Hyrule, the parallel world of Termina gave new stories and personalities to the familiar faces borrowed from *Ocarina Of Time*, with these doppelgangers adding to its otherworldly feel. Koizumi would build a bustling town, focusing on realistic depictions of the lives of the townspeople, all busy going about their day. Aonuma would design the overworld, with each cardinal direction given a different theme that tied into its dungeon and populated with different races and creatures.

At first, Termina's stories unfolded over a week of in-game time, but Aonuma and Koizumi realised that keeping track of schedules and events was too complex when spread across seven days. They were concerned that players wouldn't want to spend days waiting for a specific event to reoccur after travelling back to the start of the week. Seven days was pushed down to three, but the story and events were compressed into three days as well, forging a tightly packed world with a lot of substance. Only having to work with three days of content shortened the development time, a huge boon for a small team with a time limit.

Majora's Mask is both hailed and hated for being as stressful as it is enjoyable. Having just three days of play piles on the pressure, compounded by the many clock faces around Clock Town and the timer ticking away on-screen at all times. A fear of the passage of time is intrinsically human, conscious of our own mortality, the limited time we have and what we do with it. Time in *Majora's Mask* is utilised in such a way that you're constantly fighting against it – not just monsters and demons – and even though you alone have the power to turn back time, progress is lost and the clock simply starts winding down again. No one can escape time; it can't be defeated. This adds a sense of futility to the hero's journey – no matter how powerful Link becomes, he'll never be able to stop the march of time or help everyone in Termina in one cycle.

> "By the Final Day, Clock Town is eerily empty. Those who remain quiver in fear"

As if this isn't harrowing enough, the moon is about to crash into Termina. Time is running out for its residents, and they slowly come to terms with this over the course of the game. Upon your arrival, the people of Clock Town begin to question if it's really happening, some fearful and others in denial. With each passing hour, the falling moon becomes larger in the sky, and the atmosphere of the town changes. Fewer people go out in the streets. They'll mention their growing fears as they confront the end of the world in their own ways. By the Final Day, Clock Town is eerily empty. Those who remain quiver in fear, deny their destruction or accept their fate.

The moon falling was another of Koizumi's ideas, coming to him in a daydream. Gazing up at the sky, he wondered what would happen if the moon were to fall towards Earth and how people would react to this apocalyptic event. With a sense of impending doom a perfect fit for a game with time at its centre, the main

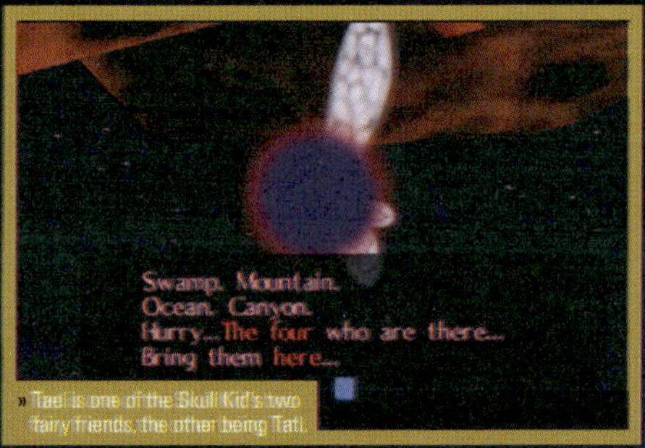

» Tael is one of the Skull Kid's two fairy friends, the other being Tatl.

» This adventure whisks us away from the familiar locales of Hyrule and into the doomed Termina.

» Mayor Dotour runs Clock Town and is faced with a bit of a conundrum thanks to that tumbling moon.

A TRANSFORMATIVE EXPERIENCE

Three core masks give you the form and abilities of a different race

Deku Scrub

YOU'RE STUCK IN Clock Town as Deku Link for the entirety of your first three-day time loop, giving you plenty of time to adjust to this form. Deku Link holds no weapons but does have a weak Spin Attack in place of a Dodge Roll when pressing A. Once Magic Power is obtained from the Great Fairy, Deku Link can shoot a Bubble Blast. His light weight enables him to hop across the poisoned swamp, and he can use Deku Flowers to launch himself into the air on petal gliders, dropping Deku Nuts to stun enemies from above.

Goron

IN GORON FORM, Link obtains all the strength of Darmani, attacking with a powerful punch and uppercut combo, though he's much slower in combat. Pressing A curls Goron Link up into a ball; pressing B while curled up will perform a slam called a Goron Pound, breaking objects, stunning enemies and activating switches. While curled, moving allows Goron Link to roll around at greater speed, increasing further and giving him damaging spikes if Magic Power is available. Goron Link cannot swim, but he can walk through lava without taking damage.

Zora

THIS ALLOWS LINK to navigate the seas with ease and expands greatly on the simple diving of *Ocarina Of Time*. Zora Link can swim in any direction, with speed increased by holding down the A Button, and can leap out of the water in a Dolphin Jump. Triggering the shield with R while swimming creates an electric barrier which can be used as an attack. Pressing B underwater has Link walk along the seafloor as if wearing the Iron Boots. Outside of swimming, holding down B turns Zora Link's arm fins into twin boomerangs.

story and sidequests were designed around a world about to meet a terrible fate. Though early concept art showed a moon with no features, the final version's pained expression adds further discomfort, constantly looking down on Link with those haunting eyes as he makes yet another attempt to stop its deadly descent. And here the hero can fail. Without player input, the world still progresses, the moon growing ever closer, the clock ticking away. The Final Day ends, and the world with it in a fiery blaze.

The downfall is depicted beautifully in Koji Kondo's soundtrack. Clock Town has a different arrangement each day. It starts cheerful and joyous, the town still gearing up for the festivities. By the Second Day, uneasiness has crept in. The pace has picked up and fewer instruments are featured. The tones of the ocarina stand out against the more muted backdrop. There's a slight sadness to it, especially against the rainfall. On the Final Day, the pace is frantic. There's a sombre string motif behind it that compounds feelings of anxiety – something about it doesn't sound right. But it's the music in the Final Hours that's truly chilling: slow, sorrowful strings that pull at your heart as you wait for it all to end.

» The Happy Mask Salesman returns in a more prominent role compared to *Ocarina Of Time*.

» While *Majora's Mask* is less combat-focused, there are still many enemies to defeat.

O*carina Of Time* had dark moments, but can't compare to the despair, distress and desperation woven throughout *Majora's Mask*. While designed for returning players – hence the complete lack of a tutorial – the sequel levels the playing field by ripping away everything that made Link special. You begin the game absolutely powerless: a lone child lost in the woods, robbed and cursed by a mischievous imp. Though memories of Hyrule make this all the more impactful, *Zelda* veterans will feel just as lost and confused in a new body and a new world. Adjusting to his transfiguration into a Deku Scrub, the fallen hero soon finds purpose upon meeting the Happy Mask Salesman, who offers a deal Link can't refuse.

Opening the doors of the Clock Tower to uncannily familiar faces in an unknown setting, it sinks in that you're a foreigner in this land. Link was destined to save Hyrule, but in Termina, he's simply passing through. Exploring the ill-fated Clock Town, you'll find that people are too preoccupied with their own anxieties to give you much consideration, especially while you're trapped in a childlike wooden body. Even after you regain your true form, not many people outright ask for your help. You infer their troubles and simply decide to help because it's the right thing to do. You want to see if you can help… to heal this cursed world.

It's apt that Clock Town runs like clockwork. Everyone sticks to their schedule unless you choose to intervene, but you have to be in the right place at the right time, sometimes needing a specific item or song. If you miss or fail an encounter, you'll have to take what you've learned and try again. Interacting with some of the citizens is entirely optional, though there's a lot to gain from helping them – and not just through rewards. *Majora's Mask*'s many sidequests expand its small world exponentially. Exploring the personal stories gives you all the more reason to save Termina because these characters feel real: they have fears, hopes and feelings. Koizumi built his real-life experiences into them, giving them heart. You can also be confronted by the consequences of your inaction, guilt spurring you to want to help next time around.

To experience the full spectrum of emotions here, you'll need to collect masks – an element that was present, but not fully realised, in *Ocarina Of Time*. In Termina, masks are given deeper meaning and grant a host of abilities. While some citizens of Hyrule would react to Link wearing different masks, here he uses them to elicit the feelings of others and break the many curses afflicting the land. Each mask Link receives is bound with the feelings and memories of the person who entrusted it to him, reminding him of those he aided even when he returns to a time before he solved their problems.

The three transformation masks contain the very essence of a departed soul. Link soothes the restless dead with his song, allowing them to move on. Wearing the masks they leave behind, he's flooded with their regrets, of things they didn't manage to accomplish in life and the friends they left behind. He takes up the mantle of the deceased, vowing to right the wrongs they failed to fix in their stead. Transforming into shades of their former selves, he selflessly saves each corner of Termina while wearing another's face – once again, Link won't be remembered as the hero. Each race is liberated by its own masked champion, but because of this, none of them realises they've lost someone dear to them.

Pain and loss are found wherever you go in Termina. The Southern Swamp of the Deku is toxic and its princess is missing. Snowhead is trapped in an eternal winter and the Gorons are freezing to death. Great Bay is under threat from climate change and Zora-egg-stealing pirates. Ikana Canyon is a place cursed with undeath. In each direction from the terminal that is Clock Town, there are self-contained problems to solve on top of the threat of the moon. Navigating each locale successfully will require you to master your masks, seamlessly blending in with the people who dwell there and gaining their trust in order to access their sacred temples.

While *Majora's Mask* only has four major dungeons, reaching them is a challenge in itself, preparing you for the puzzle themes you'll discover within. All four are masterfully crafted, making excellent use of three-dimensional space. You'll need to understand the very architecture of the temples, with a good grasp of spatial reasoning required to best them. Exploration is key, traversing interlinking rooms and learning the layout, but doing so against the clock makes it all the more difficult. Woodfall requires mastery of Deku Link. Snowhead needs you to visualise how each room connects to the central pillar. Great Bay has you paying attention to pipe colours and changing water currents. In Stone Tower, you must map out both the floor and ceiling, but it also tests you on your transformations, bringing together every part of your journey.

Though it would have been easy to follow *Ocarina Of Time* with another heroic tale, the courage of the team to try new ideas and weird concepts ensured that the game was far from a cheap imitation, and that it was compiled in a year using borrowed assets makes that all the more impressive. *Majora's Mask* certainly stands out as a black sheep of the series, with not even *Twilight Princess* coming close to its level of darkness. It's a divisive entry, with many complaining about the punishing difficulty and focus on side stories, but it has gained a cult following from those looking for a little existentialism in their adventures.

What's so captivating about *Majora's Mask* is the many mysteries it leaves behind. Even after multiple playthroughs, you're still left with questions you'll never get an answer to, daring you to come back to the game to see if you can finally uncover all of its secrets. It's the kind of game that will occupy your mind for years after you put down the controller, be it in frustration or completion. But whether your parting with the game is forever or simply for a short time… that is up to you.

» The Skull Kid is a mischievous creature, most Terminians dislike him thanks to the pranks he pulls.

» Playing until the last second sees you suffer the fiery end of the world.

MAJORA'S MASK 3D

The 2015 3DS remake lost some of the original's mystery

AS WELL AS adults returning to a game they remembered from childhood, the remake would be many people's first encounter with *Majora's Mask*. Nintendo saw this as an opportunity to improve upon the rushed Nintendo 64 iteration, and Aonuma put together a list of things he considered to be too punishing or that he was ashamed of to be reworked. Many players loved the original for its weirdness, difficulty and lack of guidance, worrying that these elements would be stripped back in favour of mass appeal. Unfortunately, this wasn't completely off. Boss fights were overhauled, requiring specific mechanics and in some cases having entire extra stages. They were also given obvious weak points. While some battles were now more dynamic, not all were improved, with Odolwa and Twinmold suffering somewhat.

The clock is less dominant, featuring all three days along the very bottom of the screen and presented digitally over analogue. The Bomber's Notebook is improved but much more intrusive, and the Bombers themselves will bombard you with hints, chasing Link around. The restriction of only being able to save by using the Song Of Time was removed entirely, with players able to save at any Owl Statue as desired. These changes made *Majora's Mask* less unique, with elements shared by other *Zelda* titles bringing this strange sequel more in line with the status quo. While the over-brightened graphics looked the part, they didn't lend themselves to the game's dark and doomed atmosphere, lessening its impact.

Source: Wikipedia Commons © Public Domain

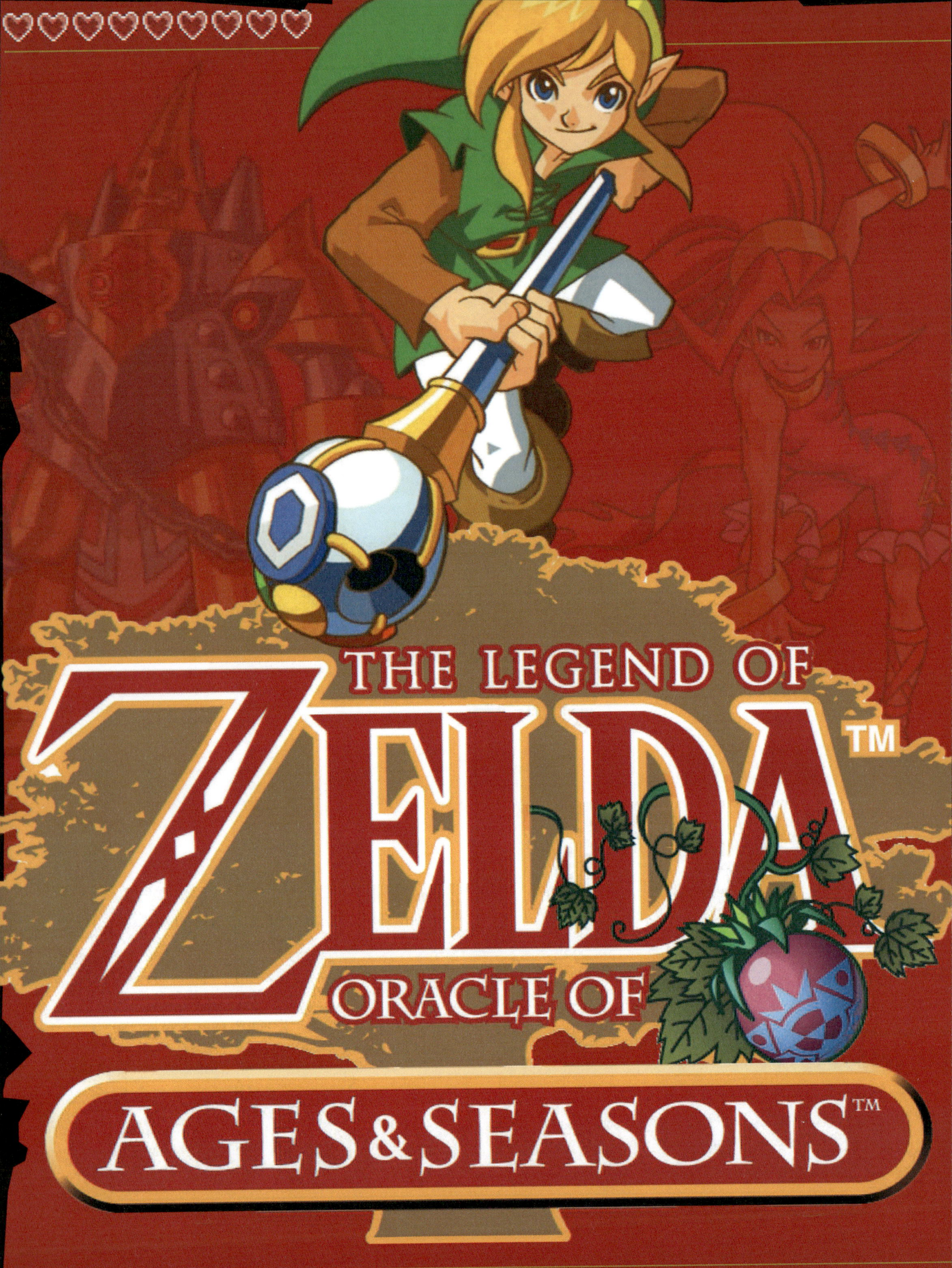
THE LEGEND OF
ZELDA™
ORACLE OF
AGES & SEASONS™

How Capcom's first field trip into the world of Zelda left a lasting influence on the series that can be felt today

WORDS BY MATTHEW PELLETT & DREW SLEEP

Think of gaming pairs and the mind immediately goes to the likes of *Pokémon Red & Blue*: one core game released as two titles thanks to a few small additions and omissions in each version. Outside of *Pokémon*, however, the concept can appear to be quite rare, and for good reason. Making two games, however similar they might be, to release on the same day is a tall order for any game developer.

Not content to take an easy option, Capcom's first-ever contributions to *The Legend Of Zelda* series were not only a dual-release but they were also two unique games. *The Oracle Of Ages* and *Oracle Of Seasons* were an ambitious set of titles that rewarded completionists and could be linked up for a grander adventure after the two were finished.

In 1999, Flagship (a subsidiary studio of Capcom) was looking for work. Studio head Yoshiki Okamoto met with *Legend Of Zelda* creator and Nintendo luminary Shigeru Miyamoto and proposed that Flagship remake the original *Legend Of Zelda* for the Game Boy Color, bringing Link's first adventure to a new audience. Okamoto left discussions with Miyamoto with an order of six *Zelda* games – two based on existing games and four original titles.

Okamoto proceeded with his original plan of remaking *Zelda* first as it would be a fertile proving ground for his team to learn the ropes. As work began, the team led by director and designer Hidemaro Fujibayashi found that the remake wouldn't be the easy job that Okamoto envisioned. By 1999, the original *Legend Of Zelda* was a hugely difficult game compared to modern releases at the time, and the team discovered that a litany of changes was needed that would be nothing short of a complete overhaul. Fujibayashi petitioned Okamoto that the team wanted to skip the remake and create an original *Zelda* title instead.

Flagship returned to Miyamoto, asking for guidance on what to do next, and Miyamoto proposed a trilogy with each game focusing on different elements of gameplay. This overall project was to be called the *'Triforce Trilogy'* with each title representing one of Courage, Wisdom and Power.

Bolstered by this exciting new premise, Flagship returned to work incorporating elements – such as a link-up feature conceived by Okamoto – that bridged the games and tied them together into a cohesive theme. The development team's large ambition resulted in the cancellation of the third game, which was perhaps a wise choice in retrospect when you consider the wealth of love and attention that went into what are now titled the *Oracle* games. The two titles were released together in 2001, at the twilight of the Game Boy Color's lifespan, and what a swan song for the system they are.

Oracle Of Seasons and *Oracle Of Ages* see the Hyrule hero Link journeying to two very different lands and vanquishing two new foes, Veran and Onox. In *Oracle Of Seasons*, that new region is Holodrum, and it's there that Link meets the dancer Din. In *Oracle Of Ages*, meanwhile, Link visits Labrynna, where he encounters a singer named Nayru. Secretly, both Din and Nayru are also Oracles – the Oracle Of Seasons and Ages respectively – and when both are kidnapped, Link ▶

» Link is well-versed with shoving boulders, but he might have to come back to this early-game conundrum later.

» Obtaining the Poe Clock in *Oracle Of Ages* kicks off a trading quest. We're sure there's a clueless postman that might need it...

> "The games were released together in 2001, at the twilight of the GBC's lifespan"

embarks out on two wildly different journeys to rescue them.

The first port of call for both games involves tracking down the Maku Tree. Portrayed as male in *Seasons* and female in *Ages*, like Hyrule's Deku Tree this ancient shrub acts as each world's guardian, but they can only help once Link has found all eight of the Essences Of Time/Nature scattered about the worlds' deepest, darkest dungeons. Flagship's ambition was astounding: each game boasts unique lands and dungeons too, but more than that, they – quite brilliantly – also feature very different game mechanics.

» Both Nayru (pictured) and Din share the same colour association as the Hylian deities of the same names.

It's here where the *Oracle* series truly stood apart in *Zelda* lore. Sure, the foundations for the adventures are immediately familiar. Especially to those who had played *Link's Awakening* on the original Game Boy. The UI is strikingly familiar, as is the sprite art and general control scheme where you can assign items in Link's inventory to the A and B buttons. However, while bearing a resemblance to past games, this duo of Game Boy Color titles – unlike the *Pokémon* games which consistently dole out dual versions with small distinctions – are remarkably different to each other. *Oracle Of Seasons* was an action-focused game with plenty of combat for Link to sink his sword into. Meanwhile, *Oracle Of Ages* was a far more puzzle-heavy affair, throwing the plucky hooded hero up against some deviously designed conundrums. You can still see that original *Triforce Trilogy* design concept here, with *Seasons* embracing Courage or Power, where *Ages* is clearly championing Wisdom.

Thanks to the Harp Of Ages and the Rod Of Seasons (no prizes for figuring out which item belonged to which game), the twin adventures are even more distinct from one another. Using the Harp in *Oracle Of Ages* opened any hidden time portals in the on-screen area, letting Link jump between past and present versions of Labrynna to alter events in history. The timelines feature unique worlds, and combined, they make for one gigantic adventure.

» Vasu will appraise your magic rings and even let you trade them between *Seasons* and *Ages*.

Oracle Of Seasons, meanwhile, doesn't have two worlds, though. It effectively has *five*. The Rod Of Seasons grants its user the power to usher in new seasons, which means that Link could travel between Holodrum's spring, summer, autumn and winter incarnations once he unlocks the Rod's full power. Each season brings in new environmental features. In certain situations, Link will have to travel to winter to pass by a giant tree that is far too leafy to squeeze past at all other times of the year, or switch to summertime to dry up a lake and enter a cave that was otherwise submerged. The fifth world is the subterranean land of Subrosia: a lava-filled underground universe filled with secrets and mysterious Subrosian people. Those two standalone games might have satisfied most *Zelda* fans, however, Capcom and Flagship innovated further than anyone would have expected them

DYNAMIC DUO

Explore the key elements from the Oracle games

Din

THE ORACLE OF Seasons is blessed with the power of controlling the flow of seasons, which is why General Onox targets her for imprisonment to throw the world into chaos.

Nayru

PROTECTED BY CHILDHOOD friend Ralph, the Oracle Of Ages controls the flow of time. When she's possessed by antagonist Veran she travels back in time and destroys history.

Onox

THE GENERAL OF Darkness works for Twinrova in the quest to revive Ganon. He attempts to capture Din and submerge the Temple Of Seasons.

Veran

BY BRINGING SORROW to the world of Labrynna, this sorceress aids Twinrova in resurrecting Ganon. Though normally a fairy, she morphs into beetle, bee and spider forms in combat.

Magnetic Gloves

THIS ITEM IS found in *Oracle Of Seasons*. It lets Link cross chasms, rip armour off Iron Masks, flip Magnites, solve polarity puzzles and use giant weapons to defeat bosses.

Switch Hook

ONLY AVAILABLE IN *Oracle Of Ages*, the Switch Hook is essentially a Hookshot with the distinction of switching Link's place with that of the item he latches onto.

» Ricky is a boxing kangaroo which can be summoned using Ricky's Flute in each game.

» In both titles, the environment will slightly change depending in which age or season you are in.

to. Individually, the *Oracle* games were as big and as classy as any other *Legend Of Zelda* game, but the pair were designed to interact through either the Game Boy Link Cable or a built-in password system. There are four key reasons to join the games. One, to trade the 64 stat-boosting rings hidden across the two games. Two, to carry over plot elements, meaning certain characters remembered Link's actions in the previous title. Three, to unlock new items and gain extra-powerful gear. And four, to play a remixed story, fight extra bosses and see the true ending.

Despite the developmental rethink of first ditching an original *Zelda* remake and then scaling a trilogy down to a duet, the *Oracle* subseries is still one of the franchise's most complex chapters. More than that, these games were both a critical and commercial success. The likes of *IGN* and *Nintendo Power* both granted the games perfect scores, while *Famitsu*'s jury awarded 31/40 for *Seasons* and 30/40 for *Ages*. Although it is extremely close, the consensus is that *Oracle Of Seasons* offers the better experience of the two, with its easy-to-grasp focus on action and its quartet of seasonal changes presenting more opportunities for the Game Boy Color's graphical capabilities to shine.

The *Oracle* games also made an impressive impact on the *Zelda* series as a whole. Pleased with how the games turned out, Nintendo continued its relationship with Capcom and produced a port of *A Link To The Past* for the Game Boy Advance in 2002, with a new multiplayer component: *Four Swords*. The creative pairing reached its zenith with *The Minish Cap*, also developed for the GBA and released in 2004. You can read more about that on page 82.

While Nintendo decided to cease its partnership with Capcom, Hidemaro Fujibayashi – the director of the *Oracle* games – remained close to *Zelda*. He is now the creative mind behind some of the series' modern highlights, having helmed *Minish Cap*, *Phantom Hourglass*, *Skyward Sword*, and most crucially, *Breath Of The Wild* and its follow-up *Tears Of The Kingdom*.

The next time you find yourself figuring out that "aha!" moment of a shrine puzzle, or revelling in the many ways to approach a Moblin encampment in *Breath Of The Wild*, you will do well to remember that the highs of *Zelda* today can be directly traced back to the ambitious *Oracle* games on Game Boy Color.

» Overall, the core gameplay resembles *Link's Awakening* on the original Game Boy.

"These two standalone games might have satisfied most Zelda fans, however, Capcom and Flagship innovated further than anyone would have expected them to"

Twinrova

THE FORCE BEHIND both games' mishaps, Twinrova only shows its faces once both games have been beaten as it attempts to revive Ganon once and for all.

Magic Rings

SIXTY-FOUR PIECES of jewellery that give Link bonuses when worn. Some of these are only obtained through trading or by playing the games on a Game Boy Advance.

» Just like Hyrule, Labrynna and Holodrum are a joy to explore and have enticing items hidden just out of reach.

THE MAKING OF THE LEGEND OF ZELDA® the Wind Waker™

Some still write it off as the franchise being all at sea, but look deeper and you'll find a Zelda game far closer to the original than any that have come since. Let's set sail in search of the surprising truth…

WORDS BY LUKE ALBIGÉS

» Sailing is relaxing, at least until the sun goes down...

So you most likely already have your favourite *Zelda* game locked down. Everyone does, it seems. Many cite the exceptional 3D rebirth of the franchise that is *Ocarina Of Time*, 16-bit purists wouldn't dare name anything other than *A Link To The Past* while many newcomers adore *Breath Of The Wild*. A far less popular choice, however, would be the ambitious GameCube outing, *The Wind Waker* – liberties were taken with structure, mechanics and style that meant that this particular game sticks out like a toon-shaded sore thumb alongside the rest of the series. But does that make it a bad choice? Does it heck. If anything, there's more of the NES original in *The Wind Waker* than there is in any *Zelda* game, although it might not be immediately apparent through the distinct visuals and the soaked setting.

Speaking with Eiji Aonuma, we learn that Link's primary companion on the vast open seas was written from experience. "We were working on *Wind Waker* right around the time that my son was born," he recalls. "Having just become a father, I wrote the text for the King Of Red Lions, the talking boat who takes Link on his adventure, as if I was talking to my own son." It's a beautiful sentiment, but one with which Aonuma isn't entirely happy. "Looking back over that text now, I felt as if he had a really self-important attitude and was forcing Link to go along with him. I regretted that a bit and changed the way he speaks to be a bit more mild in the remake."

But rewind to before that and you'll see a developer in a tight spot. After blowing minds and dropping jaws with *Ocarina Of Time* and its ambitious follow-up *Majora's Mask*, Nintendo found itself in a tricky situation. A new console meant all the old faces had to come back out to play – Mario had to bolt on a superfluous jetpack while we'd see the world through Samus' eyes for the first time, but what of Link? "Right when *Majora's Mask* ended, we knew that GameCube was going to be our next platform, so we had to begin planning for that," explained Shigeru Miyamoto in a 2004 interview. "The reason we were able to show you the more realistic-looking *Zelda* battle at Space World 2000 was because we had been doing some preliminary experiments with the console prior to completing *Majora's Mask*. That's why that video existed. It wasn't until afterwards that we began working with the director and the programmers to go ahead and create *The Wind Waker*."

IN THE KNOW

PUBLISHER: NINTENDO

DEVELOPER: NINTENDO EAD

RELEASED: 2002

PLATFORM: GAMECUBE

GENRE: ADVENTURE

» Training with Orca gets Link his first sword. Lovely.

» Might want to avoid that big, glowy orange patch.

"I wrote the text for the King Of Red Lions as if I was talking to my own son"

Eiji Aonuma

But there was quite a difference between the Space World demo and the game that was actually in development. "That announcement was shocking to *Zelda* fans," recalls Nintendo's Satoru Iwata. "Many were surprised and puzzled." Indeed they were – the Space World tech demo (for that's all it turned out to be) showed off a mature Link, while the game itself would take a decidedly different tack. "When I first saw the toon-shaded *Zelda*, I was very surprised and excited by it," admitted Miyamoto. "However, I was startled by the response we got from the press when we showed it off the first time. They all said, 'Oh, so is Nintendo now taking *Zelda* and trying to aim it only at kids?' Really, the whole concept we had behind it was that we thought it was a very creative and new way to show off Link. All of a sudden it had been interpreted as Nintendo's new strategy, and that was a shock for us."

» Not that we need to be told how swords work...

And just like that, a change in art style divided a fanbase almost overnight. "When something unexpected happens, the first reaction people have is to be wary," Aonuma tells us. "We expected a negative reaction at the show. Although I don't regret anything, part of the reaction was that this version of *Zelda* looked 'kiddy' and we weren't able to shake that off with any of the PR we did later. We encountered an awful lot of problems from the drastic leap we took with *Wind Waker*."

Miyamoto also wanted it to be known that this was not just change for change's sake. "When it comes to Nintendo strategy, it's not that we want to make games for kids," he explained. "It's that we want to make them creative while appealing to a wider audience. Obviously, we see games as entertainment, and ▶

▶ we want to find the best way to make the gameplay experience entertaining for everyone." But it was too late. Already, many of the *Zelda* hardcore had jumped ship based on the cartoon-style visuals of the new game, while yet more of the unconverted chased the impossible dream of photorealism on PS2 and Xbox. Hindsight is Link's best friend in this respect. *Wind Waker*'s look is timeless, as evidenced by the updated HD version on Wii U – a spot of tidying up and it's instantly the best-looking game on the GameCube's upgraded cousin, whereas any PS2 game from the same era would take tens of thousands of development hours to scrub up to the same level.

And in that respect, we have our first analogue with the series' origins. No matter how many photorealistic games are released from now until the rest of forever, *A Link To The Past* will *still* look good. And with Link's colourful and relatively basic look in *The Wind Waker*, we see exactly the same thing. It's a timeless art style, not one hung up on chasing the latest tech or trends and as such, it's one that still looks amazing today. But by Miyamoto's own admission, it's not the style that saw *Wind Waker* get the green light so much as the inherent practicality.

"It's not so much that we wanted to go with the toon shading as it is that we are really happy with the proportions of Link in the game," he recalls. "We liked the fact that we can have the package art match the artwork in the game. In the past, you'd have a Game Boy *Zelda* game and a home console *Zelda* game where the art styles didn't match. On top of that, the art style on the boxes didn't match the art style in the games. We've really tried to cut back on that, so you can see the same Link across the different platforms."

It's here that design manager Satoru Takizawa jumps in. "We had been trying to figure out which graphical direction to take for the next *Zelda* game. And we wondered whether continuing the path taken by *Ocarina Of Time* and evolving upon it by giving it more detail was really the right path," he revealed in that same 2004 interview. The Space World demo had inadvertently shown

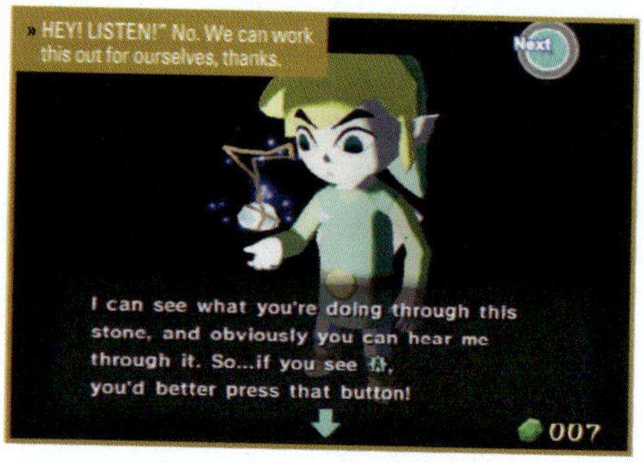

» HEY! LISTEN!" No. We can work this out for ourselves, thanks.

A WHALE OF A TIME

There are many highlights in Link's maiden maritime adventure. Here are just a few of the absolute finest...

The Story So Far

■ NOT ONLY IS *The Wind Waker* one of the few games in the series to acknowledge Link's previous adventures, it also manages to do so in a striking way. The game begins with the history of Hyrule told through woodcarving pictures and subtitled folklore (for those who don't speak Hylian). This adventure's mythology is forged by Link's exploits in older games. Genius.

Time To Say Goodbye

■ YOU CAN'T STAY on Outset Island forever, you know. After Aryll's kidnapping and Link's rather brief training in swordsmanship, it's time to leave your home and set out in search of adventure and your missing sister. Townsfolk gather on the beach, but it's the final shots of Link's gran watching from afar that really give you a kick in the tear ducts.

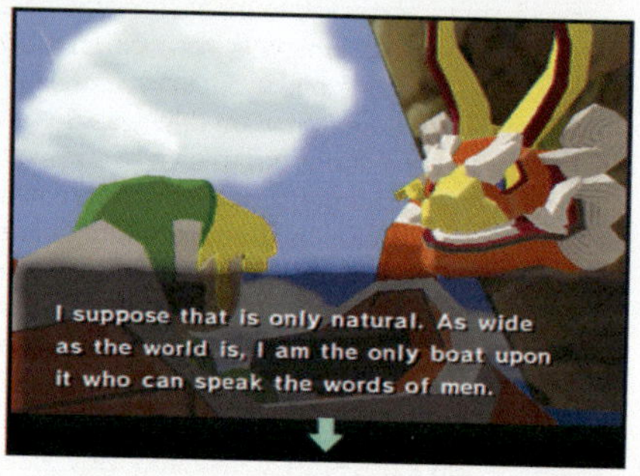

The Boat Can Talk?!

■ BOTH THE SETTING and the game's cover gave away the fact that Link would take charge of his own boat, but we weren't expecting it to be alive. That's just weird. The King Of Red Lions proves to be a good friend to our hero, although we can't say we appreciated him stopping us from exploring the world early on...

My First Sunken Treasure

■ SAILING AROUND WITH glowing plumes erupting from under waves is frustrating early on but, once you get the grappling hook, all that booty can be yours. There's enormous satisfaction to be gleaned from using clues and logic to find a treasure map's big score, but even the regular treasures are a nice little touch.

Sunk Cost

■ WITH THREE ORBS under your belt, you're able to unearth the game's first big secret – the Tower Of The Gods. Survive its trials and you're ready to take a trip through time, venturing into the submerged Hyrule Castle to get a glimpse at what this world was like before the sea claimed it. It's both a novel twist and a way to excite fans of the series, of which there are quite a few.

The Showdown

■ THERE IS NO shortage of great boss battles across the *Zelda* series, but *Wind Waker*'s final battle with Ganon sits comfortably in the top flight. It's an epic encounter the likes of which few modern games can touch, the music and the setting lending brilliantly to the sense of occasion and importance. But how do you beat him? Well now... that would be telling.

the world a *Zelda* game it was not to receive any time soon, but Nintendo was confident in its decision both on visual and gameplay levels. "Another benefit of those visuals was how we could represent the mechanisms and objects for puzzles in a more easy-to-understand way," Takizawa continued. "When the visuals are photorealistic, it had the adverse effect of making information difficult to represent game-wise."

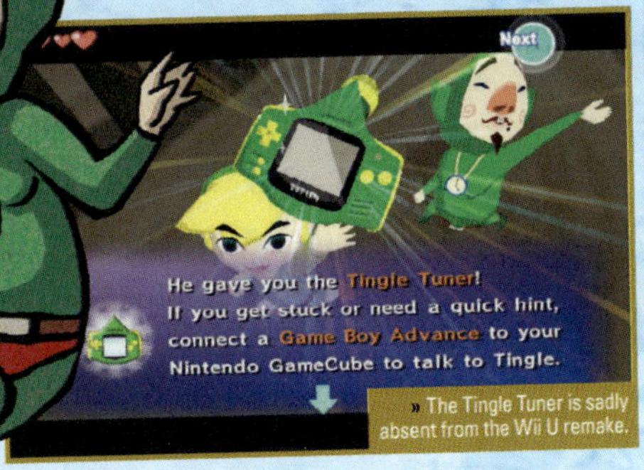

» The Tingle Tuner is sadly absent from the Wii U remake.

» Carrying a really big pig. Just another day at the office...

But it wasn't just the style that would prove to be a sticking point for *The Wind Waker* – it was the setting itself. The rolling hills of *Ocarina Of Time* were shunted aside for rolling waves in a controversial twist. But again, it's one that harks back to the series' earlier adventures more than most. *Ocarina* and *Majora* both do a decent job of presenting the illusion of freedom, but with your own ship (and once the good ol' King Of Red Lions allows it), the rolling waves are your very own playground. In earlier games, breaking the sequence would simply result in a dead end. Here, the main path may be blocked but there are still other things to investigate and explore – each of the 49 main islands on the map offers something to do whether you're a keyholder or not, some offering extra goodies while others purely tease great rewards once certain critical equipment is obtained. Just mapping the whole seascape is its own reward, feeding the fish to fill out the map and make mental (or, if you're proper hardcore, graph paper) notes of what else lies in store once certain gear has been unlocked.

One of the prerequisites for exploring the entire map was having the wind on your side, which was apparently something that Nintendo had been meaning to offer players for some time. "For a long time we'd wanted to be able to use wind in games," said Miyamoto. "We'd had windy stages in the *Super Mario* games before, but really it wasn't until we were able to use the technology of the GameCube and some of the visual styles possible with it that we were able to really show wind blowing in a videogame. So, that was one of the things we decided to challenge ourselves with, which made it a driving force behind *The Wind Waker*."

But while other games were roping in voice actors to help flesh out their characters and stories, *The Legend Of Zelda* would remain one told through body language and subtitles. "We obviously carried this on from the previous *Zelda* games," explained *Zelda* veteran Eiji Aonuma. "We can express what we want within the game without having to use a lot of voice acting. While I can't say for certain it will always be like that with *Zelda* games, the way we did it for *The Wind Waker* is suitable for the world. Also, as people have played *Zelda* over the years, they have formed their own ideas of how Link might sound. If we were to put a voice in there that might not match up with someone's image, then there would be a backlash to that. So we tried to avoid that."

In fact, the real beauty of *Wind Waker* is that so little of it even needs explaining, to the point where we were comfortably able to finish it in Japanese back in the day. This is not a complex story, but rather one made interesting by the characters and the life breathed into them by new hardware. "Once we decided to go in the toon shading direction, we thought it would be important to use the technology as much as possible so we could draw out the natural features of the world," revealed Aonuma. "We wanted to ▶

ZELDA HIGHLIGHTS

A LINK TO THE PAST (PICTURED)
SYSTEM: SNES
YEAR: 1991

LINK'S AWAKENING DX
SYSTEM: GBC
YEAR: 1998

OCARINA OF TIME
SYSTEM: N64
YEAR: 1998

» Mad Maestro, eat your heart out. Link's a pro when it comes to music.

» Yeah, running away here might not be a terrible plan...

show Link's expressions, and the eyes became very important. Gradually, as we managed to program the movement of the eyes, we began to look at different ways we could make use of that. It became part of the natural process of figuring out how to make Link feel more alive and aware of his surroundings. It was through this natural process that we began to put in items that would attract Link's attention."

And though some feat of game development witchcraft, this relatively simple feature would change the entire game. Link's awareness of his own surroundings became a hint system of sorts, his gaze wandering towards key objects, nearby enemies or puzzle items. It all feels incredibly natural but also helps out on a gameplay level without the need for any intrusive HUD elements or similar modern conventions. "When we decided to use the eyes in this way, we considered changing Link's eye colour throughout the game," Miyamoto mused. "There were points in the game where we programmed it so his eyes were bright red while he was fighting, and there were some different opinions on that. Obviously, one of the concerns was that you could only see the colour of his eyes if the camera was looking at him from the front. But, even if you could see his eyes we thought it felt a little strange. So, ultimately we decided not to do that."

» Link's gadgets work differently when used on the boat.

Even so, the wandering eyes and increased emotion evident on Link's face proved to be one of the most popular and memorable features of the game – it isn't often that such emotion can be so easily conveyed by a game character and being able to read and identify with the protagonist so easily and universally was something we had never really seen in a game before. It was an ingenious system, both making the main character seem aware of the world around him while offering gameplay advice at the same time – pause to survey the scene and Link will glance at key objects with the very same eyes that were just surprised by a rogue Moblin, his gaze clearly drawn to the most important thing at that time. Even without the proposed colour changes, it's a mechanic that works brilliantly.

Wind Waker had it all: exploration, innovation, freedom, looks... it's crazy that people aren't falling over themselves to proclaim this the best *Zelda* game, though nostalgia dictates that popular vote *Ocarina Of Time* must be crowned king. But for all the risks it took

WIND WAKER HD

How Nintendo updated the best GameCube Zelda for a new generation of gamers

AFTER SUCCESSFULLY BRINGING *Ocarina Of Time* to a whole new audience with the 3DS remaster, Nintendo's decision to do the same on Wii U didn't come as much of a surprise. Its choice of game, however, did. As much as we love *Wind Waker*, most rumours and speculation pointed towards *Majora's Mask* being next in line for the HD treatment. But we're glad this was the game that won, if only because the art style lends itself perfectly to a 1080p transition. While *Ocarina* looks great on the smaller screen of the 3DS, the work that would need to be done to get the same clarity on a large television screen would basically amount to remaking the game from scratch. But with *Wind Waker*'s stylised look, all it takes is some edge smoothing and a few fancy new effects and it looks every bit the modern classic.

So it looks the business in HD – almost exactly as you remember the original looking, in fact – but there has been some tidying up on a gameplay level as well. One of the lengthier fetch quests has been streamlined to improve pacing and flow, while upgraded sails allow users to sail at a much greater pace regardless of wind direction. You can still use the basic sail if you'd rather but, once you've already covered most of the map, it's actually quite nice to have the option of an extra burst of speed – it can even make sailing an enjoyable alternative to simply abusing the fast-travel magic, which has to count for something. There's even a new Hero Mode – in which Link takes double damage and health hearts can't be earned by searching containers or slaying enemies – if you fancy putting your skills to the test.

We can only hope Nintendo chooses to port this excellent remaster to the Switch.

» Cunning swordplay can help to undress armoured guards.

EXTREME MAKEOVER

Other franchises that underwent dramatic changes in look and feel

Castlevania

BEFORE: SUPER CASTLEVANIA IV
AFTER: CASTLEVANIA: SYMPHONY OF THE NIGHT

■ WITH A SUCCESSFUL string of hardcore action-platformers under its belt, Konami took the brave decision to bring in RPG elements for the series' PlayStation debut. Between stat growth, inventory management and a *Metroid*-style map that promotes backtracking and exploration, it's little wonder this became the template for most *Castlevania* games that followed.

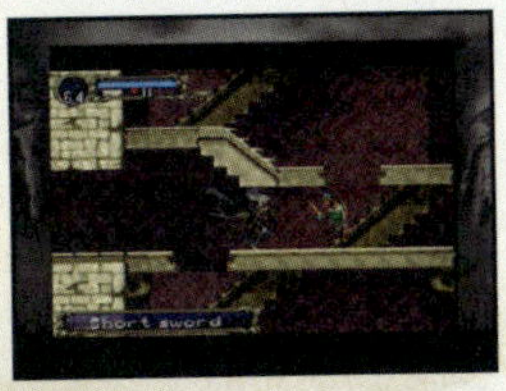

Bomberman

BEFORE: SUPER BOMBERMAN
AFTER: BOMBERMAN: ACT ZERO

■ THERE ARE FEW franchises that stand to benefit from a gritty reinvention less than *Bomberman* – you might as well make a new *Mario Kart* where Toad drops nailbombs out the window of a stretch Hummer. This grotty Xbox 360 reboot was an utter mess in every respect – it even had a mode called First Person Bomber, which, inexplicably, was third-person. Absolute rubbish.

R-Type

BEFORE: R-TYPE
AFTER: R-TYPE TACTICS

■ *R-TYPE* IS WIDELY regarded as one of the greatest horizontal shooters of all time, delivering fantastic visuals, freakish bosses and exceptional level design. Sequels followed and stuck to the same path, until Irem decided to turn the series into a turn-based strategy game for the PSP in 2007. It feels odd at first, but ends up working well. A sequel, also on PSP, followed in 2009.

Resident Evil

BEFORE: RESIDENT EVIL 2
AFTER: RESIDENT EVIL 4

■ STATIC BACKGROUNDS, ZOMBIES and hammy horror were all staples of the series until it was time to leave the 32-bit consoles behind. Although *Resident Evil 0* stuck largely to the same formula, *Resi 4* went for an over-the-shoulder camera and made things grittier and more cinematic (not to mention more action-heavy), paving the way for the franchise's current Hollywood-friendly style.

Mario

BEFORE: SUPER MARIO BROS
AFTER: SUPER MARIO 64

■ NINTENDO'S MASTERY OF 2D platforming is hard to dispute. But for a launch title to sit alongside its new 64-bit hardware, that wasn't going to cut it. The solution? Borrow *SMB3*'s hub-based structure, befriend the third dimension and both create and define a new genre in the same breath. Yeah, that'll do it. Outside of the *Galaxy* games, it's still the pinnacle of 3D platforming.

> **"For a long time, we had wanted to be able to use wind in games"**
> **Shigeru Miyamoto**

and innovations it made, we can't see *Wind Waker* as anything less than a prince, and a bloody good-looking one at that. Ultimately, the style is what put many people off and Nintendo knows it. But the risk paid off and Aonuma was so taken with the look that it was his go-to style for Link's Wii U debut. "When we were discussing what kind of graphical style to use for the new *Zelda* game on Wii U we looked at a variety of past games as reference. *Wind Waker* was the game that had the most innovative graphics and yet, due to the capabilities of the hardware at the time, it was not able to fully achieve that potential," he tells us. "Thanks to the HD version the developers can now finally make it look like it was always meant to. We decided to release this version because we thought that users would also be able to share in that feeling."

And this, apparently, was the first choice for a remake. "The game that I most wanted to go back to and make it more accessible was *Wind Waker*," Aonuma reveals to us. "I'm really glad that I was able to do that." More remasters have, of course, followed in the *Wind Waker HD*'s, err, wake. *Majora's Mask* was remixed for Nintendo's 3DS, while *Twilight Princess* and *Skyward Sword* found their own HD updates and *Link's Awakening* was fully remade with a gorgeous diorama aesthetic.

"I think we will be a bit more careful in future, but if we find a new approach that not just the developers, but also the users would enjoy then I think we will want to break new ground again," Aonuma concludes. "But we haven't found such an approach yet..."

6
1
15
20
10
4
8
2
14
16
7

A LINK TO THE CAST

Meet the bizarre bunch of folks that call the Great Sea home

1

Link

■ IF YOU DON'T know this guy, you're probably reading the wrong magazine. The Hero Of Time reborn, rocking a slick, yet practical green ensemble.

3

King Of Red Lions

■ A MAGICAL BOAT with a talking figurehead. Still, at least this particular *Zelda* companion doesn't shout 'HEY! LISTEN!' at you every three seconds.

5

Grandma

■ HAS GAMING'S DEPICTION of the elderly sunk so low that we don't need to give them names any more? Apparently so. Still, Link's granny is a star.

7

Makar

■ THIS LITTLE *PRINCESS Mononoke* extra plays a mean violin, but that's not the extent of his powers. And no, we don't just mean the cool leaf mask...

9

Fado

■ THE WIND SAGE, and the only Kokiri representative to appear in *The Wind Waker*. Apparently he's friends with the original Hero Of Time.

11

Valoo

■ A DRAGON WITH an island named after him and the Rito looking out for him, Valoo has it pretty good. Well, apart from the centipede thing that won't leave his tail alone...

13

Cyclos

■ THE SECOND FROGGY cloud-rider isn't quite so kind – Link has to try and defeat him amid a hurricane in order to learn the Ballad Of Gales.

15

Tingle

■ THE MIDLIFE CRISIS, personified. This fairy wannabe just so happens to be really good at deciphering maps, although his rates border on the extortionate.

17

Fishmen

■ THERE'S ONE OF these talking fish for every square of the map. Track them down and give them some dinner and they'll map the area out for you.

19

Nudge

■ TETRA'S PERSONAL BODYGUARD and the crewman who knows her best. He's also apparently stronger than Gonzo but we've seen no proof to that effect.

2

Aryll

■ LINK'S LITTLE SISTER, who gets kidnapped by a giant bird at the start of the game. Still, at least she gives you her telescope before she gets carted off...

4

Tetra

■ THE SPUNKY PIRATE that goes easy on Link. She was supposed to have her own game called *Tetra's Trackers*, which only surfaced in Japan and under a different name.

6

Ganondorf

■ AGAIN, YOU'VE LIKELY had a few run-ins with this dude in the past. In keeping with the swashbuckling theme, he seems to prefer swords over magic this time out.

8

Medli

■ THERE AREN'T MANY characters in *Zelda* canon that you get to throw around, so Medli will be remembered for this if nothing else. The young Rito girl is Valoo's attendant.

10

Laruto

■ YOU'D HAVE THOUGHT the Zora would be okay after Hyrule was flooded. You'd have thought wrong. The Earth Sage only appears to Link in spirit form.

12

Zephos

■ THE MORE LEVEL of the two Wind God siblings, this frog helps Link out by making sure he learns the Wind's Requiem. And by pointing out that his brother is a bit mean.

14

Komali

■ A TIMID RITO prince who is particularly attached to an orb that makes him feel better. An orb that you probably want to get him to part with, somehow...

16

Beedle

■ A SALESMAN WHO roams the seas plying his trade. He doesn't often have much of use beyond extra bait, although his friends occasionally carry some useful gear.

18

Gonzo

■ THE MUSCLE OF Tetra's pirate crew. Don't expect much in the way of insight from him but if you ever need anything bashing to bits, he's not a bad person to know.

20

Quill

■ A RITO DELIVERY man who offers a few pieces of sage advice to Link over the course of his journey. When he should probably be delivering letters. The slacker.

THE LEGEND OF ZELDA® FOUR SWORDS ADVENTURES

This evolution of Capcom's multiplayer mode in the GBA's A Link To The Past is one of the highlights of the GameCube

WORDS BY DARRAN JONES

Revealed in 2003, *Four Swords Adventures*, alongside *Tetra's Trackers*, highlighted the connectivity between Game Boy Advance and GameCube. Nintendo and Capcom had already proven the merits of a four-player *Zelda* game thanks to the addition of *Four Swords* to the GBA version of *A Link To The Past*, which enabled four Links to team up and solve dungeons while they competed against one another for rupees. It was a great idea, if a little rough around the edges, and was obviously the inspiration for Nintendo's new GameCube project.

Several months later, Nintendo announced that the two games (*Four Swords* was now known as *Hyrulean Adventures*, while *Tetra's Trackers* had changed to *Navi Trackers*) would be included on the same disc and joined by a third title, *Shadow Battle*. *Navi Trackers* sounded particularly intriguing at the time because it featured a speech navigation system that would recognise a player's name and notify them when it was their turn to play. Unfortunately, only Japanese gamers got to experience it. However, even with just two of the proposed games, the western version of *Four Swords Adventures* proved an essential release for any *Zelda* fan.

The meat of *Four Swords Adventures* is the excellent '*Hyrulean Adventures*', which expands magnificently on Capcom's original GBA multiplayer effort.

Unlike the vast majority of *Zelda* games, *Four Swords Adventures* takes place over eight distinct worlds, broken down into three smaller levels featuring such well-known locations as Lake Hylia and Kakariko Village, and always culminate in an exciting boss encounter. It was a massive step away from the traditional sprawling worlds of *Ocarina Of Time* and *The Wind Waker*, but it perfectly suited the more arcade-style trappings of *Four Swords Adventures*' gameplay mechanics.

When playing on your own, you typically control one Link, with the other three following you (don't worry; you can control each one independently when needed). When using linked-up Links, you'll need to master four different formation styles, which cover everything from defence to setting up attack strategies and solving puzzles. While initially tricky to get to grips with, you soon get used to the new mechanic and, before long, will be activating switches, swapping attack formations and lobbing huge boulders many times your size without a second thought.

The arcade-style pace only increases further when playing with friends; while you need to work together to progress, the inclusion of Force Gems allows for plenty of squabbling between teammates. At certain points of the game, the

» It's great fun teaming up with friends, but by requiring one GameCube and at least three GBAs, it's a big ask.

» Link's regular spin attack is great fun, but a four-fold one? Magnificent.

» If you're playing on your own, you can snap the quartet of Links into various formations.

» Bosses are, naturally, a highlight of the game, as are the showering of gems that come at each victory.

screen can become filled with a showering of gems, which immediately cause a frantic fracas as you rush to collect them all. Collecting gems grants its own rewards, as it greatly powers up your sword and enables you to break the seal at the end of each stage.

This tense competition between friends is further fuelled by the inclusion of eight fun minigames that range from racing horses to collecting monsters. Additionally, we shouldn't forget about the separate game *'Shadow Battle'*, which pits you against your mates until only one Link is left standing. In fact, the only downside to the multiplayer was its reliance on four Game Boy Advances and GameCube-to-GBA adaptors to play it.

Luckily, while *Four Swords Adventures* benefits greatly from playing with friends, it is still a superb adventure when playing in single-player, where you are tasked with taking control of all four Links at once. Admittedly, the story is a little twee – and the ending is something you'll probably be able to see coming a mile off if you've ever played a *Zelda* game before, but it's assembled with so much love and attention that you won't mind.

Thanks to its unique design, you can only play the original game which means the game has risen in price in the retro gaming marketplace (especially the more lavish box set that comes with a Link Cable). And that's before you consider you'll need to pick up extra GBAs and Link Cables if you want to play with friends.

The reason why we're still thinking of this unique arcade-style trip into Hyrule is that it's just an amazingly charming little game that offers endless replay value. While there's no denying that the main joy of *Four Swords Adventures* comes from playing with up to three other friends, the single-player mode of *Hyrulean Adventures* is just as enjoyable. It features an array of clever puzzles and boss encounters that linger in the memory long after you've finished the lengthy solo quest.

Sure, the story is twee and perhaps overly familiar to any *Zelda* aficionado. The oh-so-cute visuals won't appeal to everyone, too – especially *Ocarina Of Time* and *Twilight Princess* fanatics – but the innovative gameplay mechanics, cleverly designed stages, and frantic arcade action will constantly draw you back into Hyrule's beautiful-looking world.

NO QUARTER

What made Four Swords Adventures so special?

Link me up

THE ABILITY TO link up to four Game Boy Advances wasn't just an innovative experiment but it worked very well to boot. Of course, you needed three other GBA owners first…

Old school cool

WE COMPLETELY LOVE the side-on sections that appear whenever you enter certain dungeons. They instantly remind us of the greatly underrated *Zelda II: The Adventure Of Link*.

GBA optional

IF YOU DON'T have a Game Boy Advance you can still play *Four Swords Adventures*. A mock GBA screen appears on your television whenever you enter houses or caves.

Two worlds

THE CHOSEN GRAPHICAL style acts as a bridge. It mixes the old-school visuals of *A Link To The Past*, with the cel-shaded effects of *Wind Waker*, creating a distinct aesthetic.

Go solo

WHILE A BIG box version exists, complete with a link cable, it's also possible to buy the game separately. If you're not fussed about friends, then this is your cheaper option.

THE LEGEND OF ZELDA The Minish Cap

Fewer dungeons and a smaller scale did nothing to diminish this title's enjoyability

WORDS BY NIKOLE ROBINSON

Following the dual success of *Oracle Of Ages* and *Oracle Of Seasons* for the Game Boy Color, Capcom and its now-defunct subsidiary Flagship began work on a fresh *Zelda* concept for the newly released Game Boy Advance. Hidemaro Fujibayashi would return as director of the project, while 3D *Zelda* savant Eiji Aonuma was brought in to supervise the development and ensure the game felt like it belonged in the *Zelda* series.

The first step was deciding upon a unique theme to build the world around, much like how the *Oracle* games used the passage of time and the changing seasons to harness the limited space available on game cartridges to create expansive and dynamic settings. The idea of having Link change in size was put forward as the core concept of the game, allowing the same locations to be explored in new ways and gameplay to be built around seeing the world from a tiny perspective. *Zelda* titles have always played with symmetries – light and dark, past and future, adult and child – and size was another way to bring two contrasting worlds together.

While Nintendo usually started development by creating potential game assets, Capcom approached things differently. Designers poured their passion for the project into vibrant and whimsical concept art – some showing a new race of tiny, fairy-like creatures. These were reminiscent of the brownies, sprites and pixies found in fables across the world, but also took much influence from the korpokkur of Ainu folklore. With a fairytale feel to the concept, it was decided that the colourful, cartoonish style of *Wind Waker* would be the best fit for the game; the graphical upgrades that came with the Game Boy Advance made this well within the realms of possibility for a 2D handheld *Zelda*.

Development began as early as 2001, but the project was put on hold so Capcom staff could concentrate on its *A Link To The Past* GBA port and the first multiplayer entry in the series, *Four Swords*. While never intended to become a trilogy, the simultaneous development of *Four Swords* and *Minish Cap* meant that assets and story elements were shared between the two. As *Minish Cap* was a story-led, single-player entry, the mystery behind the evil Vaati was fleshed out, with both the returning villain and the titular Four Sword being given a backstory in what would become a prequel to the much more gameplay-driven *Four Swords*.

As well as character models, items used in *Four Swords* were repurposed, such as the Roc's Cape and Pegasus Boots. The game also served as a testbed for Link's shrinking capabilities with the introduction of the Gnat Hat, though this allowed you to change size at will rather than having to find an accessible portal in the form of a stump, stone, jar or altar. In *Minish Cap*, these

SMALL WONDERS

Minish Cap featured some exciting new items along with returning classics

Gust Jar

THE FIRST NEW item is obtained in Deepwood Shrine, immediately granting you deeper access to the dungeon in a myriad of ways. Pollen and webs can be sucked up, revealing paths and switches, while mushrooms can be pulled towards you as a new means of launching yourself across gaps. Without the ability to swim yet, the Gust Jar can also be used to turn lily pads into a means of transport across water.

Cane of Pacci

ACQUIRED IN THE Cave Of Flames, this unique rod emits a beam that can flip over specific objects. This wand is key in shrinking your size as you further explore Hyrule Town, flipping over jars to reveal new Minish Portals and providing an entryway to new places. As well as being utilised against certain enemies, the Cane Of Pacci can be used to launch yourself out of holes in the ground found at the bottom of high ledges.

Mole Mitts

THE DIGGING MITTENS obtained in the third dungeon not only allow you to uncover the Fortress Of Wind's many diverging paths and secret treasures but also provide another layer to a two-dimensional Hyrule by letting you dig into caves to find new pathways lying beneath those you've already explored above ground. You can also dig into the earth in the hope of finding rupees, shells and Kinstones underfoot.

Remote bombs

OVER A DECADE before the Sheikah Slate revived Remote Bombs in *Breath Of The Wild*, the right Kinstone fusion inspires Minish inventor Belari to make some of their own. Instead of a timer, the first press of the button places a bomb on the ground, while a second detonates it, allowing you to distance yourself and avoid damage. Visiting Belari at any time gives you the option to change what kind of bombs you're carrying.

Linking up

WITH HUGE CUES taken from Capcom's previous GBA *Zelda* title, *Four Swords*, the core mechanic of duplication is repurposed here for a single player. As you collect the Elements and restore the Four Sword, you can split into two, three and finally four copies of yourself to solve puzzles both in and outside of dungeons and move previously impassable blocks – though your clones will fade if you take damage or they get stuck.

» Even raindrops are deadly when you're the size of an ant.

"The style reprises Wind Waker's cartoonish charm, but its 2D nature means that many elements were taken from A Link To The Past"

portals limit your ability to transform, but this was necessary to utilise the shrinking mechanic as a way of solving puzzles and blocking access to certain areas until the right moment.

The style reprises *Wind Waker*'s cartoonish charm, but its 2D nature means that many elements were taken from *A Link To The Past* – fresh in the minds of Capcom after working on the port. The opening of *Minish Cap* might feel like a homage for those who experienced the 1991 SNES classic, though the juxtaposition between dark storm clouds and a cheerful festival couldn't be starker. Both games begin in a small cabin south of Hyrule Town, with Link roused from his sleep by Princess Zelda. In *A Link To The Past*, she's a damsel in distress, but in *Minish Cap*, she's your childhood friend who wants to enjoy the Picori Festival with you. The main difference here is there's no peril… at least yet.

Walking into Hyrule Town, the bright colours and festival fanfare set the tone of what's to come. A chief aim in the creation of Hyrule's hub was to make it feel like a lively and bustling town, with the appearance of people going about their day. You'll notice a lot of familiar faces, and that's no accident. To populate this iteration of Hyrule, ▶

» There's a nice little reference to Capcom's previous *Oracle* games built into a sidequest.

characters were chosen from past entries who felt like they were a good fit for the game's cheery atmosphere. On your travels around the world, you run into more friendly faces, new and old, though the greatest addition can be found right atop your head after meeting Ezlo, your travelling companion throughout the adventure.

As well as giving you helpful pointers and witty dialogue, this sassy green cap has the power to shrink Link to Minish size, being a cursed member of the Picori himself. Shrinking down for the first time feels magical and exciting, as you bounce down mushrooms and into the unknown, and this change of scale is where the game really shines. Blades of grass tower over you, acorns block the way and shallow puddles become deep oceans. The world that's usually hidden beneath your feet is a small one with a big impact, and as you journey to the Minish Village you can't help but take it all in.

The first dungeon, Deepwood Shrine, is completed entirely at Minish size, allowing you the chance to get used to the new obstacles you face simply by being tiny. One of the best roadblocks here is a barrel you have to enter and rotate to open up new pathways, though the final route won't open until you claim the Gust Jar item. The final boss is one of the least threatening monsters from *Wind Waker*, a Green ChuChu, but because of your size, it's a huge challenge. This fight really highlights how different things are for a Lilliputian Link.

From here on out, you have to think before you shrink. There are visual clues like cracks in the ground and flower paths, so it's a case of looking out for little details. The overworld and most of the dungeons require you to morph in size as well as utilise a growing collection of items to progress. New items help not only in their dungeons but also in opening up more of the world. They feel less situational than in previous games, and you use them in unexpected ways – a couple even combine with sword techniques. You can also use your size creatively, like shrinking to get inside an Armos to flip its circuitry, and this mechanic is put to use fantastically in the final fight of the Fortress Of Winds.

The size-shifting makes this 2D *Zelda* feel three-dimensional by adding another layer to the world. Exploring the rafters of Hyrule Town, you can see the goings on below, adding a lot of depth – something that really impressed Aonuma. This is mirrored in the multiple tiers of the dungeons, with puzzles sometimes having to be solved across multiple planes of navigation: a key falls down a hole, light shines from above or greater heights can be reached by jumping into the clouds. All of these details help *Minish Cap* feel bigger and more expansive.

For a game with such a small world, there's a great deal of variation, from swamps and graveyards to ruins and a floating palace. Capcom certainly didn't shy away from bringing new locations and races to the world of *Zelda*, with each biome having its own atmosphere, enemies and puzzles. Each dungeon is thematically unique and has its own set of mechanics based on its design, like floating above lakes of fire in the Cave Of Flames and slipping across the ice in the Temple Of Droplets. Even with a full arsenal and an upgraded Four Sword, Dark Hyrule Castle is imposing. All the gameplay elements culminate here, putting everything you've learned to the test.

Coming at the end of the Game Boy Advance's heyday – even if the original Nintendo DS was backwards compatible – may have impacted

FINDING YOUR OTHER HALF

Unlocking secrets and upgrades with the power of friendship

ONE OF THE MOST finicky and sometimes frustrating gimmicks *Minish Cap* added to the world of *Zelda* was Kinstone Fusion. After completing Deepwood Shrine, heading back to Hyrule Town will introduce the Hurdy-Gurdy Man, who will tell you all about the wonderful world of Kinstones, as well as providing you with a sack to store them in and your first fusion. There are 100 of these spread across the game, spanning various Hylians, Minish, animals and even ghosts and walls, with 12 different types of Kinstones to find while exploring Hyrule. Green Kinstones drop from grass and enemies, while blue and red are often chest rewards in dungeons and the overworld... you can even find them in treats from the bakery! There are nine yellow Kinestones that you must find to progress at certain points, but these aren't too difficult to find.

Rewards vary, from heart pieces and item upgrades to new NPC actions and rupee riches, but there's no way of knowing if the reward will be worth the grind, as many fusions are shared between NPCs. There's also nothing worse than getting excited about a new fusion, only to find your partner wants the piece you just traded away to someone else. There can be quite a lot of back and forth with trading, and with no way to keep track of which fusions you've completed once you've reaped the rewards, even completionists may give up on finding the final few. If *Minish Cap* ever makes its way to a new generation of console, hopefully, a Bomber's Notebook-style system, which worked so well for keeping track in *Majora's Mask*, could be introduced to ease the frustration of this sidequest.

» Ezlo can be harnessed to float across gaps, a bit like using the Deku Leaf in *Wind Waker*.

» The Roc's Cape and Four Sword combine in this epic battle in the clouds.

» A Green ChuChu is much more of a threat when it's towering over you.

» The Aztec-inspired Mazaal requires size switching and sharpshooting to defeat.

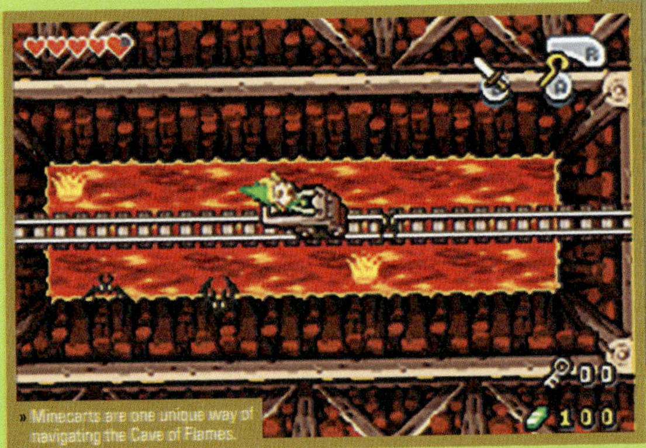

» Minecarts are one unique way of navigating the Cave of Flames.

the game's success somewhat: *Minish Cap* has the second-lowest sales of any *Zelda* title, with a modest 1.76 million. However, it remains one of the best-looking games on the GBA, with dynamic landscapes and weather effects that make it feel like an authentic world. Clouds drift overhead, water shimmers and sunbeams shine through the forest canopy. The sprites are just as spirited, with Link and Ezlo especially coming to life through their expressions and animations. And even with the limitations of the Game Boy Advance's speakers, the music manages to evoke the same feelings as those played on television.

The game's composer, Mitsuhiko Takano, was a long-time fan of the *Zelda* series, incorporating many elements from past soundtracks into *Minish Cap*'s score. Older iconic melodies were repurposed, notably 'Hyrule Castle' from *A Link To The Past*. There's a lot of familiarity here; the epic scale of 'Mount Crenel' evokes the same feelings as 'Tal Tal Heights' from *Link's Awakening*, while training with the swordmasters will take you back to the beginning of *Wind Waker* when you first learn to wield a blade. But there are plenty of new arrangements, too. All the dungeons have an ominous tone to their musical themes, but no two sound alike. Each corner of the world not only looks but sounds distinct, setting each apart as its own locale. A highlight is the Royal Valley, where the animalistic sound effects give it a truly harrowing feel, like you're being watched.

The biggest criticism about the game is that it is too short, proving that good things really do come in small packages. Much to the detriment of some, playtime was expanded with two types of collectables. Kinstones, new to the series, served almost as sidequests, while the figurine collection from *Wind Waker* returned in the form of a gacha minigame. *Minish Cap* might only have six dungeons, but each is expertly crafted. The combat and puzzles are well-balanced, even if *Minish Cap* is one of the easier games in the series, and the boss fights use interesting combinations of items and skills.

Though the *Four Swords* trilogy may remain as such, many Capcom staff who worked on *Minish Cap* now reside at Nintendo, including Fujibayashi, who directed *Breath Of The Wild* and its upcoming sequel. The Minish featured in concept art for the open-world *Zelda* but were sadly cut from the finished release, possibly due to their small size not being compatible with its grand scale. *Triforce Heroes* took the mantle of multiplayer *Zelda* on the 3DS, though there's nothing to say we couldn't see Vaati or the Four Sword return in some capacity in the future. Perhaps a modern take on *Minish Cap* could bring this smaller entry in the series back for a larger audience. ▲

> “It remains one of the best-looking games on the GBA, with dynamic landscapes and weather effects that make it feel like an authentic world”

THE LEGEND OF ZELDA® Twilight Princess

The GameCube's final bow and the Wii's launch classic would cement Zelda as a series that could both flirt with the past, and dip a toe into the electrifying future

WORDS BY DAVE MEIKLEHAM

Over the course of 130 years, Nintendo has proven itself to be a near-peerlessly pioneering company. From playing cards, to the Game Boy, to the Switch, the Japanese giant has regularly torn up the rule book when it comes to home entertainment. That's what makes *The Legend Of Zelda: Twilight Princess* a relatively rare Big N creation: it's a game that leans deeply into overtly comfortable, well-worn nostalgia.

This isn't a game that tried to chart the bold series redirection *Wind Waker* set sail for. Instead, this Wii launch title was more concerned with copying *Ocarina Of Time*'s homework in the hopes of mimicking the magic of the Nintendo 64 masterpiece. *Twilight Princess* is the ultimate act of giving *Zelda* fans what they thought they craved. Despite *Wind Waker* being a stone-cold 10/10 critical classic, those wonderful cel-shaded visuals turned many western consumers cold. With the gift of hindsight, those incredibly demanding Nintendo fans should have been a little more understanding.

After sluggish sales of the GameCube great in the US, director Eiji Aonuma told the series' original creator – and all-round Nintendo icon – Shigeru Miyamoto that *Wind Waker*'s sequel needed a more realistic look to boost its sales success. The result was a gorgeous, yet somewhat less creatively courageous *Legend Of Zelda* entry.

This being Nintendo, *Twilight Princess* is still a masterpiece. Does it come off as a slightly off-key warm-up act next to the timeless brilliance of *Ocarina*? Maybe a little. Still, there's zero shame in playing (a still amazing) second fiddle to arguably the greatest game of all time. It may not be as iconic as *A Link To The Past*, or as genre-redefining as *Breath Of The Wild*, but when it comes to classic *Zelda* design and superior dungeons, *Twilight Princess* knocks it out of the moon-worshipping park. Although unlike *Majora's Mask*, the lunar antics of that orb are limited to a bit of nighttime howling, rather than the Joker-style smiling Nintendo 64 moon crashing into Earth.

Ah yes, the wolf. Every *Zelda* needs a gimmick – *Wind Waker* had the dinky boat, *Ocarina* its time-bending instrument – and lupine Link is *Twilight Princess*'. Thanks to the titular 'Twilight', our tunic-sporting hero is turned into a cosmic canine within the first couple of hours of this adventure. Rather than eat backpackers on the moors *American Werewolf In London*-style, Link's more carnivorous tendencies are held back by the devilishly cheeky Midna. Far less annoying than *Ocarina*'s infamous Navi, the diminutive demon helps the elf navigate the Twilight area, which usually involves lock-on guided platforming sections and hunting down giant, electricity-spewing bugs.

Let's not skip past those infuriating insects. Just as with its successor, *Skyward Sword*,

» Nintendo opted for a more 'gritty' visual style for *Twilight Princess* after seeing the poor sales of *Wind Waker* in the west.

and that game's equally repetitive Silent Realm collectathons, the hunts for Shadow Insects in *Twilight Princess* quickly grow tiresome. While Wolf Link is fun to control, chasing down Tears Of Light by eviscerating paranormal creepy crawlies during the game's Twilight sections outgrows its welcome before long. It may be one of the all-time great videogame franchises, but *Zelda* has always been guilty of overusing collection tropes.

While the wolf sections are only partially successful, at worst, they're never much less than a semi-welcome palate cleanser. Where the game truly flourishes is when it focuses on being a classic *Legend Of Zelda* adventure. Wisely cutting out the open-world sailing bloat of *Wind Waker*, *Twilight Princess* instead hones in on recreating what made *Ocarina Of Time* such a success. That means the central focus is on impeccable dungeon design. While it's still a blast to gallop around Hyrule Field with Epona, the game shines at its brightest when Link is slashing beasties and solving puzzles in one of his adventure's headline dungeons.

Safe or not, leaning into the series' traditions is almost always to *Twilight Princess*' benefit. While the King Of The Red Lions sentient sailboat was fun enough to salmon through the waves in *Wind Waker*, there's something undeniably comforting about being reunited with Epona in Link's GameCube final big hit/Wii debut. Having been absent for *Majora's Mask* and the GameCube's cel-shaded predecessor, this was the first time Nintendo fans had gotten to ride the iconic equestrian in eight years. Not to miss a trick, *Twilight Princess* wisely leans into the Epona thirsting by making you herd a group of goats a couple of times within the opening act. When it comes to pitch-perfect notes of fan-pleasing nostalgia, few do it better than Nintendo.

Before we ladle heaping amounts of praise on the dungeons, Link's best four-legged girl deserves her moment in the spotlight. This is definitely *the* best version of Epona there's ever been. Not only do you unlock the majestic mount pleasingly early into the quest, but when you do, she proves more ass-kicking than ever. Link's pony pal can't just out-jump *Ocarina*'s version, she's also far more satisfying to take into combat. One of the game's best setpieces involves a protracted horseback clash with King Bulblin as he and his goblin-like goons ride fantasy warthogs into battle against Link and Epona. It's an electrifying moment, and arguably the sort of brilliantly choreographed setpiece only Nintendo, Naughty Dog and Sony Santa Monica can pull off.

One of the few (if only) criticisms you could lay at *Breath Of The Wild*'s door was the dungeons weren't quite up to scratch. For all of the Switch launch title's dizzying physics and effortless open-world inventiveness, beating the conundrums and bosses contained within each Divine Beach felt a little samey and visually uninspired. *Twilight Princess* may not be as imaginative, but hoo-boy are its dungeons ever a delight to solve. But yes, you will have to get over not preparing immaculately cooked, health-boosting stew in order to succeed.

Forget food. In *Twilight Princess*, all that matters is a degree of common sense. From beating an ape with a colossal, oh-so-red backside in the opening Forest Temple, to mastering the Double Clawshot in the City In The Sky like a gravity-defying, pointy-eared gymnast, the game's dungeons feel incredibly bespoke. Often confounding, sometimes a little frustrating, but always guaranteed to deliver satisfying 'ah ha!' moments, alongside all the boss spectacle you'd expect, *Twilight Princess* may just have the best temples in *Zelda* history. As compliments go, they don't get any loftier. Oh, and the previously mentioned City In The Sky? That's one of the all-time GOATs. Not only is its twisting labyrinth of monkey bars in the clouds a delight to navigate, but its awesome final boss takes several terrifying cues from *Metroid*'s iconic Meta Ridley.

A special mention for the Goron Mines dungeon, too. For all the times *Zelda* has so thoroughly worn out the fire world gimmick, *Twilight*'s second temple is the best roasty-toasty labyrinth Link has ever danced with. Thanks to some gleefully silly upside-down sections courtesy of Link's Iron Boots, and a sensational boss in Fyrus – who couldn't be more closely resembled with *Lord Of The Rings*' Balrog if he was spooning Gandalf while pulling him into a pit of eternal doom – the Goron Mines are *Zelda*'s ultimate take on the fire land trope. Even two decades after its initial release, the series could still pull off the definite take on dungeon ideas it had created back in the NES days.

» Wii motion controls were added in to account for the dual-console launch, and they kind of feel like an afterthought.

» It might look like a more serious *Zelda* adventure, but there's still moments of nonsense and brevity.

THE TWILIGHT SAGA

The key features of Link's lunar-inspired quest

Midna's moment

FROM A RACE seemingly named from a blend of Nintendo consoles, Princess Midna is a Twili: a demonic race who can conjure magic to help them traverse the Twilight. Midna is mercifully one of Link's least irritating companions, with the imp taking part in enjoyable platforming sections.

Tears for fears

CHASING DOWN TEARS Of Light plays a significant role in the early hours of *Twilight Princess*. These magic McGuffins are used to transport Wolf Link out of the Twilight Realm, but they can only be obtained by killing evasive Shadow Insects. Link has to slay said creepy-crawlies to earn Tears.

Natural ordon

LINK STARTS OUT his adventure in the tiny village of Ordon – a sleepy little forest community plucked straight out of classic *Zelda*. Ordon's main distinguishing features? The most terrifying collection of kids you ever did see, and a strangely boisterous goat farm that often needs herding help.

Horses for courses

EPONA MAKES ARGUABLY her best appearance in the series in *Twilight Princess*. Introduced far earlier than in *Ocarina*, Link can ride his pony pal to every corner of the map, barring those iconic dungeons. Horseback combat is a big deal too, with several major setpieces involving jousting.

Balrog me baby

TWILIGHT PRINCESS MAY have come out five years after *The Fellowship Of The Ring*, but Peter Jackson's blockbuster has a major impact on its second dungeon. The Fyrus boss is so much like that film's Balrog, the Gandalf-besting beast should probably take out a restraining order.

» *Twilight Princess* has several setpiece moments that stick in your mind long after the credits roll.

» Epona returns now that Hyrule isn't a gigantic bath, and this might be our favourite iteration of Link's faithful steed in the whole series.

It's not just the dungeons that deservedly hog the limelight. As with other all-timer *Zelda* games, *Twilight Princess* makes a habit of making its 'filler' moments truly memorable. The ultimate payoff may always be some big boss at the end of a dungeon you're three hours away from vanquishing, but it's in the knowingly silly between moments where *Twilight Princess* cements itself as one of Link's best games. Whether it's unwittingly helping catch a hungry cat its dinner during a spot of aimless fishing, using a hawk to knock off a pesky beehive, or racing a soup-loving yeti down a colossal hill, this is a game that can entrance even during its seemingly quieter moments.

Regardless of the lovely moments of random levity, the fact the dungeons are so strong doubles down on the fact *Twilight Princess* is very much *Zelda* at its most traditional. In the near-40-year history of the series, few entries in the franchise have played it quite as straightforwardly as this entry. Not that fans, or indeed critics, were complaining back then. *Twilight Princess* currently sits on a ludicrous 95/100 on Metacritic. Despite the universal praise, there's no denying this is a *Zelda* that plays it more conservatively than both what came before and after. Less visually distinctive and brave than *Wind Waker*, not as tonally interesting as *Majora's Mask*, and not as envelope-pushing as *Breath Of The Wild*, this is a safer, albeit brilliant *Legend Of Zelda* game.

It is that first and foremost, though: a fundamentally 'safe' game. Years before, Nintendo had wowed audiences with a Link-versus-Ganon tech demo that many fans had hoped would become the next proper *Legend Of Zelda* game. Then the wonderful, albeit graphically leftfield *Wind Waker* turned up, all adorable Pixar cheeriness and cherub-cheeked fun, and a significant part of the fanbase lost their collective shizzle.

In an indy-dominated era that welcomes, encourages and embraces visually distinctive looks, the backlash to *Wind Waker* looks positively bizarre all these years later. And yet, many hardcore *Zelda* fans wanted a more traditional version of Link. The sort of drop-dead-gorgeous elfin hero suggested in the dreamy art style of *Ocarina Of Time*'s manual, yet one the technically limited Nintendo 64 could only hint at, rather than actually deliver on.

Looking back, it's easy to forget just how big a deal Link's appearance in *Twilight Princess* was. After offending a fair portion of the fanbase with *Wind Winker*'s cel-shaded fairy boy, Nintendo created by far the most graphically realistic

» The Goron Mines are a dungeon-delving highlight – especially its boss, Fyrus.

> "The backlash to Wind Waker looks positively bizarre all these years later. And yet, many hardcore Zelda fans wanted a more traditional version of Link"

WATERY WOES

Why Twilight Princess caries on Zelda's problems with damp dungeons

TWILIGHT PRINCESS REALLY is the ultimate tribute act to *Ocarina Of Time*. Right down to the fact it also manages to mess up its water temple in fairly spectacular style. It may not share the quite so legendary bad reputation of the N64 dungeon, but *Twilight*'s Lakebed Temple is still a bit of a complicated stinker. Like its predecessor's submerged labyrinth, this is another head-spinning structure that bases its central puzzles around a confusing water level gimmick. If Link doesn't pull the right lever to pivot the stairs in the correct direction, he'll never get the H2O to the correct height to unlock further rooms.

Thankfully, Lakebed Temple is somewhat saved by the awesome Clawshot; a gizmo that goes on to become tremendous fun to use in the game's absolute best temple, The City In The Sky. It's just a shame that *Twilight Princess* blotches its almost-faultless run of dungeons by trying to rectify the watery woes of *Ocarina Of Time* – and even that masterpiece managed to fix its worst temple thanks to some careful tweaks courtesy of its 2011 Nintendo 3DS remaster. Let's just hope the upcoming *Tears Of The Kingdom* keeps Link away from the wet stuff as much as possible.

Link starts off as a humble villager in this entry, and he has to earn his green hood and Master Sword.

PORTS OF CALL

Looking back at TP's various console versions

WHILE IT'S AN undeniably excellent *Legend Of Zelda* entry, *Twilight Princess* hasn't always played that nicely on the three Nintendo consoles it has appeared on. Long before Nintendo hedged its bets with *Breath Of The Wild* and whether it would be a Wii U swansong or a bold, brilliant first act for Switch, *Twilight* beat Link's generation-spanning masterpiece to the punch by several years. First envisioned as one of the GameCube's last major first-party titles, the game's lengthy development meant Wolf Link would appear on both the adorable purple box and its successor, the Wii.

Sadly, the Wii port felt a little last minute, with the game's motion controls being tacked-on, lacking the nuance of *Skyward Sword*'s one-to-one motion tracking. As an introduction to the inventiveness of the Wiimote, Link's adventure pales in comparison to the likes of *Wii Sports*. Still, 2016's HD remaster on the Wii U is a handsome port, even if it doesn't do much with that console's perennially mismanaged tablet. We'd love to see an updated version on Switch – the Twilight Realm's blacks would look amazing on the OLED model – but that looks about as likely as *Breath Of The Wild* hitting Xbox Game Pass.

version of the character there had ever been. Ask *Zelda* fans which design they prefer now, and that adorable seafaring, ultra-cartoony version of the Hero Of Time probably wins the popular vote. Back in 2006 though, Wii owners couldn't have given the returning, far more traditional Link a warmer welcome.

If Nintendo played it safe with Link's look, the same is doubly true for how the company decided to tackle the Wii's then-pioneering motion controls. Despite being the only Big N franchise that can come close to going toe-to-toe in terms of prestige with *Mario*, *Zelda* has a curious recent history of being a series that hedges its bets between console generations. Just as *Breath Of The Wild* was originally a Wii U swansong that then became the glistening jewel in Switch's launch line-up, *Twilight Princess* was also a somewhat mishandled, generation-spanning title.

Years before the Wii got its MotionPlus upgrade, Link had to make do with the far less sophisticated launch Wiimote. Even then, the game barely used the motion capabilities of Nintendo's incredibly popular console. While *Skyward Sword* would implement true motion-based sword slices thanks to an upgraded controller, *Twilight Princess* was stuck with basic

Familiar Hyrule races like the Gorons return in Link's Twilight adventure.

> "This is a game solely focused on awesome dungeons and very little filler content in between"

waggle controls; an inevitable by-product of the project being a GameCube title first and foremost.

Regardless of the platform you play on though, Link's combat remains sharp. Wii-specific controls were always thin on the ground, but such is the strength of the series' core combat that the lack of waggle in the GameCube version is never an issue. Wisely adopting the Z-targeting of N64 greats like *Ocarina* and *Majora's Mask*, *Twilight Princess* presents an elegant, uncomplicated combat system that never gets bogged down in try-hard motion controls.

Seeing as the Wii was defined by legions of games where you had to waggle your limbs to near exhaustion, it's harsh to overly critique *Twilight Princess* for not fully committing to the console's central gimmick. Where other games would be summed up by a 'lightning in the bottle' electricity that would capture the world's imagination unlike almost any other console generation – we're looking at you, *Wii Sports* – Link's 2006 adventure was simply content to be

There's a lot of *Ocarina Of Time* hiding within *Twilight Princess*' DNA.

» Battles feel suitably epic thanks to the switch to a more grittier art style.

an excellent *Zelda* game. A little unambitious? Perhaps. Maybe a smidge too fan-pleasing? It could be argued. Ultimately, this is an undeniably superb videogame, purely because Nintendo had two decades to perfect the formula.

Twilight Princess also deserves credit for being one of the most focused games in *Zelda* history. Whereas past titles would force you to endure tedious sidequests just for the privilege of earning an adult-sized wallet that could hold all the rupees you needed, *Twilight Princess* is happy to let Link fill his pockets with relative ease. This is a game solely focused on awesome dungeons and very little filler content in between. In an era of offensively long *Assassin's Creed* titles, a lot of modern games could benefit from *TP*'s sub-40-hour brevity.

This structural breeziness extends to the overall game as a whole, and aside from those creepy-crawly-hunting sidequests as Wolf Link, *Twilight Princess* is refreshingly streamlined as *Zelda* games go. More than any other 3D *Zelda*, title this is the game that laser-focuses on excellent dungeons, memorable boss fights, and an iconic take on the Link-and-Zelda relationship. It may not be the boldest or bravest entry, but it is undeniably remarkable. In an age where there's an unquestionable desire to hone in on the familiar yet still marketable past of the medium, *Twilight Princess* taps into both the safe and sensational.

If you're keen on revisiting *Twilight Princess* in this modern age, your options are limited but strong. Are you still the owner of a Wii U? Then the 2016 HD remaster remains a decent option for replaying this classic on modern displays. An ever better way? If you own the disc version of said high-definition redux, you can experience Link's moon-centric quest at 4K resolution on a modern PC via the amazing Cemu emulator.

As an iconic series that does nothing but put out exceptional games, *Twilight Princess* is predictably brilliant. It's also that rare *Zelda* exception, in that it's oddly compromised. A farewell to the GameCube while also being a launch game that didn't quite do justice to the Wii's USP, this is Link playing at his most defensive. With the fullness of time, it's easier to have admiration for the likes of *Wind Waker*, *Majora's Mask*, and *Breath Of The Wild*, which all took bigger chances than *Twilight Princess*. If you're going to aim for greatness though, your sights may as well be set on the GOAT, and with *Ocarina Of Time*, Link's wolf-focused quest might just be one of the best cover acts of all time.

» Controlling Wolf Link is pleasant enough, but the insect hunts become grating.

» Move over Navi: sassy Midna is your companion throughout the adventure, and she's a big improvement.

THE LEGEND OF ZELDA®
Phantom Hourglass

With this direct follow-up to The Wind Waker, Link set sail on Nintendo's star liner, the Nintendo DS, in one of the most unique adventures in the series

WORDS BY TOM SYKES & DREW SLEEP

If you were to ever hear a criticism directed at *The Legend Of Zelda* series, it's likely an argument that they are 'all the same'. There's always a Link, there's always a Princess Zelda, and there are always puzzles, sword-swinging and nonsense involving the Triforce.

But you only need to look at *Majora's Mask*, *The Wind Waker* and its sequel *Phantom Hourglass* to know that's a load of old crap. *Wind Waker*, in particular, ditches the art style of the N64 games, most of Hyrule's landmass and even poor old Epona. *Phantom Hourglass* boldly continues this trend while adding new flourishes, making it one of the most innovative titles in the series.

The most immediate reinvention is of the traditional control scheme that had served Link so well for many years. Whether this was an attempt to make *Zelda* more accessible, or an effort to justify Nintendo's new-fangled touchscreened console, the Nintendo DS, then it's a triumph on both counts. But this fancy new control method has an invigorating effect on the game design, too.

Freed from those restrictive button shackles, Link can express himself in new ways. He can chuck boomerangs around corners, make annotations on his trusty map, and best of all, plot a course for his new paddle steamer on a series of delightful sea charts. That last part makes you feel more like a hardy sea captain than a cutlass and peg leg ever could, and it requires a great deal less hacksaw-based surgery.

Phantom Hourglass is still one of the most satisfying sailing games you can shake a spyglass at, though depressingly, it's not an overcrowded genre. Link's new vessel, the SS Linebeck, may be slightly less intimate than his tiny sailboat in *Wind Waker*, but that is easy to forgive when you consider that you can manoeuvre it across the Great Sea with greater ease. However, the best feature of the little paddle-steamer-that-could is its nifty salvage arm, which lets you plunder loot from the submerged ruins of Old Hyrule.

The innovation does not end with new controls. The game's centrepiece is the Temple Of The Ocean King: a grand multilayered dungeon you revisit throughout your adventure. Well, perhaps 'replay' is a better word, as you're charged with repeating the same sections over and over.

» The DS is a fairly primitive 3D-capable console by today's standards, but it does a grand job at replicating the 'toon' style.

» Traditional controls were cast into the sea, with the game adopting a touchscreen-focused scheme for exploration and combat.

Zelda fans are divided into those who hate the time limit and repetition of the ocean temple and those who don't mind it, but we can probably all agree that it was a novel piece of dungeon design. Link's forays inside are limited by the amount of sand in the titular Phantom Hourglass, and each time he pops out into the wide-open world to fetch more, the temple would reset. Whatever you thought of it, the recurring dungeon offered a unique challenge that hasn't been seen in the series before or since.

Not that Nintendo's own challenges were any less daunting. Until this point, most of the handheld *Zelda* games had been fun-but-simple throwbacks to *A Link To The Past*, often outsourced to the likes of Flagship/Capcom that were understandably more wary of making sweeping changes to the classic formula. In fact, development of *Phantom Hourglass* started in 2004 as a *Four Swords*-style affair until that plan was scrapped by 2006 for the game's E3 unveiling. The fertile grounds of creativity the Nintendo DS offered the team inspired Nintendo to fling the tried-and-tested formula into the ocean and try something different.

Wind Waker director Eiji Aonuma was affected by his game's sales not reaching the goals that Nintendo expected. However, he expressed a desire to create a game which utilised *Wind Waker*'s setting and unique aesthetic, giving birth to the idea that *Phantom Hourglass* should pick up where Link's first seafaring adventure ended. Aonuma chose to not direct this entry, though, instead handing the reins to long-time Nintendo programmer Daiki Iwamoto, who stepped up to the director's chair for the first time.

Following Ganon's defeat and Hyrule's sealing under the sea, Link and Tetra (the reincarnation of Princess Zelda) travel the ocean until they are separated on a ghost ship. Link then sets himself on an adventure to locate the strange spooky vessel and reunite with Tetra. The story is disappointedly barebones, and almost pulls an 'it was all a dream!' throwback to *Link's Awakening*. It's a serviceable tale, however, and works as a smaller-scale adventure that continues the *Wind Waker* iteration of Link's story.

Phantom Hourglass was acclaimed on its release, with many celebrating how the *Zelda* rulebook changed thanks to the DS's innovative features. Some criticised the return of 'toon Link' after the more serious trappings of *Twilight Princess*, as well as that infuriating Temple Of The Ocean King. That didn't dissuade over 4 million fans from enjoying Link's seafaring adventure.

While not essential, *Phantom Hourglass* proved that *Zelda* games could break their established templates and try something new. It's well worth trying for yourself if you can locate a Nintendo DS and a second-hand copy.

» The King Of The Red Lions has retired, but Link has a powerful paddle steamer as a replacement.

TIME FLIES

What made Phantom Hourglass so special

Toon Link

ARGUMENTS STILL RAGE over whether classic Link or toon Link is better – but isn't there room for both? *Wind Waker*'s cel-shaded art style looked incredible on DS, and so did Link.

SS Linebeck

THE GAME ALSO inherited the sailing aspect from *Wind Waker*, taking it to its logical extreme. In *Phantom Hourglass*, you took the wheel of a lovely paddle steamer, equipped with a ruddy great big cannon.

Phantom Hourglass

HOURGLASS DID BOLD things with its ocean temple: it put the dungeon on a strict time limit, measured by how much sand was in this magic timepiece. Helpfully, Link earned more throughout the game.

Phantoms

THESE TERRIFYING ENEMIES roamed the floors of the Temple Of The Ocean King. They were invulnerable and all-powerful, so you had to be stealthy, but they also proved a surprising ally in *Spirit Tracks*…

Ghost ship

NO PIRATE ADVENTURE is complete without a ghost ship – and *Phantom Hourglass* delivered in spades. This spectral sailing vessel kidnaps Tetra at the start of the game, and then again, near the end.

Tetra

LINK'S NAUTICAL ACCOMPLICE bears an uncanny resemblance to a certain princess. In reality, however, Tetra's nothing like the normally in-distress Zelda. Grubby and greedy, she's the perfect foil for the naively heroic Link.

THE LEGEND OF ZELDA™ Spirit Tracks

All aboard! The last train departing for Hyrule will be departing at the end of this sentence

WORDS BY TOM SYKES & BEN GRAHAM

Trains often get a bad rep thanks to price hikes, loose timekeeping and all-too-frequent breakdowns, but it's not their fault they're overseen by clown-shoed governments and corporations. Hark back to the time of steam power and it's easy to see locomotives in a better light: as the charmingly rickety coal-hungry monsters that gently wound their way across the country.

It's this nostalgic, bygone feeling that *Spirit Tracks* captures perfectly. While its predecessor, *Phantom Hourglass*, was concerned with the joys of sailing, this loose follow-up turns its steamy gaze to the glory days of public transport. Along the way, it isn't afraid to cast off traditional *Zelda* notions or reinterpret them in an engaging way.

Bolstered by the success of *Phantom Hourglass*, Nintendo was keen to create another touchscreen adventure for the Nintendo DS in rapid time. Thinking back to the short development time between *Ocarina Of Time* and *Majora's Mask*, Nintendo wanted to replicate the Nintendo 64 duo's success on its hugely popular handheld.

That didn't go to plan and *Spirit Tracks* took two years to develop. Most of the original staff from *Phantom Hourglass* returned, including director Daiki Iwamoto and producer Eiji Aonuma, and the team was keen to return to the cel-shaded style that the 'Sunken Hyrule' canon had established itself with.

At this point, you're probably screaming, "But why trains!?" That concept came from Aonuma while reading *Senro Wa Tsuzuku* to his son. This bedtime story involved children laying tracks for a magical train that took them anywhere, and Aonuma thought this could work as a keystone feature for a new *Zelda* title. Half of his development team disagreed, creating a schism between the train haters and the (ultimately successful) choo-choo champions.

Aonuma and Iwamoto wanted this to be a unique *Zelda* game, however. Just like the team had achieved with *Phantom Hourglass*. *Spirit Tracks*, therefore, feels like a verdant ground for experimentation, providing gamers with a wealth of unfamiliar traits that ultimately work remarkably well.

The first of these is its opening, the freshest in recent *Zelda* history. Set hundreds of years after *Wind Waker* and *Phantom Hourglass*, *Spirit Tracks*' iteration of Link is no mere villager waiting for his destiny to come calling. He is a lad with purpose and ambition (well, in a bumbling and slightly lazy way). He starts as an apprentice, hoping to earn the coveted green tunic that will mark him as a qualified train engineer. To do this, he has to visit Princess Zelda in her castle, and that's when the trouble kicks off.

Zelda takes a far more active role in *Spirit Tracks* than in previous titles… despite being dead for most of the adventure. Well, perhaps 'dead' is a bit strong – shortly after you meet her, a demon separates her soul from her body.

» The ghostly Zelda can possess hulking Phantoms to help Link solve puzzles and clear dungeons.

> "Zelda takes a far more active role in Spirit Tracks than in previous titles… despite being dead for most of the adventure"

» At a first glance, trains seem like a strange fit for a *Zelda* game, but they'll win you over soon enough.

In stark contrast to the victim-rescuer relationship they shared in many of the other *Zelda* titles, the pair are something of a double act in *Spirit Tracks*. Link handles all the boss-stabbing and rupee-hoarding, as usual, while the suddenly spectral *Zelda* develops the power to possess enemies.

Assuming control of one of the hulking Phantom Guardians, returning from *Phantom Hourglass*, adds a new dimension to the series' traditionally lonely dungeon raids. Your new metal friend can attack enemies, activate switches and carry you through dangerous areas, all with a quick swish of the versatile stylus on the DS's touchscreen. It's one of the few times *The Legend Of Zelda* has flirted with the mechanics of a co-op game.

Before that, however, we have a train to catch. *Spirit Tracks* transforms Hyrule into an overgrown train set, with Link as its engineer. His responsibilities include ferrying passengers, shipping cargo and – oddly most thrilling of all – sounding the whistle to frighten animals off the track. Nintendo missed a trick by not including a rope peripheral, but it's almost as exciting tugging at a little touchscreen icon.

Despite reviewing and selling commendably well, few will likely argue *Spirit Tracks* is the most outstanding *Zelda* title. Despite this, it's the only game in the series to let you indulge your inner train enthusiast (presuming you have one). After 30 years of re-assembling the Triforce, re-re-finding the Master Sword, and re-re-re-defeating Ganondorf, you learn to appreciate these unique entries. If the thought of playing with a Hyrulean train set does anything at all for you, there's still time to hop aboard the Spirit Train.

» Nintendo always keeps its armoury of items fresh and interesting for each *Zelda* game, just look at this leafy whirlwind.

» *Spirit Tracks* has a multiplayer battle mode. It's a little throwaway but still good fun.

THAT'S THE SPIRIT

The things blew our whistle

Anjean

ALTHOUGH SHE LOOKS like a genetic experiment involving an elderly woman and a teapot, Anjean is your closest advisor and never stops winking at Link.

Whirlwind

EVERY NEW *ZELDA* comes with a couple of gadgets to add to Link's armoury. The best here is the Whirlwind, which lets you blow a hurricane at enemies.

Chancellor Cole

ONE OF THE creepiest *Zelda* villains ever. Wearing two hats to conceal his demonic horns, Cole becomes close to Princess Zelda so he can steal her lifeless body.

Rocktite

THIS JERK LURKS in dark, dank tunnels, waiting for trains to approach. To vanquish it, you have to whack its gross mouth-eye a few times.

Whip

MOST WHIPS DON'T have animal heads grafted onto the end. Nintendo fixed that error, though. Thanks to its snaky bonce, it can rip the armour off enemies.

Spirit Train

THINK TRAINS ARE boring? Not when you're in control and you have a cannon with endless ammo at your disposal. *Spirit Tracks*' signature feature is *wild*.

THE LEGEND OF ZELDA™ SKYWARD SWORD

The beginning of the legend and a heroic swan song for the Wii

WORDS BY ALAN WEN

When *Zelda* games are pitched as legends retold in new eras, you have to sometimes take with a pinch of salt where in the timeline they are. Nonetheless, *Skyward Sword* is regarded as the beginning of the *Zelda* canon, set after the world's creation and the Era Of Hylia, a time before there was even a Hyrule.

Indeed, the setting here is up in the skies where the Goddess Hylia sent survivors to escape the destruction wrought on the lands below by the Demon King Demise, with descendants countless generations later living their lives amongst scattered floating islands – the largest being Skyloft – believing the surface below as nothing more than a myth. That is until one day, Link, a new knight-in-training, embarks on a quest to rescue his childhood friend Zelda (not yet a princess but the daughter of the Skyloft Academy's headmaster) who's taken by a dark tornado and whisked below the clouds.

This new chapter called for a new look and one that would best serve the then-ageing Wii console, itself already technologically behind its competitors who had taken the leap to HD. Neither sticking to the more realistic look of *Twilight Princess* nor reverting to the divisive cartoonish cel-shading of *Wind Waker* (even though in retrospect the latter is now considered timeless and beloved), *Skyward Sword*'s art style is somewhere in the middle, with a soft and vivid painterly palette that takes inspiration from impressionist painters like Monet and Cezanne – Shigeru Miyamoto himself being a huge fan of impressionist art. The reasoning behind this aesthetic was also to better exaggerate the characteristics of its characters, though you can also imagine that an art style where there's not as much focus or detail works strongly in favour of the Wii's standard definition.

A new beginning also made for the right time to pass the torch in the development team. Having been responsible for spearheading the series into its 3D era since *Ocarina Of Time*, Eiji Aonuma stepped down from the director role, though would continue to have a major involvement in the series as producer. Taking over as director was Hidemaro Fujibayashi, already an experienced developer with the *Zelda* series, although so far it had only been on a smaller scale, having directed Game Boy Color titles *Oracle Of Seasons* and *Oracle Of Ages* when he was employed at Flagship/Capcom; in fact, as development for *Skyward Sword* had begun in 2006, he was still finishing development for 2007's *Phantom Hourglass* for the DS. So having overseen *Zelda* titles that included unique gameplay features such as a diptych that interconnects and novel interactions with the Nintendo DS's touchscreen and microphone, what would be the key innovation for *Skyward Sword* in his home console directorial debut for the series?

The answer was to create a *Zelda* game that could only be experienced on the Wii, which would be a genuine tour de force showcase for the console's motion controls. It was certainly something the console needed towards ▶

» Defeating this Moblin means figuring out how to get rid of its shield first.

» There's an innocence seeing Link and Zelda together as just childhood friends, or possibly more.

» Boss fight setpieces continue to be a series highlight even if their weaknesses may be familiar.

the end of its life when the game was released in 2011. By that point, the novelty of motion controls had worn off, as the console was inundated with shovelware and short-lived gimmicks that helped coin the derisive term 'Wii waggle'. Other first-party releases like MonolithSoft's expansive RPG *Xenoblade Chronicles*, meanwhile, simply reverted to traditional control schemes that were arguably best played with the Classic Controller.

Because for all the thrill there was with swinging the Wii remote to mimic Link's sword in *Twilight Princess*, that was ultimately a GameCube title, with the Wii release bolting on motion controls as an afterthought, where your swings didn't really make a difference to how the weapon moved. It only made sense that Nintendo would want its star franchise to properly embrace the core technology of its best-selling console, because it surely couldn't leave it with just *Link's Crossbow Training*.

Coming in the latter part of the Wii's lifetime was instead to *Skyward Sword*'s benefit, as it was able to learn from other Wii titles that had come before, with ideas taken from other motion-control games and then implementing them into one cohesive package that made those mechanics feel fresh again. More importantly, it would also be able to take advantage of the new MotionPlus accessory released in 2009, which allowed for more complex and accurate motions to be interpreted than the original remote could. In other words, your swinging of the remote in your hand does have 1:1 motion with Link's sword in the game, while the secondary Nunchuk controller is held up to block with the shield, the two parts making you feel more like a hero in your living room than ever before.

It's then a surprise to learn that the team faced many difficulties implementing MotionPlus technology into *Skyward Sword* and almost abandoned it altogether. Fortunately, the release of *Wii Sports Resort*, which includes sword fighting as one of its minigames, proved to be the inspiration they needed. There's still a concession to how swordplay works, as despite

» The remote-controlled beetle is the newest item in *Skyward Sword*, and arguably the most unusual.

» Tilt the Wii remote to control where Link lands when skydiving – don't forget to open the sailcloth!

the appearance of 1:1 movement, you're still ultimately judged on eight possible directions to cut through an obstacle or enemy, as well as a forward direction by thrusting the sword. There's also a special move, the titular Skyward Strike, where by holding your sword in the air, you can charge it with the Goddess Hylia's divine power and unleash it on your enemy. In some cases, this move is essential for breaking through certain enemy defences and solving brain-teasers.

Similarly, combat itself turns into a bit of a puzzle as you parse which direction you should be slashing your sword to get past an enemy's shield instead of just mindlessly waggling and hoping for the best. This is also where the art style works effectively since the exaggerated design of characters means that from their body language you can quickly parse, for instance, which side they're holding their shield or where their weak spot is exposed so you know where to aim for instead of just an obvious glowing red spot.

Indeed, it's not just the swordplay but other minigames that also helped inspire a whole range of *Skyward Sword*'s other gameplay mechanics. Archery is another obvious example that easily translates to Link's bow skills where instead of just pointing at the screen, you're actually using the remote as the bow you hold up while you pull the Nunchuk back like the string. But then there's the way you can pick up bombs and roll them along the ground like bowling balls, and you can even angle your wrist if you want to curve them, while *Wii Sports Resorts*' Island Flyover mode surely also inspired the way you control the new flying mechanical beetle. Familiar mechanics used in sports games and other more casual pursuits are suddenly what makes you feel heroic while exploring some of the best dungeons in the whole series.

The world map has a lot in common with *Wind Waker*, if you replace sailing in the seas with random enemy outposts and islands with flying in the sky astride beasts called Loftwings. Although some of the smaller floating islands can be explored as you approach them where they might hide treasure or a minigame challenge, this isn't strictly open world since it merely places select locations that you can drop Link into before loading into another area. Yet that doesn't diminish just how expansive some of the environments below the clouds are. While the goal is usually to find the dungeon in that area, these surface overworlds are so much more involved, allowing you to make use of the many creative mechanics you have at your disposal, that they almost feel like dungeons in their own right, where you also have puzzles and challenges to overcome before you can get further in.

Using the many tools you unlock, from familiar staples like the bow and Hookshot to the rarer whip and gust bellows, already has a greater sense of immersion with motion controls. That you also have the opportunity to use them outside of dungeon puzzles also makes them feel less like glorified key cards introduced and discarded after a single dungeon, which some past instalments have been guilty of.

That doesn't make these overworlds perfect. One criticism is how you're made to revisit them in the second half of the

» Gorons are one of the few recognisable races from past *Zelda* games to appear in *Skyward Sword*.

» The lofty outdoor areas are wonderful to explore, but the dungeon design is still stellar.

» You can always rely on farming rupees the old-fashioned way.

TO NEW HEIGHTS

Features that made Skyward Sword stand out

Riding Loftwing

HORSES ARE ABSENT in *Skyward Sword* but instead of Epona, you've got a large bird to ride around the skies. Controlling this beast is intuitive as you can guide it with the Wii Remote controller, flap its wings up and down to gain altitude, and when you need to descend below the clouds, just jump off!

Dowsing

THE GODDESS SWORD can function like a fantasy metal detector, as you hold the Wii Remote in first-person mode as a beeping sound indicates if you're headed in the right direction. First used to discern Zelda's whereabouts, you can unlock a range of other dowsing targets over the course of the adventure.

Stamina

LINK HAS MANY more movesets, from running to climbing, but they require managing a stamina wheel so you have to make sure he doesn't get exhausted, though it can be upgraded over time. This mechanic carried over to *Breath Of The Wild*, while stamina management is common in other modern games.

Timeshift Stones

TIME TRAVEL HAS been a key part of the series, but having just part of a location change time is so mind-bogglingly ingenious a mechanic, as you use Timeshift Stones to move between past and present day to solve puzzles, and sometimes even transport them from one spot to another.

Upgrading items

INSTEAD OF JUST collecting hearts and rupees in the previous *Zelda* games, you can also gather other materials in the world, which could then be used to upgrade your items or even infuse your potions into stronger versions. It basically introduces a sort of crafting system in *Zelda*, if somewhat underutilised.

» After *Twilight Princess*, Nintendo decided to lean into a more stylistic art style that worked to its benefit.

» Enemies telegraph where they're blocking, making it easy to tell where to strike. However, mobs of foes still pose a challenge.

adventure, even though they have been transformed either in terms of terrain – such as how half of Faron Woods is suddenly underwater – while new circumstances mean your second visit to Eldin Volcano turns into a stealth section where you have to recover your lost items. More annoying still is when you have to enter the Silent Realm versions of these areas, tasked with collecting all the Sacred Tears without being discovered by some very stressful sentries that you can only run away from.

But of all the evolutions *Skyward Sword* takes, one of its strongest elements lies with its storytelling. Sure, you still may not get to play as Zelda in her own game, but she also has something close to resembling an arc this time around. As Link discovers each clue of her whereabouts throughout the game, you get a sense of her personal journey awakening to her destiny that we see continue in future generations of the series. In parallel to that, there is the demon lord Ghirahim who is also after Zelda and wants to use her in his plans to resurrect Demise, whose evil is hinted at being a prelude to the series' recurring big bad Ganon.

Perhaps the most memorable part of the story goes to Groose, a seemingly minor character who seems to be nothing more than a bully to Link, going as far as getting his goons to trap Link's Loftwing to stop him from passing his academy exam at the beginning of the game. Yet despite the satisfaction of seeing a vain jock eating humble pie when he realises he's not the hero in this story, it's to the writers' credit that he ends up with one of the best redemption arcs in the entire series, with still a significant role to play in the story, even getting to be one of few characters to get screen time in the ending sequence.

On the other hand, Fi, a spirit who resides within Link's Goddess Sword, is more divisive in the thankless role as Link's guide. She has a habit of coming out of the sword to give far too many hints, instructions, or reminders, at the expense of many players' patience. This wasn't limited to just Fi, since there was also a bizarre quirk where the game would repeat the same animation of Link picking up an item or material for the first time whenever you start a new play session, but it made her an easy target for frustrated players. Yet whether or not you found her annoying, it's also hard not to feel swells of emotion when the time finally comes for her to part ways with Link.

No doubt that the extra emotion felt in *Skyward Sword* was also down to it being the first game in the series to have a full orchestral soundtrack, further celebrated with an audio CD soundtrack being bundled with copies of the game. That isn't to say that the MIDI tracks in past games aren't still classics in their own right, but the themes, including the game's main theme 'Ballad Of The Goddess', truly soar to new heights thanks to live orchestration led by Hajime Wakai and supervised by Nintendo's legendary composer Koji Kondo. The work saw the game's sound team doubling from its original five-person group, the largest sound team working on a Nintendo game at the time. It's only ironic then that the in-game musical component, a harp, is disappointingly basic, where you simply wave the remote left and right at various tempos.

Officially revealed at E3 2009 and planned for a 2010 release, the game was ultimately delayed until 2011, making *Skyward Sword*'s five-year development the longest *Zelda* game in production at the time, although that meant it would arrive for the series' 25th anniversary, and for that milestone it didn't disappoint. With such immaculate polish and innovation,

SKYLOFT'S LITTLE HELPER

Gratitude for Skyward Sword's best sidequest

AS WELL AS acting as a hub you frequently return to in between your travels, Skyloft is also home to the game's most substantial sidequest. Living beneath the floating island is Batreaux, a friendly demon who more than anything wants to become human so that he can live among the other villagers who are otherwise scared by his appearance. To do this, you'll need the power of Gratitude Crystals, of which there are 80 in total. These can be gained by completing sidequests as well as exploring the world, while these crystals can also be traded in to unlock other rewards.

The majority, however, can be found on Skyloft itself, which also provides some of the most memorable missions as you help out the residents of Skyloft with their personal problems, from helping a student weakling train up his physique to finding shopkeeper Beedle's lost beetle, and even playing an unwitting matchmaker in a love triangle, while finding yourself an unlikely admirer in another. Some of these even have more than one outcome, but there's nothing better than seeing someone's gratitude towards you physically manifest as a bright glowing crystal.

» Ghirahim is an intimidating opponent, not to mention one Link finds himself facing very early on.

» Bug catching is an important pastime if you're looking to upgrade your gear.

it showed the best of what the Wii could still be, not only receiving 10/10 from *Edge*, but also earning the publication's coveted Game Of The Year award, beating the likes of *Skyrim* and *Dark Souls*. Ironically, it's the latter two that have been remembered more fondly over the years, while it didn't take long for *Skyward Sword* to be rather unfairly relegated to a black sheep status.

For many hardcore players, a *Zelda* title dedicated to motion controls, no matter how well executed, was already a deal breaker so late into the Wii's lifetime when people were ready to put it behind them. Despite the open explorable skies and fairly spacious surface overworlds, many also felt it was far too linear, exacerbated by the somewhat overbearing tutorialisation, most keenly felt in the game's opening hours. For others, despite how motion controls arguably made familiar mechanics feel new again, the formula that had been in place since *Ocarina Of Time* was beginning to wear thin, with fundamentally not enough that felt genuinely new while also being too repetitive in places (the less said about recurring boss The Imprisoned, the better).

While some of these criticisms are valid and would be addressed in its remaster (see the box on the right of this page), it doesn't diminish how *Skyward Sword*'s story and dungeon designs remain the very best in the series – two elements that fans retrospectively cherish, given their reduced appearances in the otherwise game-changing masterpiece *Breath Of The Wild*, also helmed by Fujibayashi. The two are of course very different games, but we can see ideas from the former being reworked into the latter, from Link's stamina wheel gauge when performing certain actions to his sailcloth, restricted for a few functions like riding certain updrafts or breaking his fall, evolving into a paraglider that has far more traversal possibilities. Even with the huge land mass of Hyrule at your feet, *Tears Of The Kingdom* looks set to take us back to the skies again too, perhaps to fulfil the potential when we first looked beyond the clouds in Skyloft. The Wii may have revealed that the sky did actually have a limit, but even within those limits, *Skyward Sword* aimed high and smashed it out of the park.

SOARING HIGH AGAIN

Skyward Sword comes to Switch

TEN YEARS AFTER its Wii release, *Skyward Sword* came to Nintendo Switch with a high-definition remaster. While the original's aesthetic, designed with standard-definition screens in mind, doesn't really benefit from sharper visuals, this was ultimately a way to encourage *Zelda* fans who had passed on it to give it a second chance.

While the best way to play is still arguably with the motion controls, refined for the console's split Joy-Con controllers, players can now opt for traditional buttons and stick controls, for instance using the right stick to control the direction the eight-way direction of sword strikes or pressing the stick to thrust.

More importantly, the pacing of the game was improved by allowing you to skip dialogue and cutscenes, while you'd finally stop getting a message about picking up a new item or material every time you started up the game again, while Fi also doesn't bother you so much, though she still resides in your sword for when you want to ask for help. In other words, *Skyward Sword HD* is the definitive version of the game, though the release still garnered controversy over a limited-release Amiibo of Zelda and her Loftwing, which provided an exclusive way to fast-travel between the sky and surface overworld anywhere and anytime.

» Enemies in *Zelda* games tend to have gigantic 'hit me' targets, which is helpful in this entry when you factor in the motion controls.

THE LEGEND OF ZELDA: A LINK BETWEEN WORLDS

A successor to a 16-bit classic that dramatically shakes up the traditional series structure

WORDS BY ALEN WEN

» Long-time *Zelda* iconoclast, Eiji Aonuma, together with Shigeru Miyamoto, proposed the idea of a *Link To The Past* successor.

The *Zelda* series has had its share of direct sequels over the years. *Majora's Mask* takes place a couple of months after *Ocarina Of Time* while the DS titles *Phantom Hourglass* and *Spirit Tracks* follow on the path set by *Wind Waker*, including its cartoon art style, meanwhile, of course, the newest entry, *Tears Of The Kingdom*, follows directly on from the events of *Breath Of The Wild*. However, while these are narrative continuations, they also take place in new settings. *A Link Between Worlds*, on the other hand, is a more curious case in that it is a direct sequel to the SNES classic *A Link To The Past* – in Japan, the 3DS game is called *Triforce Of The Gods 2*, *Triforce Of The Gods* being the Japanese title for *A Link To The Past* on Super Famicom – but also a spiritual successor.

The story is set untold years after that game's events, but the Hyrule we're in is undeniably the same one from the SNES game. The connection is clear when the game starts up, greeting you with the iconic fanfare of *A Link To The Past*'s opening theme, while the camera pans over familiar landforms, only rendered in 3D instead of the original 2D sprites. Indeed, glance at the two games' world maps and it's surprising to see how alike they are, and there's a delight knowing that some things haven't changed – for instance, you'll still find a man camped beneath the castle bridge who'll also give you a bottle if you talk to him.

There's a difference in tone for how the story begins. Unlike its predecessor which begins on a stormy night, when our hero is thrust into a quest to save Hyrule after witnessing his uncle's death, *A Link Between Worlds* commences on a regular sunny day. Link, a humble blacksmith's apprentice, is tasked with making a delivery to Hyrule Castle before the plot thickens. But on the surface, there's a lot that's identical: again, Link must find three pendants, retrieve the

» The 3D visuals mean some cutscenes shift away from the top-down perspective.

Master Sword from the Lost Woods, and rescue seven sages to rescue Princess Zelda. Once again, the antagonist is an evil sorcerer who's out to resurrect Ganon, while there are also two different worlds, Hyrule and Lorule, which Link can traverse between. You'd be forgiven for thinking this was just a bit of a glorified remake when the 3DS had already enjoyed a handsome enhanced port of *Ocarina Of Time*.

Revisiting *A Link To The Past*, however, wasn't what the developers had in mind initially. Following the release of *Spirit Tracks*, members of that team had originally planned on a 3DS *Zelda* game that was built around the theme of 'communication', only for the concept to be rejected by Shigeru Miyamoto for being outdated. It was then that the idea came that Link would be able to merge into walls, switching the game between 3D to 2D perspectives, which was also well-suited to showcasing the handheld's stereoscopic 3D capabilities.

This concept was approved and remained as one of the key gameplay features of *A Link Between Worlds*, which is also how Link can traverse between the game's two realms by squeezing his flat form in between fissures in the world. It was then later that Miyamoto suggested basing this title on *A Link To The Past*. *Zelda* series producer Eiji Aonuma proposed it use the same landforms and top-down viewpoint, and also retire the *Wind Waker* cel-shaded aesthetic ▶

OFF THE WALL

Five new features in A Link Between Worlds

Wall-merging

WITH THIS NEW ability, Link can merge into walls to traverse previously inaccessible areas – including navigating around ledges, torches and traps, while it also makes enemies oblivious to the hero. Just make sure you're not forced out of the wall into an awkward situation when your energy gauge runs out.

To rent or buy

RENTING ITEMS FROM the start means you can journey to dungeons in any order you want, though you'll lose your access to them if you're defeated. Better yet, why not save up rupees so that you can outright buy these items to keep them permanently? More importantly, only items you own can be further upgraded.

Touchscreen inventory

ITEMS CAN NOW be used or equipped with an intuitive drag-and-drop inventory system using the 3DS touchscreen, made possible by also having 60fps performance. A similar touchscreen feature is also utilised in *Wind Waker HD* and *Twilight Princess HD* using the Wii U's gamepad.

Stereoscopic 3D

AS A FIRST-PARTY release, there's an extra effort in taking advantage of the eye-popping 3D effects of Nintendo's 3DS handheld. It's most pronounced when there are actions that make Link or enemies jump as if they're popping out of the screen. The height and depth of environments are even more distinct than before.

Hint Ghosts

WHILE LESS ANNOYINGLY handholdy than in previous games, help is there if players need it. By acquiring Hint Glasses from the fortune teller early on in the adventure, Link can see Hint Ghosts in the world who'll offer guidance when you're stuck in exchange for Play Coins earned by walking with the 3DS in sleep mode.

» Wall-merging in dungeons may also help you find new solutions to otherwise familiar puzzles.

» Sticking to tradition, Link can fire a sword beam when at full health.

» Thanks to Ravio's bracelet, Link can control between turning into a painting and re-emerging.

that the DS titles had continued. Although this resulted in somewhat bland low-poly visuals that replicate but fail to capture the timeless sprites they are based on, the game's art style is just about rescued by the 2D version of Link being given a unique design as if he's a living mural painting moving through walls. This led to the creation of the game's villain Yuga, a sorcerer who traps people inside artwork, including the sages and Zelda, an idea apparently also inspired by *Ocarina Of Time*'s Phantom Ganon, who would attack you by leaping out from canvases.

This familiar and nostalgic setting also served as an opportunity for the team to rethink and subvert *Zelda*'s traditions, notably the way dungeons were structured so that you'd find a new item and then move onto another dungeon that requires the new item to access, and so establishing a linear sense of progression. But for the first time since the original *The Legend Of Zelda*, dungeons in *A Link Between Worlds* can be completed in any order you wish. The gating of progress with items is done away with, owing to how you now have all the items available from the start that you can rent from a mysterious rabbit-headed merchant called Ravio.

Unlike the NES title, which nonetheless had a hidden order based on their difficulty, these dungeons are balanced so that you can freely go to any as your first and not immediately come out with your tail between your legs. To that end, this game doesn't even have a canonical sequence unless players refer to the dungeons from *A Link To The Past* (many sharing the same names like Turtle Rock and Swamp Palace) to figure out a 'classic' route.

Knowing which item you need to overcome a dungeon and then renting it may mean there's a loss of the surprise of finding a new tool in a treasure chest and figuring out how to use it (although series veterans will always know what to do with a Hookshot or a bomb), where solutions to puzzles may seem more prescriptive, however, the nonlinearity offered nonetheless meant *A Link Between Worlds* was a breath of fresh air when *Skyward Sword* on Wii had been criticised for being too linear. This freedom also meant less handholding, without an irritating guide popping up to tell you what to do every few minutes, although you'll find an eccentric witch who can help you fast-travel around Hyrule while also throwing in a few snarky remarks along the way. Nintendo would continue in this direction for great player freedom and nonlinear progression with the even more ambitious *Breath Of The Wild*.

Of course, what the Wii U and Switch title was lacking was dungeons, and *A Link Between Worlds* has them in spades, cleverly concocted conundrums where you're playing with light and dark, fire and ice, or even cooperating with another character. In terms of sheer creativity, these are arguably the best dungeons in a top-down *Zelda* title, even if its 3D visuals mean it isn't a 'true' top-down perspective, with the camera slanted at an angle so that character faces and bodies could actually be visible.

Where *A Link To The Past* introduced multiple floors to give a sense of 3D depth and scale to the dungeons, the 3DS game goes further, with Link able to traverse along the walls in mural form. There's also a much greater sense of depth thanks to the stereoscopic 3D effects that make this adventure another showstopping first-party title for the handheld alongside *Super Mario 3D Land* and *Luigi's Mansion 2*. That said, the release of the 2DS that same year meant the team had to revise the designs to ensure puzzles could be completed without the 3D features enabled.

At the same time, it also restored a tradition that would be a relief for many players: the return of button controls. While the touchscreen was used to control Link in *Zelda* games for the DS and arguably made the game more accessible, it wasn't embraced by the hardcore traditional fanbase. This control scheme was wisely ditched for the 3DS titles, especially since this new handheld had a circle pad that allowed for intuitive 360-degree movement, and now you can just see Link and all the action on the top screen without your finger or stylus getting in the way. A more reliable and satisfying control method was matched by a buttery-smooth 60fps performance. The touchscreen could be used as inventory management instead, adding immediacy to the gameplay that felt as fluid as *A Link To The Past*.

Without the gimmick of touch controls or multiplayer, *A Link Between Worlds* was at once

» *A Link To The Past* players will find this first boss familiar in more ways than one.

a back-to-basics top-down *Zelda* game not seen since 2004's *The Minish Cap* that also opened up how you could go about exploring the world. It was met with universal acclaim, even if some critics did find that the over-familiarity with *A Link To The Past*'s map and landforms meant a loss of surprise, despite having the freedom of when and how you can explore certain places. This is nonetheless still a bit gated since you can't rent select traversal items, such as the Zora Flippers for swimming in deep water.

It's only really let down by an unmemorable art style that would also be used in *Tri Force Heroes*, although *Smash Bros* creator Masahiro Sakurai liked this game's iteration of *Zelda*, using it for *Super Smash Bros Ultimate*. Yet one might look at its simple polygons and consider it a prelude to the much more inspired diorama aesthetic for 2019's *Link's Awakening* remake, made possible with the Switch's HD-quality graphics. Indeed, a remake in that style for a modern platform is precisely what Nintendo should consider, as the best handheld *Zelda* game's legend deserves to endure for future generations.

LORULE AND HILDA

An alternate world with a different tragic story

THIS ADVENTURE SHARES a similar twist to *A Link To The Past* where it's revealed that Hyrule has a dark mirror version that Link can travel between, where much of the second and more expansive half of the game takes place. But Lorule isn't just another Dark World showing a parallel of what could be if the hero was to fail his task. Instead, it's a kingdom that did fall into decay long ago, but its world still has its own character, including its ruler, Princess Hilda, and its own incarnation of the Triforce.

There's a greater tragedy to Lorule as its downfall was due to its people warring amongst one another for power, with Hilda's ancestors choosing to destroy its Triforce rather than let anyone have it, but also causing the kingdom to crumble. What's more, it's revealed that the real culprit behind Hyrule's problems isn't actually Ganon or Yuga but Hilda, who has used these malevolent forces in a desperate bid to use Hyrule's Triforce to restore her own. It's a surprise revelation that makes Hilda a relatable tragic figure, quite unlike other princesses we've seen before in the *Zelda* series.

» Link can create whirlwinds with the new Tornado Rod to help with traversal.

THE LEGEND OF ZELDA™ Tri Force Heroes

Channelling the DNA of Four Swords and Spirit Tracks, this multiplayer follow-up to A Link Between Worlds is a madcap adventure

WORDS BY CHRIS SCHILLING & DREW SLEEP

It's not often you can say this about a *Zelda* game, but *Tri Force Heroes* is a good old-fashioned romp. Here is a series kicking back, letting its hair down, taking a break from the deadly serious business of saving the world and throwing a costume party. Yes, there are forces of evil to fight. And yes, there is a princess to rescue. But in this case, she needs saving from a fashion fate worse than death, as a witch curses her to wear a dull brown unitard in a style-obsessed kingdom. Link's job, then, is to venture into the aptly-named Drablands to obtain a brand-new outfit. The story setup says much for the overall tone: this is a more light-hearted adventure than most *Zelda* titles, with a rich vein of comedy running through the entire story.

Despite being a follow-up to *A Link Between Worlds* in terms of story and real-life chronology, the inspiration for *Tri Force Heroes* actually came from an earlier title. "I was the lead game designer on *The Legend Of Zelda: Spirit Tracks*, and within that game, we had the phantom-Link element where you switched back and forth between controlling the phantom and Link, and I was always interested in that type of gameplay, but not with a person switching between two, but with two people," director Hiromasa Shikata told *Game Informer* in 2014.

While working on *A Link Between Worlds*, Shikata revived that idea and optioned a 3DS follow-up to *Four Swords* to Nintendo. That plan was reworked and the game was reimagined as a standalone affair that championed three characters instead of four. "We played around with the idea of four players, but to be honest, it just seemed too high," Shikata admitted to *Game Informer* in the same interview. "It was a little difficult to see and it just didn't quite get what we were going at, so we reduced it down to three."

Another plan that was revised was to restrict the game to multiplayer only. The leadership at Nintendo pushed back, though. Long-time

» Dungeoneering with friends never gets old, especially when something goes comically wrong.

» The overall game design is reminiscent of *Four Swords* and *Four Swords Adventures*.

Zelda producer Eiji Aonuma pressed the importance of including a single-player mode, highlighting that solo players shouldn't be left out of the adventure. Shikata later revealed that not including a single-player component would have been disastrous.

The game itself is a fascinating outlier rather than a classic, a cooperative adventure designed to unite a trio of heroes to conquer a series of dungeons, fighting alongside or even on top of one another, as they formed totems to reach higher ground or to stand tall against bosses.

» Each outfit provides you with a different ability to get to grips with.

Each bite-sized mission requires three Links, which rules out a two-player mode, though solo adventurers can bring two doppelgängers with them, switching control between the three to solve puzzles and aggro enemies.

Alone, you are never quite given enough to think about, the awkwardness of manoeuvring three characters separately causing more headaches than any of the puzzles. Ostensibly adding two others to the mix should only have made things easier, but successfully co-ordinating a plan was never quite that straightforward – proving the old maxim about threes and crowds.

Still, with local partners, ensuring everyone is on the same page eventually makes things easier. It is when you take *Tri Force Heroes* online that it springs to life. Nintendo at the time was often bemoaned for its tendency to leave out voice chat in online games, but here its absence is the making of the game. Instead, it limits communication options to a set of cute pictorial icons, which you tap whenever you need your partners to follow you, throw a bomb, or give you a piggyback to reach a treasure chest. Until *Tri Force Heroes*, few games had ever quite managed to capture the exquisite frustration of trying to communicate effectively without the tools to do so. The confusion that often results is usually entertaining and frequently hilarious – particularly with room to play pranks on impatient players by deliberately misinterpreting their desperate attempts to direct you.

Players might be empowered by forming a totem, but *Tri Force Heroes* never stacks up to the sublime *Four Swords Adventures* on the GameCube. Its dungeons are compromised by having to simultaneously cater to lone players and groups while forcing players to share a single life bar neutering the playful competitive element that enlivened the GameCube favourite. Still, if four swords ultimately proved better than three, *Tri Force Heroes*' infectiously breezy, fashion-forward pleasures often prove difficult to resist.

TRI-HARDS

What made Tri Force Heroes special?

Stacking links

ALL IN THE name of teamwork, the trio of Links can stack up to reach three times an individual's height. What this means in gameplay terms is that you can get closer to interactive objects that are otherwise inaccessible – such as a door switch or an enticing poppable balloon.

Communication chaos

NINTENDO *COULD* HAVE implemented full voice chat into its multiplayer game, but instead it went for something a bit more chaotic. The limited communication options are endearing and are comical when a well-intentioned plan breaks down.

Dress for success

INSPIRED BY *ZELDA*'S phantom possession abilities in *Phantom Hourglass*, the development team wanted to give its trio of Links an array of swappable abilities. This comes in the form of different outfits, which fits neatly into the fashion-forward setting of Hytopia.

Mission-based mayhem

TRI FORCE HEROES was designed as a multiplayer adventure. As much as we'd want to, it's hard to have a sprawling interconnected *Zelda*-style epic with three players. So, a more bite-sized, multiplayer-friendly level structure was implemented instead.

Triple threat

THREE PLAYABLE CHARACTERS is a bit of a odd number, right? Well, there is some logic to that. You see, when testing the game, the team learned that four Links are one too many and would make the action on 3DS's small screen seem a bit too busy.

THE LEGEND OF ZELDA™ BREATH OF THE WILD

Breath Of The Wild director Hidemaro Fujibayashi tells us how Link embraced the open world

WORDS BY CHRIS SCHILLING

Under ordinary circumstances, Hidemaro Fujibayashi (pictured below) could be considered something of an industry veteran. He has, after all, been making games since 1995, when he joined Capcom – and he's been a level designer, after a fashion, for even longer, having previously been responsible for planning the layouts of haunted houses for theme parks in Japan. Indeed, his ties to *The Legend Of Zelda* alone stretch back over 20 years, to the two *Oracle* games for Game Boy Color.

However, Nintendo is no ordinary company, and so it is that Fujibayashi finds himself thrust into the spotlight after more than two decades in the wings, as the old guard of Miyamoto, Aonuma, Tezuka et al take a step back. Alongside the likes of Yoshiaki Koizumi, Shinya Takahashi and *Splatoon* producer Hisashi Nogami, Fujibayashi represents the new face of Nintendo – even if 'new' is a bit of a stretch for such long-serving employees.

A relatively sprightly 44 years of age at the time of the game's release, the *Breath Of The Wild* director's first entanglement with *Zelda* came during the development of *Oracle Of Ages & Seasons*, where he was responsible for collating game concepts from Capcom's team and reporting back to Miyamoto. His organisational skills must have impressed his superiors, since he was appointed the role of director and co-writer. Fujibayashi conceived the password system that connected the two games for a special ending.

Who better than a man responsible for a link between Links to helm a new *Zelda* game designed both to span two hardware generations and to bridge the gap between established ideas and brave new horizons? And yet Fujibayashi says it took some time to find a fresh point of focus for *Breath Of The Wild*. "It didn't come to me right away as a fully formed idea," he recalls. "For a long time, I went from idea to idea before I finally reached what I think are the very roots of *Breath Of The Wild*'s gameplay: the idea of cliff climbing and paragliding back down, the keyword 'survival', and the idea of 'creativity of combination' whereby players make use of things that happen when their actions interact with objects placed on the map – for example, lighting wood with fire to create a bonfire. It was this root gameplay that I then submitted."

» Items you gather on your journey can be thrown into a cooking pot to make stat-boosting dishes that also restore your hearts.

» Link awakens after a hundred-year nap to find his beloved Hyrule is in ruins, thanks to Calamity Ganon.

HYLIAN USUAL

Fujibayashi offers insight into Breath Of The Wild's story

THE CHALLENGE OF telling a compelling story within an open-world framework is not necessarily a new one, but it is new to *Zelda*. How did Fujibayashi and his team handle that? "This is something I did a lot of work on with the development staff, but I can't say too much because I don't want to spoil anything," he says. "With regards to the actual story, what I can say is that the game starts with Link waking up in a cave with amnesia, not knowing why he's doing anything. Likewise, the player doesn't know why Link is there either. Link and the player have exactly the same level of knowledge. What would you do if it were you in that situation? How would you go about finding out who you are and about the world?

"Your answer to that question might be the solution to the system that lets you experience a rich story in an 'open-air' game like this."

01

02

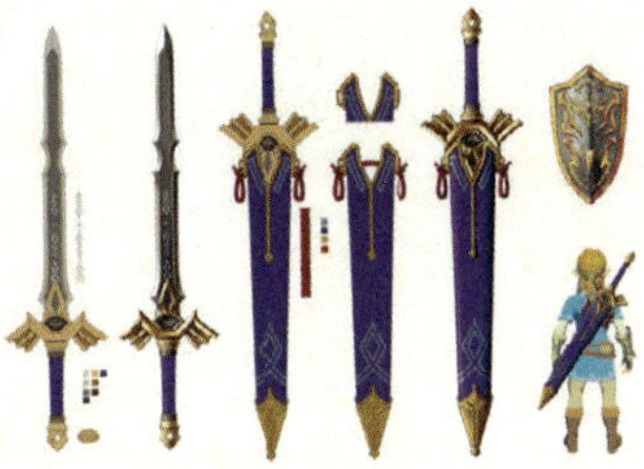

» 01 - Each Divine Beast holds the spirit of a champion that fell to Ganon 100 years ago, such as Daruk.

» 02 - These swords may look great, but don't get too attached – they'll all break.

» 03 - You can swap out Link's gear and clothing to suit your needs..

03

"I don't think the core gameplay of the series has changed at all compared to that of 30 years ago"

For Fujibayashi, *Zelda* is, first and foremost, a puzzle game. Whether it's one of the many shrines (self-contained miniature dungeons, essentially) scattered throughout the land, or even a cluster of Bokoblins blocking your path, *Breath Of The Wild*, like previous entries, is designed around a series of situations that require the player to come up with a hypothesis and then test it out. That has, he says, been central to the appeal of *Zelda* since the beginning – back when he was part of its audience rather than its creative team. "The look and feel of the game has changed with the times, [but] I don't think the core gameplay of the series has changed at all compared to that of 30 years ago," he explains. "I feel that's because even though the puzzle-solving element of the series changes with the times in how exactly players interact with it, the fun of it – the fun I experienced for the first time myself as a child – is still there in more recent *Zelda* titles, completely unchanged."

So long as that core – or 'rule', as he calls it – is intact, Fujibayashi believes, then there are no limits to what can surround it. He is, it's fair to say, an ideas man – keen to stuff as many as he possibly can into each new entry for which he's responsible. "Whenever we get a new piece of hardware, or a ▶

new feature, or a new development environment, I just want to tell people about the ideas I have for getting that same feeling of fun I felt way back into a game, but in a new way," he says. "What I've learned from working on *Zelda* games is that you will never run out of ideas if you ask yourself what you can mix together with this rule."

In the case of *Breath Of The Wild*, there are lots of new ingredients to stir in, from crafting to cooking, degradable weapons and gear to physics-based conundrums and realistic weather with tangible environmental effects. No sweat for a pioneer such as Fujibayashi, who's overseen Link acting as an advocate for a host of Nintendo hardware features, such as the Game Boy Advance Link Cables in *Four Swords*, the DS touchscreen and microphone in *Phantom Hourglass*, and Wii MotionPlus in *Skyward Sword*. In that sense, the series' heroic lead isn't just a mascot for Nintendo, but for its ideas. What is it about Link, we wonder, that makes him so ideally suited to showing off the capabilities of Nintendo hardware?

"Actually, I don't really think of only *Zelda* games being especially appropriate for drawing out the abilities of Nintendo's hardware," Fujibayashi says. "However, solving puzzles is at the root of *Zelda* games, so maybe it is this way simply because the puzzle-solving gameplay allows us to show off new features in a very easy-to-understand way." He follows up with the mildest of spoilers: "In this story Link wakes up at the outset wearing only underwear. I think, as the avatar of the player in this world, he's able to take on all these different roles precisely because we made him as a character so neutral."

If Link is adaptable, the same could be said for a series that has never been content to stay in one place, even as some features have remained constant. *Majora's Mask*, for all its recycled assets, adopted an entirely different structure to its immediate predecessor; *Spirit Tracks*, too, borrowed a control scheme from *Phantom Hourglass*, but approached navigation in its own distinct way. The Fujibayashi-directed *Skyward Sword* left little room to explore outside its dungeons and hub areas, while its successor's expansive world stretches as far as the eye can see, and beyond. Fujibayashi has his own theory for why *Zelda*, unlike so many of its peers, has been so open to change.

"The history of the *Zelda* series is very long, so I should note that a lot of what I'm about to say includes some speculation of my own," he begins, cautiously. "But I think that perhaps it's because throughout the series, even though directors have changed, I feel like we've made the games to allow players to get one specific sensation or experience. A universal experience, a feeling that exists in everyone no matter the time period; something that's not really affected by a difference in views you hold or the culture you come from. There can be a language barrier, but it's not an absolute. Anyone would be excited when they manage to get the ring out in one of those metal-wire puzzles, right? That's the kind of experience I'm talking about. I think it's because the *Zelda* games are built to treasure that feeling that makes it so adaptable."

Exhibit A: tasked with negotiating a frigid river, Link must cut down a tree and push its trunk into the water in order to cross safely. This is just one example of what Fujibayashi calls

» The kingdom may have fallen, but its varied races endure and Link journeys to the lands of the Zora, Rito, Gorons and Gerudo.

"I thought it'd be fun not to make the system too complex, and instead try to recreate the entertainment and enjoyment of the first Zelda game"

SOFT LAUNCH

How playtesting was used to keep the team co-ordinated

BREATH OF THE WILD was Nintendo's most ambitious project at the time, and the company's own staff required some assistance to get it finished. Around 100 staff from *Xenoblade Chronicles* developer Monolith Soft helped out. Marshalling a workforce of that size is no mean feat, particularly when you're making a game with so many variables. But this was less of a problem than you might assume, as Fujibayashi explains. "Since this was a rather large-scale project, we were coming up with a lot of ideas for features and gameplay at the same time as we were creating the game," he says. "When doing this it's impossible to avoid some inconsistencies in terms of development decisions and what's actually being made. So at milestones during development, we were sure to have all of the development staff take plenty of time to play the game that had been made so far and understand the problems we had."

This might sound time-consuming, but Fujibayashi says it became a useful shortcut, ultimately cutting down development time rather than extending it. "By repeating this process, the director just has to define the problem, and the staff working on the game can then easily understand what the issue is, avoiding any differences in key areas in terms of decisions, or the direction we should go. Also, by understanding the game as a whole by playtesting it, our developers were able to understand what the colleague next to them was working on. It's horizontal information sharing. We overcame the boundaries of roles, which often isolates information."

This collaborative approach allowed staff to easily exchange information with colleagues, encouraging ideas to be shared. "It may seem obvious, but this had quite a huge effect on the project," Fujibayashi says. "For example, the enemies in this game really have lots of unique actions. If you throw a bomb, they may kick it or throw it back to you, or they might pick up and use weapons dropped by others. These actions were created by staff working on all kinds of other areas finding things that could be fun and bringing up those ideas."

The ruined Hyrule tells a story through its environment alone, leaving you to piece together what happened to certain areas.

Instead of Epona, Link can train a stable of different steeds.

The climbing mechanic is simple, but elegant. You can climb almost anything, as long as you preserve your stamina.

WEAR IT'S AT

LINK HAS BEEN able to increase his health, stamina and/or magic gauges throughout the series, but *Skyward Sword* introduced a series first: upgradeable gear. Crafting has been significantly expanded in *Breath Of The Wild*, encompassing a *Monster Hunter*-like cooking system that lets you combine ingredients – from food to plants to monster parts – and there are various items of clothing, such as a quilted shirt that protects Link against the cold.

Like the open world, these features are designed to give the player a greater feeling of freedom, Fujibayashi explains. "It's up to you how you want to play *Breath Of The Wild*. These systems, such as ability boosting, items and equipment, are there for that purpose. This quality also means that different people might experience the game very differently. There will be players who might gather lots of food and potions to recover hearts and stamina, so they can recover from any mistake. Other players might try to overcome difficulty by improving and strengthening their clothing and equipment." So players can exert a degree of control over the challenges they face according to their own style of play – and Fujibayashi is well aware that will include an audience that would rather raise the difficulty than lower it. "Some may rely on their bow-and-arrow technique and complete the game wearing just underwear!" he says. "*Breath Of The Wild*'s systems make all of these approaches possible."

Breath Of The Wild's "sensory and intuitive" puzzle solving. His team has worked hard to fill the game with such moments.

Problem solving is inherent to game design, of course: part of Fujibayashi's job over the past decade and a half has been finding inventive ways to use hardware, just as Link must dig into his backpack to find the right kit for his current predicament. What's different this time is that *Breath Of The Wild* is a crossplatform game, built for two formats – and, as such, couldn't realistically be bound to any specific hardware features. Rather than looking back through his own *Zelda* games for inspiration, Fujibayashi opted instead to study one he'd always enjoyed as a fan.

"There was no need for us to build the gameplay around a certain special game mechanic," he says. "This heralded a return to our roots. I thought it would be fun not to make the system too complex, and instead try to recreate the entertainment and enjoyment of the first *Zelda* game using our current platforms. When looking into the idea, I realised the original *Zelda* allowed users to freely explore an expansive world; players would search for the dungeon they were

HERO OF TIME

A game-by-game journey through Hidemaro Fujibayashi's Zelda career

The Legend Of Zelda: Oracle of Ages/Seasons

(GAME BOY COLOR, 2001)

FUJIBAYASHI'S FIRST *ZELDA* game was developed at Capcom subsidiary Flagship. Conceived as a triumvirate – representing the three parts of the Triforce – one game was cancelled, leaving the puzzle-led *Ages* and the more action-focused Seasons. The two could be connected to form a single plot, leading to an extended ending.

The Legend Of Zelda: Four Swords

(GAME BOY ADVANCE, 2002)

FROM LINKING GAMES to linking players: Fujibayashi's next project was this multiplayer adventure, which was bundled with the GBA remake of *A Link To The Past*. It blended co-op and competitive play: collaboration was required to progress in its randomised puzzle dungeons, but the player with the most rupees would earn an extra reward.

The Legend Of Zelda: The Minish Cap

(GAME BOY ADVANCE, 2004)

THE FINAL CAPCOM *Zelda* title saw Link don the titular garment to shrink down to the size of an insect – as a result, regular enemies such as Chuchus became towering bosses. It also saw a return for *Four Swords* antagonist Vaati, while the Gust Jar – later seen in 3DS multiplayer entry *Tri Force Heroes* – made its debut.

after and look for a way to reach it. This was a theme that fit exceptionally well with *Breath Of The Wild*." It's appropriate, really, that for a series whose timeline is so hotly debated, *Zelda*'s future should be so deeply rooted in its past.

Still, the presence of the Sheikah Slate, a multi-faceted tool shaped suspiciously like a Wii U GamePad, is a lasting reminder that *Breath Of The Wild* was originally built around a single piece of hardware. It was spring of 2016 when the decision was made to develop and release the game for Switch, too. Eiji Aonuma has already spoken of the "large extra burden" it placed on the shoulders of the development team: the move from two displays to one enforced a shift in the way the game controlled. Fujibayashi, however, reflects on this unusual situation with great diplomacy. "Of course, we didn't have a huge amount of leeway in terms of time," he recalls. "But as director I wasn't particularly fazed by this. I have a very strong impression that work proceeded without panic under the specific instructions of our producer, Mr Aonuma. Personally, when I started thinking about what kind of features the Nintendo Switch hardware had, I ended up thinking about whether we could add in any new ideas, which looking back on it now was probably not the best thing to be thinking of at the time!"

Fujibayashi's past experience perhaps made for an easier transition than would otherwise have been possible. Having previously directed handheld and home-console *Zelda* titles, he now found himself helming a game that would, in its Switch incarnation at least, function as both. The key difference between the two types, he says, is an obvious one: horsepower. "The *Oracle* games and *The Minish Cap* were 2D pixel-art games released on the Game Boy Color and Game Boy Advance. Compared to the Wii, Wii U or Nintendo Switch, graphically they can't even begin to match up – the kinds of animations, the text we can show, the audio, and storage space are definitely not comparable. The most notable difference is simply that we can no longer 'fudge' things when it comes to anything graphical. What we have previously left up to players' imaginations can all now be shown for real, so continuing to use our previous methods of expression would lead to some very odd experiences for players."

» Combat is very standard *Zelda* fare with embellishments such as breakable weapons and harder-hitting enemies.

» Puzzle-box-like shrines are scattered throughout Hyrule, posing you with a self-contained conundrum to solve.

The Legend Of Zelda: Phantom Hourglass

(NINTENDO DS, 2007)

AFTER CAPCOM CLOSED Flagship, Fujibayashi began working for Nintendo. Borrowing the cel-shaded aesthetic (and sailing elements) of *The Wind Waker*, *Phantom Hourglass* featured ingenious stylus controls and a central dungeon, the divisive Temple Of The Ocean King, to which players had to repeatedly return.

The Legend Of Zelda: Skyward Sword

(WII, 2011)

FUJIBAYASHI'S FIRST HOME-CONSOLE *Zelda* took five years to make – and the stresses of development pushed him into throwing a sickie so he could write the game's scenario in a day while cloistered at home. Its motion-controlled combat didn't sit well with everyone, though plenty appreciated its breaks with series tradition.

The Legend Of Zelda: Breath Of The Wild

(NINTENDO SWITCH/WII U, 2017)

FUJIBAYASHI SAYS THAT *Breath Of The Wild* was built with the notion of rethinking series conventions, but he hasn't simply gone back to the drawing board. "We're not changing the true nature of *Zelda* games," he says. "We're just changing our approach to it." Discounting *Four Swords Adventures*, it's the first mainline *Zelda* to use auto-saves.

The Gerudo desert is extremely hot, so dress – or undress – accordingly when exploring its expansive sands.

> "More than anything, what's influenced my understanding of what a Zelda game should be has been the teachings I've received from Miyamoto"

Otherwise, he says, the process is remarkably similar. His approach to crafting the foundational play logic that underpins *Breath Of The Wild* hasn't really changed a great deal since *The Minish Cap*. Rather than elucidate, he says, "It might be more fun for players to see how we maintained a balance [between the two styles] by playing the game and seeing for themselves."

Talking of playing, Fujibayashi naturally hasn't had an awful lot of free time in which to play videogames. A couple of years ago, however, a pair of indie successes in particular managed to capture his imagination. "I was rather inspired by playing *Minecraft* and *Terraria*," he tells us. "I was able to learn from the gameplay and the possibilities found in [those games]. I could learn from the sense of adventure, exploration and how it inspired curiosity."

These virtual realms may have offered some pointers, but the real world has had a much greater impact on the direction of *Breath Of The Wild*. Fujibayashi excitedly reveals that he's part of an adventure club, in which he regularly engages in outdoor activities alongside other Nintendo staff. "[We do] things like cave diving where you actually go down into the water to get into the cave, as well as rafting tours and so on," he elaborates. "I know this may not be such a big deal in the west, but in Japan it's quite an adventure!"

The director's embrace of the great outdoors is most clearly expressed through Link himself, but it's apparent in *Breath Of The Wild*'s expansive environments, too. This may be a fantasy setting, but it's the first *Zelda* world that bears close comparison with our own. It's tempting to view the size and openness of that world as a reaction to *Skyward Sword*'s more compact spaces, but while Fujibayashi acknowledges that fan feedback is always taken into consideration, such a marked shift in the construction of its environments has little to do with criticisms aimed at the 2011 Wii *Zelda* game.

"We weren't looking back on *Skyward Sword* ourselves all that much, although we did add on some parts that worked well in the development of *Skyward Sword*, and revised some parts that we had concerns with," Fujibayashi says. "Something else we've done now is make it so you can climb walls basically anywhere, and you can jump off from high places and glide where you want. We had to consider what kind of landscape would work for that. In the game, it's even possible to dive straight towards a lake from a cliff so high that the surface of the water looks hazy due to the distance. How can we create a thrilling adventure in a place where you can go anywhere you want? That is the kind of question we were considering as we made *Breath Of The Wild*."

Talk of cliffs and lakes reminds us of an anecdote from one of Fujibayashi's mentors. Always a man to draw inspiration from his hobbies rather than other games, Shigeru Miyamoto once recalled how a hiking trip near Kobe, one of Japan's largest cities, saw him discover a large lake at the top of a mountain, and how he drew upon such moments when creating the original *Legend Of Zelda*. With Fujibayashi citing both the first game and his love for the great outdoors as key inspirations for *Breath Of The Wild*, it's as if the series has come full circle – only now Nintendo has the technology to recreate that sensation without having to fudge anything.

It's a reminder that despite this symbolic changing of the guard, as Nintendo's veterans make way for a new generation of designers – and, perhaps, future mentors – that the legacy of those who have gone before is just as vital as it has ever been.

"More than anything, what's influenced my personal understanding of what a *Zelda* game should be has been the teachings I've received from Shigeru Miyamoto in the years since the *Oracle* games," Fujibayashi concludes. "I really feel that it's not because of knowledge or experience that I'm here working as a developer for *Zelda*, but because of the people."

» Elemental effects interact with the world in surprising ways, providing players with a proving ground of experimentation.

» One notorious segment has link infiltrating the all-female Gerudo tribe by adopting their clothing.

ONE LINK TO RULE THEM ALL

SHIGERU MIYAMOTO HAS talked about a shift in Nintendo's development philosophy for *Mario* games: where recent titles have focused more on welcoming new players, *Super Mario Odyssey* marks a return to the days of *Super Mario 64* and *Sunshine*. Is *Zelda* likely to follow a similar path? Did Fujibayashi set out to aim *Breath Of The Wild* at experienced players? "It's true that we do, for example, have lots of tribes that people familiar with the series will know, such as Goron, Zora, Rito and Gerudo," Fujibayashi begins. "There's a story revolving around the legendary Master Sword, and you'll hear the keyword 'Ganon' too. There are lots of things like that, but these are just meant to entertain players who've supported the series a long time.

"[But] with regards to the gameplay, we wanted to try something new and simplify the puzzle solving, so we did a lot of work on the themes of breaking the conventions of previous *Zelda* games, and going back to our roots. As a result of this, the game is accessible to even people who haven't played a *Zelda* game before. It definitely isn't a game made only for those who are experienced with the series."

THE LEGEND OF ZELDA™ TEARS OF THE KINGDOM

The return of true dungeons and an even more inventive power set makes this remixed Hyrule feel equally as joyous

WORDS BY AARON POTTER

Only a company as innovative and madcap as Nintendo could find itself in the unique position of needing to surpass what many people consider to be one of the greatest games of all time. Its own, in fact. That's exactly the prospect Eiji Aonuma, Hidemaro Fujibayashi, and the rest of the team at Nintendo EPD faced when wanting to follow up 2017's *The Legend Of Zelda: Breath Of The Wild*, a game that itself had blown expectations out of the water by taking the franchise back to its roots while remoulding what its ideas of adventure and discovery meant for a new generation of players. How do you begin to tackle doing this? The answer, it turns out, is not by rewriting the entire rulebook, but by flipping the script.

Tears Of The Kingdom isn't your average direct *Zelda* sequel. Rather than wiping the slate clean and starting totally from scratch, you see, it elects to take a familiar version of Hyrule that worked so beautifully to instil a sense of wonder before and then builds upon it by sprinkling in even more opportunities, stories and secrets for players to uncover. Sceptics may argue using an existing framework in this way was done to prevent pushing the ageing Nintendo Switch hardware past breaking point. However, a generous six-year development cycle between the console's first and latest mainline series entries says otherwise, suggesting Nintendo always had a lot more planned than simply remixing the same map. Fortunately for all of us, it absolutely did.

True, as before you play as a newly awoken version of Link, tasked with exploring several mysterious regions in an attempt to bring peace back to the land and reunite with your beloved Princess Zelda. So far, so standard. As well as looking inward at the franchise's own past for inspiration, though, *Tears Of The Kingdom* also looked above and below – literally! The big new gimmick heading into the adventure (or so we thought) is the addition of sky islands, as first evidenced by the game's reveal trailer which saw Link leap from a stratospheric platform and down into the clouds beneath. In truth, the amount of territory available to explore ended up being threefold, much like the Triforce.

In fairness, creating a whole new map high above the one we knew from *Breath Of The Wild* would have been a triumph in its own right. And even the Great Sky Island, as this game's tutorial area, deceptively evokes such sentiment. It's here where you'll get to grips with Link's brand-new toolset and learn how to navigate *Tears Of The Kingdom*'s various sky-level archipelagos, which most players had assumed would be just as lavish and endless as Hyrule itself. Before you know it, however, Link is cast back down to ground level soon after Ganondorf's evil is reunleashed, where before long yet another new map reveals itself in the form of the Depths, a cavernous underground location.

It's here where the true magic of *Tears Of The Kingdom* begins to be fully unveiled, and any belief that it's merely an expanded DLC-like

» Dungeons wouldn't be anywhere near as memorable were it not for Link's companions, like the returning Prince Sidon.

» Almost any item or material can be fused to another. Attaching a flame emitter to a shield creates a flamethrower while defending.

» *Tears Of The Kingdom* never goes the easy route, and so places the Water Temple in the sky. Of course!

FLIPPED SCRIPT

Some key highlights from Link's latest quest

Companion abilities

IT'S NOT JUST Link's new stone arm that grants useful abilities, but also those gifted to you by the companions, who aid you in each of the game's dungeons, too. The Rito Tulin, as the Sage Of Wind, grants you one of the most useful, allowing you to create gusts to make for an effective sky boost.

Hudson Construction

ONE OF THE most fun sidequests relates to a guy named Addison. In random locations you'll find him struggling to keep signs upright on behalf of Hudson Construction. This proves tough for him but it's a perfect excuse to put your Ultrahand skills to the test, helping him prop up the sign using surrounding materials.

Hidden caves

WHILE THE LAYOUT of Hyrule is remarkably similar to *Breath Of The Wild*'s landscape, one major change is the inclusion of 140 or so caves sprinkled throughout that can hide chests and precious rewards. It's only in these where you find Bubbul Gems, for example, which are useful for obtaining cool costumes and creature masks.

Zonai devices

NINTENDO'S *ZELDA* SEQUEL expertly fuels your ability to be creative with the introduction of Zonai devices, which come in all shapes and sizes. These are best found from dedicated Zonai dispensers, dishing out everything from sleds to flame emitters to springs, which can then be combined to overcome challenges in the overworld.

Geoglyphs

LEARNING THE SECRET past of ancient Hyrule and Zelda's ultimate whereabouts requires you to find all 12 different geoglyphs spread throughout the kingdom. Most are easy to spot from high up, luckily, but most will take you to the far reaches of the map. Discovering each unlocks a hidden memory core to the overall story.

update for *Breath Of The Wild* melts away. Because unlike the challenge-based sky areas, the Depths acts as a hard mode, a place Link can explore to find precious resources while battling toughened-up enemies and (in a not-so-surprising turn for a location situated underneath Hyrule) the darkness. Doing so successfully means finding ways to illuminate the space, either by firing Brightbloom seeds from your bow or discovering the 120 Lightroots littered around.

All three present levels in *Tears Of The Kingdom*'s world are in constant dialogue with one another in ways that frequently delight, serving to emphasise the interconnectedness of the adventure far better than *Breath Of The Wild* ever could. Armour collected from a chest up in the sky, for instance, can be upgraded by any one of the four Great Fairy locations on the ground, which will make your time in the Depths far less devastating. This is but one of countless other examples where diving into each of the kingdom's different tiers can greatly pay off for anyone brave enough.

Luckily, helping Link navigate these vastly more complex locations is a completely fresh toolbox of abilities: Ultrahand, Fuse, Ascend, and Recall. Some are more powerful than others, sure, but all four have their uses that rapidly change the way you're able to interact with your surroundings, be it in terms of traversal, combat, or building. Indeed, being able to craft gadgets and contraptions serves as a core part of the gameplay loop in *Tears Of The Kingdom*. To the extent that it makes *Breath Of The Wild*'s abilities appear vastly underpowered by comparison, and you'll wonder how you were ever able to cope without it before.

> "Being able to take any object, large or small, and attach it to another is game-changing"

Being able to take any object, large or small, and attach it to another is game-changing. And sure, you'll start with simple Ultrahand experiments like attaching logs to form a raft needed to cross a river. It isn't that long after, however, that more of the newly arrived Zonai devices make themselves known, and you're combining a glider and a fan to form an airship, a cannon and a cart to create a turret, a shield and a rocket to make a hoverboard and so on. Ultrahand is by far the most inventive ability gifted to you (thanks to Link's new stone arm) in this sequel, outright breaking the game in ways arguably Nintendo wouldn't have imagined by saying 'yes' to players' ingenuity at every turn.

This isn't to discount the usefulness of *Tears Of The Kingdom*'s three other main powers, though. Far from it. Fuse, as an example, is a direct response to many people's previous frustrations with the previous game's weapon degradation system, by letting you create your own extremely durable objects of destruction. A Soldier's Broadsword and Bokoblin Horn might be limited in strength alone, but not together. The last two abilities, meanwhile, remove climbing's few annoyances tied to stamina or time required present previously, with Ascend letting Link melt through any above surfaces while Recall makes rewinding time on a fallen stone double up as an elevator to the sky.

While Hyrule is packed full of scenarios and instances designed to put the full capabilities of these sandbox-style powers to the test, it's really

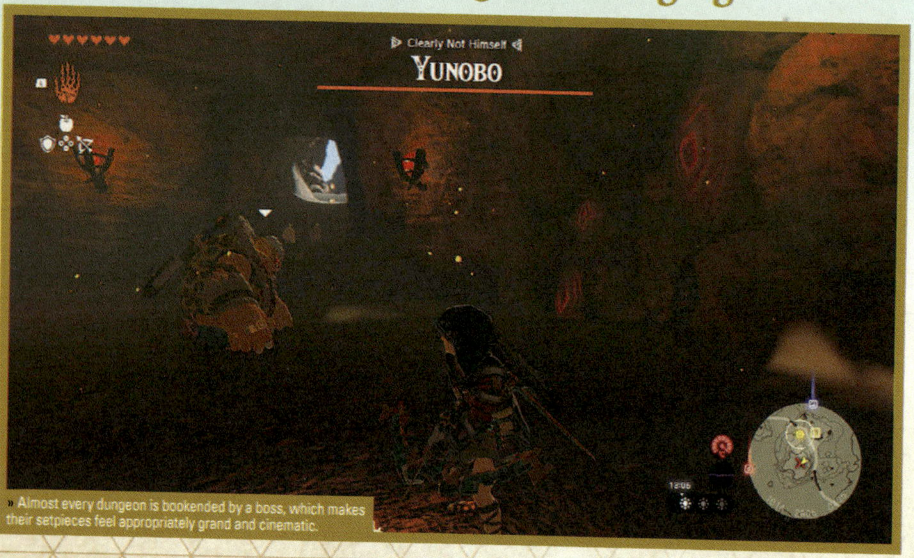

» Almost every dungeon is bookended by a boss, which makes their setpieces feel appropriately grand and cinematic.

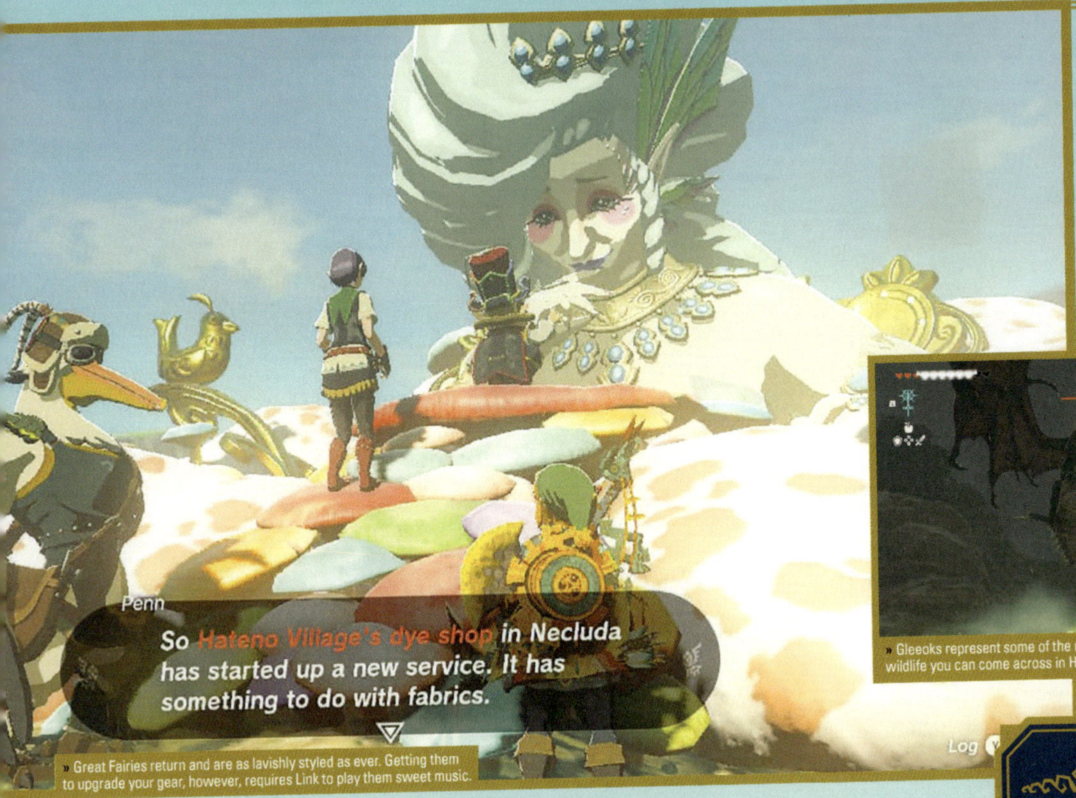

» Great Fairies return and are as lavishly styled as ever. Getting them to upgrade your gear, however, requires Link to play them sweet music.

» Paragliding now represents an opportunity to flaunt your love for previous *Zelda* games with new dyes.

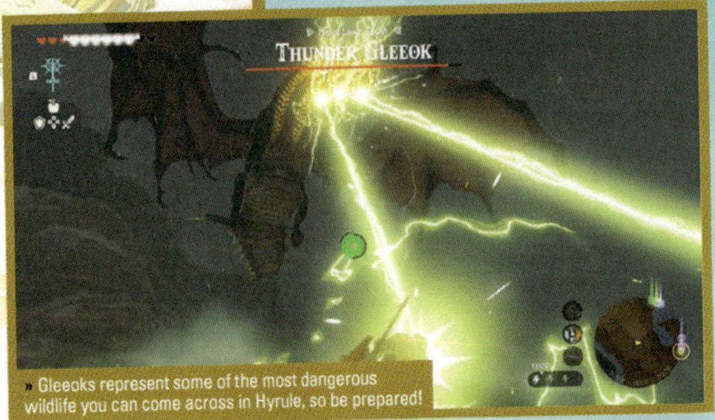

» Gleeoks represent some of the most dangerous wildlife you can come across in Hyrule, so be prepared!

in the returning shrines where you're afforded the chance to fully hone them. Whereas in *Breath Of The Wild*, there was some wiggle room for experimentation in terms of how Link was able to solve these intricate, bite-sized puzzle rooms, *Tears Of The Kingdom* presents them in a way where it's clear there's rarely a wrong or right solution. Do you attach wheels to a board using Ultrahand to cross a river of lava, for example, or do you stick enough plinths together to create one high up enough for you to paraglide down and fly over? It's up to you.

For as great as shrines are at testing your wits, *Tears Of The Kingdom* purposely goes out of its way to let players have their cake and eat it, combining the strengths of both new and classic eras by reinstating a tentpole feature of *Zelda*'s more linear entries. Because yes, traditional dungeons (of a sort) make their return here, once again geared around elemental themes and capped off with a memorable boss battle to make completing them feel truly cinematic. It helps that Nintendo kept their existence a surprise right up until the day of launch.

Whether it's using giant, air-based trampolines to dodge cyclones to stay high enough to reach the wind temple, or navigating the winding routes of underground rail tracks to smash the fire temple's five gongs, all four dungeons have you using Recall, Ascend and especially Ultrahand in ways you previously thought not possible. What's more, each one is broken up and designed in pieces, coming together to create a giant puzzle box setpiece that really hits home just how much the previous game's Divine Beasts lacked in such grandeur. Similar to the sky archipelagos, getting to the dungeons and then solving them proves to be a true event to the point it's worth savouring them.

» Great Sky Island serves as this sequel's tutorial area, letting you get to grips with almost all of Link's new powers.

The most impressive aspect of *The Legend Of Zelda: Tears Of The Kingdom* is that, much like *Breath Of The Wild* before it, the world is totally yours for the taking – only to a far higher degree. True, certain threads are more obvious to pull on than others because they have to be, but by and large this more in-depth and expertly crafted version of Hyrule is one that will reward you for exploring in whatever direction you see fit. It's rare to have a videogame come along that not only encourages your ingenuity at every turn but actively approves of it like few other games attempt to.

As for the future of *The Legend Of Zelda*? It almost certainly lies beyond Nintendo's current hybrid console. And with *Tears Of The Kingdom* releasing so close to the tail-end of the Nintendo Switch's life cycle (and outright making the prior release look like a dry run) the next logical step is surely to reinvent this franchise's wheel yet again on whatever brand-new hardware Nintendo is cooking up. Aonuma has been clear that an open-world system will be "the new format to proceed from" going forward, indicating that Nintendo's creative sandbox approach to the series won't be going anywhere anytime soon. Regardless of whatever form the next *Zelda* takes, Nintendo can be confident it sent the Switch off with a bang with yet another candidate for one of the greatest games of all time.

TIMES GONE BY

The world and people of Hyrule move on

AS ONE OF the rare direct sequels to an existing *Zelda* game, similar to *Majora's Mask* or *Spirit Tracks*, there's an acute joy to *Tears Of The Kingdom*'s world in that you get to reacquaint yourself with familiar characters, discover how events have progressed and how locations have changed following the Upheaval that occurs when Ganondorf returns. Purah no longer conducts her research within Hateno's Ancient Tech Lab, for example, having decided to set up shop at Lookout Landing under the shadow of Hyrule Castle. Impa has similarly retired from her role as Kakariko village's elder, now dead set on helping Link find the geoglyphs in her air balloon.

In terms of locations, the journey heading up Death Mountain now feels different due to the lava slops that have been lost. Gerudo Valley, meanwhile, is arid no more and suddenly has a large water flow running through it. Anyone who skipped *Breath Of The Wild* won't notice these small instances of change, but each tell a story about the way the world has moved on. It's yet another way Nintendo uses the existing map to the game's benefit. Something only possible by making *Tears Of The Kingdom* a direct sequel.

THE ORACLES SPEAK

The people behind the world's greatest adventure series tell us why The Legend Of Zelda is so special

WORDS BY LEIGH LOVEDAY

The development of *Zelda* games has changed: not only from a team of 20 developers to hundreds, but from simple 2D environments to jaw-dropping 3D worlds. Three key figures have, since *Zelda*'s earliest days, masterminded the steps Link takes: Shigeru Miyamoto, the series creator; Eiji Aonuma, the director of many 3D *Zeldas*; and Takashi Tezuka, a Nintendo stalwart who has directed and produced more than half of the games in the series. Here, these luminaries will provide insight on the series they created.

SHIGERU MIYAMOTO

Nintendo's most-storied developer now oversees every game the company produces, but retains a special fondness for *The Legend Of Zelda*. He came up with the concept for the first game while trying **to think of something** different to *Super Mario*, his inspiration **an adventurous** childhood and an insatiable curiosity. Ever since, Miyamoto has stewarded the *Zelda* games – though the last he outright directed was *Ocarina Of Time* – and is responsible more than any other for their grand ideas and attention to detail.

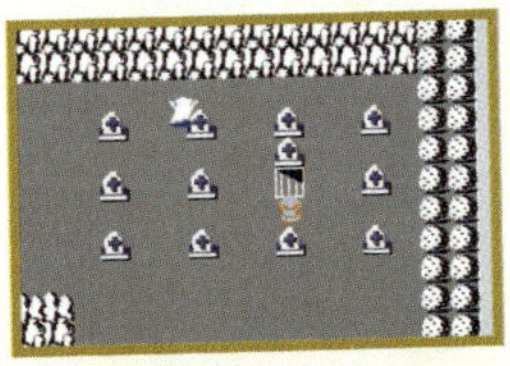

DID YOU KNOW?

Shigeru Miyamoto is ambidextrous, but prefers using his left hand – and Link, until Twilight Princess and the Wii motion control scheme, was always left-handed.

MIYAMOTO ON...

The first Zelda

"When I was making *The Legend Of Zelda*, it was very plain. I didn't think that genre would be seen as something so mainstream. I really didn't expect the response I got: a world of swords and magic really wasn't considered mainstream at the time."

Curiosity

"What if, on a street, you look up and see something appear that should not, given what we know, be there? You either shake your head and dismiss it, or you accept that there is much more to the world than we think. Perhaps it really is a doorway to another place. If you choose to go inside you may find many unexpected things."

Fear

"Throughout the *Zelda* series I have always tried to make players believe they are in a kind of miniature garden. So my challenge is always how to make people feel comfortable and also very scared at the same time. That's the big challenge."

Secrets

"Because *Zelda* is an adventure game, you have to find many things, and many of them may be hard to find. In the game's fishing pond, something might happen if you're playing there for a long time or are trying to do many things there. You can find Gold Skulltulas. You may want to search for them where you would find bugs and insects. Sometimes, if you have a Deku Stick and you find some butterflies flying about, you can make them follow you and something special could happen..."

The formula

"It has to do with balance. My formula for success is that 70% of the game should have to do with objectives and the rest should be secrets and exploration, things such as burning trees to find a hidden dungeon entrance like in the first game."

The future

"I'd like to create a totally realistic atmosphere. For example, if you went to a dungeon, you could almost smell it [laughs]. Or even within the same body of water, you could see differences between cold water and hot water. That would be my dream."

EIJI AONUMA

Compared to Miyamoto and Tezuka, Eiji Aonuma is a sort of latecomer to the *Zelda* series. He began as the dungeon designer for *Ocarina Of Time*, and impressed Miyamoto enough to be given the role of director on the next *Zelda* title, *Majora's Mask*. Ever since, Aonuma has directed a remarkable number of titles in the series and acted as producer for many more. He is currently adding the finishing touches to *Tears Of The Kingdom* with director Hidemaro Fujibayashi.

AONUMA ON…

The first time

"When I joined Nintendo, *A Link To The Past* was launched – so my first encounter with *The Legend Of Zelda* was not as a designer but a player. I realised it was doing many things other games did not do, and it became the game that gave me the framework for how I think about videogames."

Exploration

"To me, *Zelda* has always been an exploration game. You believe that you know everything – but you are wrong. In the worlds we choose to create, there is always something hidden somewhere that you are unaware of, and where you can find out new things, explore something for yourself. It's a very pleasant type of surprise."

Zelda's items

"Sometimes we use the same items, and sometimes not. It depends. In the case of *Phantom Hourglass*, for example, we were able to utilise the boomerang once again – but it's manipulated on the touchscreen with the stylus. So even when we use an old item, if we cannot come up with a new way of utilising it, we should definitely say no – this isn't final, it's not unique, it's not good enough for *Zelda*."

Working with Miyamoto

"In one of his emails, Miyamoto-san wrote: 'We're supposed to be creating something for people's entertainment. This part won't do at all.' That has really stuck in my mind. He went on to say: 'We want people to enjoy the game, but how on Earth are they going to enjoy what you've done here?' The fact that we're making something to entertain people is completely obvious when you stop to think about it, but what he said made me realise it afresh."

His favourite Zelda game

"My strongest personal attachment is to *Ocarina Of Time*. That game was something really special for me, it was the first *Zelda* game that I worked on, the first to create a 3D universe for *Zelda*, and I was able to learn an awful lot from working with such a hugely talented team. Even today, when making new *Zelda* games, what we did on *Ocarina Of Time* can give me feedback on what we're doing now."

© Alamy

DID YOU KNOW?

In his last year at university, Eiji Aonuma studied mechanical design inside 3D objects – and credits this with Ocarina's complex dungeon interiors.

TAKASHI TEZUKA

Takashi Tezuka is the least-known of the 'golden Triforce' behind *Zelda*'s history – yet he has worked on every single *Zelda* game ever made, and is credited as either director or producer on over half of them. Tezuka has worked on the series since the first game, though he was first given charge of one with the Game Boy title *Link's Awakening*. "Tezuka-san did whatever he wanted with it," explained the late Nintendo president Satoru Iwata. That made the game a fan favourite, as well as a big influence on the future of the series, and Tezuka's impact on *Zelda* is even wider than that.

DID YOU KNOW?

The first game Takashi Tezuka worked on, with Shigeru Miyamoto, was Devil World for the NES – which was released in Japan in 1984, and in Europe in 2008!

TEZUKA ON...

Zelda's concept

"We basically decided to do a real-time adventure game. No one wants to do physical things like pushing and pulling by selecting them from a menu. If they're going to push something, they want to put some force behind it."

Link's Awakening

"We weren't particularly planning to make a *Zelda* game for the Game Boy, but we thought we'd try it out to see how it would work. So at first there was no official project. We'd do our regular work during normal work hours, and then work on it sort of like an after-school club activity. We moved along at quite a good speed in a relatively freewheeling manner. Maybe that's why we had so much fun making it. It was like we were making a parody of a *Zelda* game."

Characters

I was talking about fashioning *Link's Awakening* with a feel that was somewhat like *Twin Peaks*. At the time, *Twin Peaks* was rather popular. The drama was all about a small number of characters in a small town. After that, in *Ocarina Of Time* and *Majora's Mask*, all kinds of suspicious characters appeared. I didn't tell them to do it that way, but personally I did find it considerably appealing."

Difficulty

"We want *Zelda* to be a game you can play over and over again. Beating it once, for example, and then challenging yourself to see how fast you can beat it again. There are lots of things to discover, even just walking around the overworld."

Change

"You mess up if you put in lots of effort to do better than before but throw out some good things because they're old, and just indiscriminately add new things. Just because something is new, you can't guarantee it's good."

LEGENDARY SPIN-OFFS

We've covered every main Zelda game, but what about beyond that? Let's explore the franchise curios that exist on the periphery

WORDS BY DREW SLEEP

No videogaming series can exist for over 35 years and not be part of a crossover or spin-off. Take Nintendo's other flagship series, *Super Mario*, for example: we can see that the powerhouse plumber has been in everything from tennis showdowns, kart racers, paper-themed role-playing games and so much more.

The Legend Of Zelda is no different. While not as prolific as Mario, Link, Ganondorf and Zelda have ventured beyond the safe confines of their main series of games and into worlds beyond Hyrule. Link has even crossed over into the universes beyond Nintendo's grasp with Namco's *SoulCalibur* – a feat very few Nintendo characters have achieved.

Over the following pages, we'll explore how *The Legend Of Zelda* evolved beyond the borders of its main series and into side-games and crossovers, as well as the unfortunate experiments that weren't the Triforce's finest hour. From crossbow training to over-the-top battles, let's enter the world of *Zelda* spin-offs.

SUPER SMASH BROS

» *Super Smash Bros* is simple to grasp but difficult to master, meaning anyone can jump in and join the fracas.

This crossover fighting series has evolved from its humble party game origins and has become a shining jewel in Nintendo's crown with a loyal community bolstering it. The most recent game in the series, *Super Smash Bros Ultimate*, has a remarkable 82 fighters in its roster from franchises including *Super Mario, Dragon Quest, Fire Emblem, Final Fantasy, Banjo-Kazooie* and, of course, *The Legend Of Zelda*.

The original game was a lot more modest, however, with only eight characters available to choose from, and Link was there at the very beginning. Hyrule's champion is a versatile fighter, with his sword adding extra reach to his attacks, while his bow, bombs and spin attack make him one the most well-equipped characters in the game.

For the 2001 sequel, the character list expanded to throw Zelda, Ganon, Sheik and Young Link into the fray. The new additions are great, especially Zelda/Sheik as she can freely transform between her Princess and Sheika forms mid-fight. Young Link and Ganondorf, meanwhile, have cloned movesets from Link and Captain Falcon respectively, but that doesn't stop them from being monsters on the battlefield.

Young Link didn't survive the move to *Brawl* in 2008 and was replaced by Toon Link to represent the distinctive GameCube title *The Wind Waker.* Toon Link's moveset is almost identical to his Young Link predecessor, but if anything, this cartoon iteration is more nimble. The following two entries in the series, *Super Smash Bros For Wii U/3DS* and *Ultimate*, didn't add any new *Zelda* characters, however, *Ultimate* did restore Young Link to the roster.

We would wholeheartedly recommend picking up *Super Smash Bros Ultimate*, as it's the best game in the series by a massive stretch. Plus, Link usually finds himself in the upper section of tier lists for the best fighters in the game, which is a fitting place for the hooded do-gooder.

» That's right: you finally get to find the answer to the age-old question, "Who would win in a fight, one Link or 18 Yoshis?"

HYRULE WARRIORS

» The first *Hyrule Warriors* acts as a multiversal battle for the ages, drawing in *Zelda* characters across its entire history.

» If you enjoy hack-and-slash action games, you'll absolutely love *Hyrule Warriors*.

Omega Force's *Dynasty Warriors* series is known for its larger-than-life, over-the-top battles. At their core, they're (loosely) historic hack-and-slashers that see the likes of Lu Bu, Guan Yu, and Zhou Yu decimate entire armies with one sword combo. If that sounds a little absurd, it is. But it's oh-so-satisfying, and you can't help but grin as your hero performs elaborate genocidal sword-slinging in the name of escapist fun.

In recent years, Omega Force has been let loose on other beloved gaming franchises, adapting its *Dynasty Warriors* game design into the worlds of *Dragon Quest, Persona* and *The Legend Of Zelda.* While the main *Zelda* games are often quiet adventures, *Hyrule Warriors* is a loud and proud celebration of the series.

The first game, *Hyrule Warriors* for the Wii U, is a timeline-spanning adventure that assembles characters across the entire *Zelda* story to defeat Ganon and a sorceress called Cia. The 3DS port, *Hyrule Warriors Legends*, is notable for introducing a new female character, Linkle, who dual-wields crossbows and bares a striking resemblance to Link. Linkle was positively received by fans, so much so that producer Eiji Aonuma had thoughts about including her in a future *Zelda* game.

Based on the success of *Hyrule Warriors*, a sequel was greenlit, and *Age Of Calamity* arrived on Nintendo Switch in November 2020. This follow-up serves as a prequel to *Breath Of The Wild*, retelling the war that swallowed Hyrule before Link was placed in stasis. While it takes liberties with the story, it acts as a satisfying companion to *Breath Of The Wild* and performed well enough to receive two DLC packs. Remarkably, *Age Of Calamity* is the greatest-selling entry in the entire *Warriors* series. No doubt *Zelda*'s loyal fans warmly embraced Omega Force's carnage in their millions.

» Link has a strong advantage over the regular *SoulCalibur* roster as he has a bunch of projectile attacks.

» Press any button on this face-off screen to make Link yell at his enemy.

LINK'S CROSSBOW TRAINING

Nintendo's Wii was a machine that made bank on its peripherals. The Wiimote, Nunchuk, Classic Controller, Wii Motion Plus, Wii Wheel... it was dizzying to be a Wii owner in its heyday. The Wii Zapper was just one of these add-on controllers, and it was a peripheral Nintendo felt would be perfect for shooter-style games. To demonstrate this to consumers, the company needed a killer title to highlight the Zapper's potential.

Link's Crossbow Training started life as an original 'Introduction to Wii Zapper' game before adopting the *Zelda* name. It was given its simplistic 'Crossbow Training' moniker to manage expectations as something epic-sounding might have given fans the wrong idea.

Bundled with the Zapper, it sees Link attempt to hone his sharpshooting skills by taking on a series of challenges. These range from target practice to defending a point from foes and, finally, directly taking control of the hooded hero and assaulting an encampment.

Link's Crossbow Training certainly achieved its goal of demonstrating the Wii Zapper's appeal, especially when you consider it as a bundled game for the add-on. When examining it today, however, the game doesn't add much to the epic mythos of Hyrule.

» The target practice mode is good to start with, but we doubt you'll return to it.

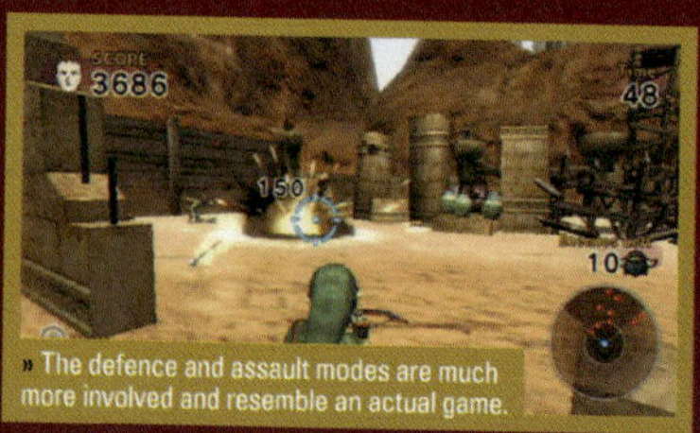

» The defence and assault modes are much more involved and resemble an actual game.

SOULCALIBUR II

Namco and Project Soul's *SoulCalibur* series of arcade fighting games sets itself apart from your *Tekkens* and *Street Fighters* by being weapons-focused. Its characters wield oversized zweihanders, bladed tonfa or deadly bo staffs to create battles with exciting spectacle. When it came to porting *SoulCalibur II* to the PlayStation 2, Xbox and GameCube, the team decided to add guest characters representing each console. The PlayStation 2 got Heihachi from *Tekken*, Xbox got the comic book character Spawn, and the GameCube's candidate was obvious, right?

Link enters the battleground wielding his Hylian shield and Master Sword, and like his *Smash Bros* incarnation, once again proves himself to be a fearsome competitor. He has an edge over the other characters in the game thanks to his projectile attacks. His bow and arrow, boomerang and bombs make him an excellent zoner, while his shield and sword fighting stance give him excellent close-range options.

His appearance went down well with both the *SoulCalibur* and *Zelda* communities. Link has only appeared in the second instalment, but his impact was huge. *SoulCalibur* is known for its guest characters, and in a poll by *IGN*, he was ranked at the top of the lot, beating the likes of Darth Vader and Yoda. It's official: Link is better than a Jedi Master.

LINK: THE FACES OF EVIL, ZELDA: THE WAND OF GAMELON AND ZELDA'S ADVENTURE

In 1989, Nintendo began talks with Sony to develop a CD-ROM add-on for the SNES. This 'Nintendo Play-Station' would be capable of full-motion video and more ambitious games. However, in a poor business move for the ages, Nintendo snubbed Sony and partnered with Philips instead. Sony didn't back down and created its own PlayStation console to world-conquering success, which later became a thorn in Nintendo's side. Meanwhile, Nintendo and Philips's machine didn't work out but Philips retained some rights to use Nintendo characters in games for its CD-i console.

Philips created three *Legend Of Zelda* games for the CD-i, and they're let's say 'distinct' from Nintendo's output. *Link: The Faces Of Evil* and *Zelda: The Wand Of Gamelon* are side-scrollers that star Link and Zelda respectively. While not hitting the highs of Nintendo's games, modern reassessment has determined they're 'not *that* bad' despite some grating cutscenes. Plus, it's nice to see Zelda take a more active role in the action.

That 'not that bad' ruling is probably because they often get compared to Philips's final title, *Zelda's Adventure*, which is notoriously awful. Not even Ganon would wish a fate this bad upon poor Princess Zelda, who is trapped inside a static-looking game with poor controls and unfair difficulty, along with those god-awful FMV moments from the prior games.

The *Zelda* CD-i games are entertaining, but for all the wrong reasons. It's probably best to avoid seeking them out and perhaps look up a let's play video on YouTube for a quick giggle and move on to something worth experiencing.

» While we don't *hate* the art style, it does leave a lot to be desired.

» Hey, at least Zelda broke out from her damsel-in-distress stereotype...

» You have to time your movement and attacks to the beat of the music, which gets difficult when things are hectic!

CADENCE OF HYRULE

Nintendo is a company that protects its properties, and you can't blame it for doing so. It knows all too well what happens when you lend your beloved characters to a developer or publisher and that partnership doesn't work out. That's not to say Nintendo is a hoarder of its own copyright, though. Some of the most memorable adventures featuring Link and Zelda were born from a partnership with Capcom; both the *Oracle* games and *The Minish Cap* are some of the most well-regarded entries in the series.

During a March 2019 Nintendo Direct, Nintendo unveiled news that surprised many watchers: a *Legend Of Zelda* spin-off with independent developer Brace Yourself Games at the helm. This Canadian studio won fame in 2015 with *Crypt Of The NecroDancer*, an excellent game where you have to navigate a dungeon while timing your steps and weapon strikes to a thumping synthwave soundtrack.

Based on *NecroDancer*'s success, Brace Yourself started planning DLC for its Nintendo Switch port of the game. "Originally Spike Chunsoft (our publisher in Japan for *Crypt Of The NecroDancer*) was speaking to Nintendo about the possibility of including Link and Zelda as playable characters in a *Crypt Of The NecroDancer* DLC," director Oliver Trujillo tells us. "While that would have been a fun project in its own right, we decided to ask about our ideal situation of creating an entirely new *Legend Of Zelda*-themed *Crypt Of The NecroDancer* game. To our surprise and delight, Nintendo was receptive to the idea, and so we started working on the design docs, art mockups and music remixes that eventually turned into *Cadence Of Hyrule: Crypt Of The NecroDancer Featuring The Legend Of Zelda*."

The idea developed fast, and the partnership worked smoothly. "It was excellent overall, and an interesting insight into different game development methods," Trujillo elaborates. "It is probably no surprise that Nintendo's approach to game development differs from ours at Brace Yourself Games, them being a large Japanese studio, and us being a small North American studio, but their feedback was always on point and incredibly beneficial for us. Nintendo was also very helpful in providing support in the form of outstanding QA testing and localisation. Oh, and it was certainly a fun and illuminating experience to be able to visit Nintendo HQ in Kyoto and meet some of the *Legend Of Zelda* developers that we have so much respect for!"

The star of the show was, of course, the music by Danny Baranowsky which delivers pulsing remixes of *Zelda* tunes. "I sort of split the difference between *Crypt Of The NecroDancer* and *The Legend Of Zelda*," Baranowsky says. "Some tracks are wholly *Crypt Of The NecroDancer*, like Ice Palace and Lost Swamp, but some are wholly *Legend Of Zelda*, like 'Overworld' and 'Gerudo Valley'. 'Overworld' and 'Gerudo' are just legendary, and the musical identity of *The Legend Of Zelda*, for me, is so strongly linked to them that it seemed like even with these worlds commingling, they would retain their identity."

» You will encounter iconic *Zelda* items, along with some *NecroDancer* favourites.

» From the screenshots alone, it's obviously a *Zelda* game, but the music takes it to a new level.

Printed in Dunstable, United Kingdom

91342773R00076